W9-CSU-829

BLACK SISTER

BLACK SISTER

POETRY BY BLACK AMERICAN WOMEN, 1746–1980

EDITED WITH AN INTRODUCTION BY

Erlene Stetson

INDIANA UNIVERSITY PRESS

BLOOMINGTON

To
Anne Spencer (1882–1975),
who
represents a long tradition of unsung
black women poets
and to
Margaret Goss Burroughs
who
writes still, having always known the beauty
of
our blackness

Copyright © 1981 by Erlene Stetson

All rights reserved

No part of this book may be reproduced or utilized in any form
or by any means, electronic or mechanical, including photocopying
and recording, or by any information storage and retrieval system,
without permission in writing from the publisher. The Association
of American University Presses' Resolution on Permissions constitutes
the only exception to this prohibition.

Manufactured in the United States of America

Library of Congress Cataloging in Publication Data

Stetson, Erlene, 1949-
Black sister.

Bibliography: p.
1. American poetry—Afro-American authors.   2. Ameri-
can poetry—Women authors.   I. Title.

PS591.N4S75   811'.008'09287   80-8847
ISBN 0-253-30512-8   AACR2
ISBN 0-253-20268-X (pbk.)   9 10 11 12   99 98 97

CONTENTS

PREFACE   xiii

INTRODUCTION   xvii

I. EIGHTEENTH- AND NINETEENTH-CENTURY POETS   1

LUCY TERRY

Bars Fight, August 28, 1746   12

PHILLIS WHEATLEY

Selection from "Liberty and Peace, A Poem"	13
To a Gentleman and Lady on the Death of the Lady's Brother and Sister, and a Child of the Name Avis, Aged One Year	14
To S.M. A Young African Painter, On Seeing His Work	15
On Imagination	16

ADA

Lines, Suggested on Reading 'An Appeal to Christian Women of the South,' by A. E. Grimké.	17
[Untitled]	19
Lines	20
To the Memory of J. Horace Kimball	21

CHARLOTTE FORTEN [GRIMKÉ]

A Parting Hymn	22
Poem	23
To W.L.G. on Reading His 'Chosen Queen'	24

SOJOURNER TRUTH

Ain't I a Woman?   24

FRANCES E. W. HARPER

A Double Standard	26
Vashti	27
Learning to Read	29
An Appeal to My Countrywomen	31

She's Free!   32
The Crocuses   33
The Mission of the Flowers   34

HENRIETTA CORDELIA RAY

Robert G. Shaw   37
Idyl: Sunrise   37
Idyl: Sunset   38
To My Father   38
Milton   39
The Dawn of Love   39
Antigone and Oedipus   40

CLARA ANN THOMPSON

His Answer   42
Mrs. Johnson Objects   42

ANN PLATO

The Natives of America   43
To the First of August   45
Reflections, Written on Visiting the Grave of a Venerated Friend   46

II.   TWENTIETH-CENTURY POETS   49

ROSALIE JONAS

Ballade des Belles Milatraisses   55
Brother Baptis' on Woman Suffrage   56

LUCY ARIEL WILLIAMS

Northboun'   57

GEORGIA DOUGLAS JOHNSON

I Want to Die While You Love Me   58
The Heart of a Woman   58
My Little Dreams   59
Smothered Fires   59

ANGELINA WELD GRIMKÉ

A Mona Lisa   60
At April   61
To Keep the Memory of Charlotte Forten Grimké   61
For the Candle Light   63

Contents

JESSIE REDMON FAUSET

Touché	63
Oriflamme	64

ALICE DUNBAR-NELSON

Sonnet	65
I Sit and Sew	65
Snow in October	66
Music	67

ANNE SPENCER

At the Carnival	68
Before the Feast of Shushan	69
Letter to My Sister	70
Substitution	71
Lady, Lady	72

GWENDOLYN B. BENNETT

Fantasy	72
Hatred	73
Song	73
Secret	74
Advice	75
To a Dark Girl	76
To Usward	76
Heritage	77

HELENE JOHNSON

Bottled	78
Magalu	79
The Road	80
Trees at Night	81
Summer Matures	81

CARRIE WILLIAMS CLIFFORD

The Black Draftee from Dixie	82

BESSIE CALHOUN BIRD

Proof	83

PAULI MURRAY

Dark Testament	84
Inquietude	92
Song	93

CONTENTS

MAE V. COWDERY

I Sit and Wait for Beauty 93

MARGARET WALKER

Lineage 94
Kissie Lee 95
Molly Means 96
Ballad of the Hoppy-Toad 98

GWENDOLYN BROOKS

The Mother 100
The Bean Eaters 101
The Birth in a Narrow Room 102
The Anniad 102
Appendix to the Anniad 111

MAY MILLER

Gift from Kenya 112
Not That Far 113

MARGARET GOSS BURROUGHS

To Soulfolk 118
Black Pride 118
Only in This Way 120
Everybody But Me 121

GLORIA C. ODEN

This Child is the Mother 123

NAOMI LONG MADGETT

Deacon Morgan 127
Exits and Entrances 128
Midway 128
Nomen 129
New Day 130
Black Woman 130

MARGARET DANNER

A Grandson is a Hoticeberg 131
The Rhetoric of Langston Hughes 133
At Home in Dakar 133

Contents

KATTIE M. CUMBO

Nocturnal Sounds	134
Domestics	135
Black Sister	135
The morning after . . . love	136
I'm a Dreamer	137
Ceremony	137

SARAH WEBSTER FABIO

Back into the Garden	139
To Turn from Love	140
All Day We've Longed for Night	141

MARI EVANS

Daufuskie (Four Movements)	142
Jake	143
The People Gather	143
Janis	144
How Will You Call Me, Brother	144
. . . And the Old Women Gathered (The Gospel Singers)	146

ALICE S. COBB

The Searching	146
Angela Davis	147

JUNE JORDAN

Poem for Nana	148

JAYNE CORTEZ

Orisha	151
Phraseology	152
Orange Chiffon	153
Under the Edge of February	153
So Many Feathers	155
In the Morning	157
Grinding Vibrato	160

DELLA BURT

Spirit Flowers	161
A Little Girl's Dream World	162
On the Death of Lisa Lyman	163

FAREEDAH ALLAH

Hush, Honey	164
Cinderella	167
Funky Football	170
You Made It Rain	173
The Generation Gap	174
Lawd, Dese Colored Chillum	175

CAROLYN M. RODGERS

Poem for Some Black Women	176
Masquerade	178
Jesus Was Crucified or: It Must Be Deep	180
U Name This One	183

LINDA PIPER

Sweet Ethel	183
Missionaries in the Jungle	184

CAROLE C. GREGORY

Love Letter	185
Revelation	185
A Freedom Song for the Black Woman	188
The Greater Friendship Baptist Church	190

JO ANN HALL-EVANS

Cape Coast Castle Revisited	191
Seduction	192

JOHARI M. KUNJUFU

Ceremony	192
Return	194
The Promise	195

IRMA McCLAURIN

The Mask	195
To a Gone Era	196
I, Woman	197

AUDRE LORDE

Coal	198
Chain	199
Summer Oracle	201

Contents

Harriet   202
Naturally   203
The Woman Thing   204

GAYL JONES

3-31-70   205
tripart   209
Satori   210
Many Die Here   210

ALICE WALKER

Revolutionary Petunias   212
Once   213
Early Losses: A Requiem   223

PINKIE GORDON LANE

On Being Head of the English Department   228
When You Read This Poem   229
Sexual Privacy of Women on Welfare   230
Migration   231
Who Is My Brother?   232
Nocturne   233

NIKKI GIOVANNI

Nikki-Rosa   233
Woman Poem   234
Mother's Habits   236
Knoxville, Tennessee   237

PATRICIA PARKER

From the Cavities of Bones   238
I Followed a Path   239
there is a woman in this town   240

SONIA SANCHEZ

Memorial   242
poem at thirty   245
summer words for a sister addict   246

LUCILLE CLIFTON

The Lost Baby Poem   247
My Mama Moved among the Days   248
Miss Rosie   248

xii   CONTENTS

PATRICIA JONES

i done got so thirsty that my mouth waters at the thought of rain   249
Why I Like Movies   251

SHERLEY ANNE WILLIAMS

The Empress Brand Trim: Ruby Reminisces   253
Say Hello to John   254
The House of Desire   255
Driving Wheel   260

MAYA ANGELOU

Woman Me   264
Still I Rise   265
My Arkansas   266
Sepia Fashion Show   267
On Diverse Deviations   267

NTOZAKE SHANGE

nappy edges (a cross country sojourn)   268
Dark Phrases   270
No More Love Poems #1   272
frank albert & viola benzena owens   273

THADIOUS M. DAVIS

It's All the Same   276
Remembering Fannie Lou Hamer   277
Double Take at Relais de L'Espadon   277
"Honeysuckle was the Saddest Odor of All, I Think."   279
Asante Sana, Te Te   280

MELBA JOYCE BOYD

Sunflowers and Saturdays   281
Why?   283
Beer Drops   285

COLLEEN J. McELROY

Ruth   286
Caledonia   288
Looking for a Country Under Its Original Name   290
A Woman's Song   291

BIBLIOGRAPHY   295

PREFACE

Inevitably I am tempted by renewed insight, self-conscious corrections, and momentary retrospection to tamper extensively with what I have written. One is naturally assailed by self-doubt when confronting a task that no one else has successfully completed. The recent publication of several anthologies of "black" poetry and "women's" poetry compels me to try. Although both kinds of collections were designed to fill a void, the same few black women poets—and all too frequently even the same poems—are anthologized repeatedly, while entire periods and many individual poets are still ignored. One gets the impression that only the work of white poets and black male poets deserves critical attention, while black women's work takes the back seat as a minor variation of "black" poetry or of "women's" poetry. The result is that the poetry of black women has not been seen as a complex whole that can be analyzed in terms of style, structure, and a coherent tradition.

Black women poets have made a unique contribution to the American literary tradition. This contribution is shaped by their experience both as blacks and as women, an experience whose pressure they have resisted at the same time they have recognized its strategic survival value in life and exploited its symbolic power in their art. This contribution begins with their arrival as reluctant African immigrants three hundred years ago and spans their transformation from Negro slaves to free women of color.

Black Sister includes the work of representative poets from 1746—when sixteen-year-old Lucy Terry wrote her poem—to the present. In order to be comprehensive and at the same time maintain economy, the collection is divided into two sections: the Eighteenth and Nineteenth Centuries (1746–1899) and the Twentieth Century (1900–1980). In the Introduction I place the poets within a theoretical framework that stresses the unity of this tradition. Over the centuries, the problem of establishing an identity in a hostile environment has drawn women poets to similar themes, and even to similar imagery. On the other hand, in the essays that introduce the poetry selections, I discuss the work of a few major poets, allowing the part to speak for the whole. And it is in these essays that I take up issues that are unique to each time period, that distinguish the poets of the earlier and later periods. For one thing, the earlier poets were effectively silenced by a publishing industry that would not print the work of black women in book form. In the twentieth century, black women began to break through that resistance, and their poetry has developed and matured, with the help of symbols taken from black musical culture.

Because of the range and power of her work, as well as its sheer volume, I chose Phillis Wheatley (ca. 1753–1784) to represent the eighteenth century. White public reception of Wheatley was ambivalent: she was honored for the accomplished virtuosity of her scholarship at the same time she was considered an oddity and a freak, a member of that unheard-of category—black lady poet. Since then she has been put forth as an example of what black women should strive for and yet unfairly presented as a mere imitator of the neoclassical Alexander Pope. Thus, she has become a prophetic symbol of the dilemma facing the black woman poet: Wheatley embodies both her possibilities and her limitations, as others perceive them. Briefly popular during her lifetime, Wheatley, like numerous other black poets, died in poverty and obscurity.

Frances E[llen] W[atkins] Harper (1825–1911) represents the nineteenth century. Her poetry is stylistically diverse and reverberates with a creative tension between her polite Victorian style and a socio–political content concerned with slavery, temperance, and suffrage. Harper's poetry bridges the gap between the syncretic poetic style of Wheatley and the rhetorical and political tones of contemporary poets like Jayne Cortez, Mari Evans, and Nikki Giovanni. It goes beyond Wheatley's formalist poetry and for the first time portrays strong and revolutionary black women in the tradition of African female warriors and Western heroines: Harper's proud Vashti (the queen banished by the king who later took Esther as a concubine) reappears in Anne Spencer's "Before the Feast of Shushan" (1920) and Gwendolyn Brooks' "The Anniad" (1949); her heroines from recent history like Sojourner Truth, Harriet Tubman, and Mum Bett are literary antecedents of Margaret Walker's characters in *For My People* (1942).

Poets of the modern period present multi-dimensional images. Unlike their sisters Wheatley, "a devoted servant" who favored the aristocracy and persons of known stature, and Harper, the popular Christian poet who appealed to white Christians to do their "duty" and love the least of their fellows—that is, blacks—modern black women poets are heretics who symbolically slash at the "soft white flesh" of their oppressors. They are not satisfied with Harper's use of the metaphor of the rebel—they are rebels themselves. They are not waiting for the reciprocity between blacks and whites that Wheatley and Harper hoped for. Whether it is bold and strident or calm and introspective, their poetry proclaims "a new day" and celebrates their collective and individual dark-skinned selves. Twentieth-century black women poets have used a new resource: music, particularly the blues, has provided themes, images, structures, and poetic devices unavailable to poets before this century. The poetry of Nikki Giovanni illustrates all of these trends.

Despite the great differences in tone and the centuries that separate them, black women poets from Terry to Giovanni are literary sisters. They share an autobiographical consciousness and an appreciation of their troubled history as blacks and as women. They are all sensitive to change, revolution, and rebellion; and they have created symbols—like Vashti—that are uniquely black and female. Above all, they share the drive to define and redefine themselves in the past, present, and future. The careful reader can hear this sisterhood even in the patterns of contradiction, ambivalence, and studied omission in this poetry. These poets have infused Afro-American history with a sense of their living presence, and their poetry leads us directly into the experience of black women during the diaspora, under slavery and peonage, and in the Great Migration that followed.

Black Sister documents this black feminist poetic tradition. I want to make the poetry of black women visible and accessible to black and white sisters everywhere, to scholars in high schools, colleges, and universities, and to the casual reader. Black women's poetry must no longer be viewed as having recently sprouted, fully-grown, from the ghettos and barrios with contemporary revolutionary poets. I hope that *Black Sister* challenges academics, critics, and publishers who have defined American literary tradition by their inclusions and who have denied importance and validity to the poets in this collection by systematically excluding them from the official canon.

INTRODUCTION

For black women creativity has often been a survival tactic. Their poetic heritage has not been one of smooth continuity, with new poets reading earlier poets' work and then sharing support with a community of contemporaries. Nor is their poetic tradition based on style: from Lucy Terry's poetic account of an Indian raid, through the formalist syncretic poems of Phillis Wheatley and the race-conscious, woman-centered prose poems of Frances E. W. Harper, to the choreopoems of Ntozake Shange, their poetry shows wide variation in form and technique. Their themes and subjects have developed over the generations out of common historical experiences.

As a logical result of the social forces in their lives, carried on under the practical travesty of "liberty and justice for all," black women poets in the United States have been driven into a compelling quest for identity. The fundamental differences between Western and non-Western cosmologies—both part of the American black heritage—and the psychic hell of existing where cultural wholeness is denied have given further impetus to this search for personal and collective integration. These poets have brought to their quest a perception of reality that is subconscious and subversive. It is a perception rising out of their disenchantment with the emptiness of American life. It recognizes that appearance is not reality, but only a partial and ineffective semblance of reality. And finally it is a perception of reality as unified and dialectic rather than fragmented and disjunctive. Subterfuge and ambivalence arise as active strategies for living and for creating art where more direct means for survival and self-expression have been denied. And these strategies are the key to understanding the nature and function of black female identity.

Because of this underlying unity of theme, strategy, and symbol in the poetry of black women, and their external diversity of style, in my teaching I have chosen to present this poetry thematically. The three key concepts—a compelling quest for identity, a subversive perception of reality, and subterfuge and ambivalence as creative strategies—have provided a versatile analytic framework for evaluating the literary quality and creative achievement of the works, as well as for organizing their themes and metaphors.

Black women poets have addressed two questions: How do we assert and maintain our identities in a world that prefers to believe we do not exist? How do we balance and contain our rage so that we can express both our warmth and love and our anger and pain? Wheatley's poem "To the King's Most Excellent Majesty. 1768" (1773) openly acknowledges her submission to her masters. She uses this pose to seek concessions for Africans like herself, and thus she becomes the trickster, the cunning underdog who disguises her real message behind innocuous "appearance." Her elaborate praise of King George fulfills the customary ritual: "Your subjects hope, dread Sire—/The crown upon your brows may flourish long,/And that your arm may in your God be strong!" By applauding his repeal of the Stamp Act she seeks a favorable hearing for her personal plea for the abolition of slavery:

> Great God, direct, and guard him [King George] from on high
> And from his head let ev'ry evil fly!
> And may each clime with equal gladness see
> A monarch's smile can set his subjects free!

Margaret Danner (1915) in "The Elevator Man Adheres to Form" (in Langston Hughes and Arna Bontemps, eds., *The Poetry of the Negro*, 1949) speaks to the reality of being "black" as opposed to the appearance of acting "white":

> I am reminded, by the tan man who wings
> the elevator, of Rococo art. His ways
> are undulating waves that shepherd and swing
> us cupid-like from floor to floor.

The elevator man embodies the American Dream and its superficialities with "His greetings, God-speedings, display his Ph.D/ aplomb." Nevertheless, his blackness and his career connect him in the poet's mind to an original underground self:

> instead, I vision other tan and deeper much than tan
> early-Baroque-like men who (seeing themselves still
> strutlessly groping, winding down subterranean
>
> grottoes of injustice, down dark spirals) feel
> with such torturous, smoked-stone greyed intensity
> that they exhale a hurricane of gargoyles, then reel
> into it.

Frances E. W. Harper and Anne Spencer (1882–1975) demonstrate their estrangement by deliberately juxtaposing their energetic cultural images against those of popular and classical male poets. Harper's *Idylls of the Bible* (1901) satirizes the idealized concept of white female purity glorified in Alfred Lord Tennyson's *Idylls of the King* (1859). Harper uses Bible heroines as models for her rebellious, recalcitrant black women activists, antidotes to Tennyson's vision of pale "courtly love." Spencer's "Lady, Lady" (see p. 72) parodies Tennyson's "A Dream of Fair Ladies" and mocks his masculine fantasy of an idealized womanhood:

> Lady, Lady, I saw your hands,
> Twisted, awry, like crumpled roots,
> Bleached poor white in a sudsy tub,
> Wrinkled and drawn from your rub-a-dub.

The poems of Gwendolyn Brooks (1917) fuse the Western literary aesthetic to a non-Western one, and in this process they reveal an inadequacy of the former to treat the black experience. The "Womanhood" section of *Annie Allen* (1949) consists of four Italian sonnets. The fourth sonnet contrasts two cultures and therefore two approaches to the cultural role of music. In this poem, violin music represents the Western ideal of contemplative music, while the thuggee—a frenetic, nineteenth-century Hindu rite of ritual murder offered up to the goddess Kali—represents an active and communal tradition. Placing classical violin against thuggee, Brooks highlights the fundamental antagonism between a philistine "high art" designed to be appreciated passively and a functional folk art that demands collective response. By judging the traditions in terms of the role of the audience and the cultural function of the art form, Brooks also demonstrates that Western art forms demand an analytic and overly intellectual response.

Above all, however, this sonnet requires that strong, secure, and independent black cultural bonds be established before Western culture be savored:

> First fight. Then fiddle. Play the slipping string
> With feathery sorcery; muzzle the note
> With hurting love; the music that they wrote
> Bewitch, bewilder. Qualify to sing
> Threadwise. Devise no salt, no hempen thing
> For the dear instrument to bear. Devote
> The bow to silks and honey. Be remote
> Awhile from malice and from murdering.
> But first to arms, to armor. Carry hate
> In front of you and harmony behind.

Though it is rendered with finesse, her preference for the thuggee over the violin is clear, and her message prefigures the revolutionary artistic consciousness of the 1960s.

Her sonnet "The Egg Boiler" (*The Bean Eaters*, 1960)—after the style of John Keats and Robert Frost—achieves irony by weighing the value of abstract beauty against the value of utilitarian fact. It explores counter-bourgeois values while it applauds the achievements of the black homemaker:

> Being you, you cut your poetry from wood
> The boiling of an egg is heavy art.
> You come upon it as an artist should,
> With rich-eyed passion, and with straining heart.

Boiling an egg is a simple and yet rich metaphor for the world that women inhabit.

If some black women have written themselves into Western literary history by taking on the bogies of Tennyson and Keats, others have written about the psychic hell of cultural fragmentation. Georgia Douglas Johnson (1886–1966) was a poet of the Black Renaissance and the third poet after Wheatley and Harper to receive public acclaim. She relied on the literary stereotype of the mulatto to define her themes of struggle and identity. "Mulatto," which comes from the Spanish and Portuguese, means "young mule," the mule being the usually sterile hybrid of a horse and an ass. Johnson's mulattoes often seek meaningful reciprocity between the races. Some find communication with either race next to impossible; their ambiguous race can render them impotent and isolated from both the black and white traditions. On the other hand, the mulatto image has a positive strength as Johnson shows in "Cosmopolite" (*Bronze*, 1922):

> Not wholly this or that,
> But wrought
> Of Alien bloods am I,
> A product of the interplay
> Of traveled hearts.
> Estranged, yet not estranged, I stand
> All comprehending;
> From my estate
> I view earth's frail dilemma
> Scion of fused strength am I,
> All understanding,
> Not this nor that
> Contains me.

The mulatto thus becomes a focus for the conflict between blacks and whites. Disguise is another way of negotiating between these worlds. Veil, mist, and the deceptive smile that hides and lies and reveals are common in Johnson's work, as in "Aliens" (*Bronze*, 1922):

> They seems to smile as others smile, the masquerader's art
> Conceals them, while, in verity, they're eating out their heart,
> Betwixt the two contending stones of crass humanity
> They lie, the fretted fabric of a dual dynasty.

Johnson is also troubled by the similar disjuncture between the worlds of men and women, and again she sees disguise as women's way of reconciling the two. Masking and concealment are basic elements of women's dress and can be found in the features of their faces, in eyes and tears, in mouths and smiles. Johnson uses these images to suggest women's bondage and their confinement to a narrow role in "A Paradox" from *An Autumn Love Cycle* (1928):

> I know you love me better cold
> Strange as the pyramids of old
> Responselessly.
> But I am frail, and spent and weak
> With surging torrents that bespeak
> A living fire.
> So, like a veil, my poor disguise
> Is draped to save me from your eyes'
> Deep challenges.

Later, in "Far from Africa: Garnishing the Aviary" (in Arna Bontemps, ed., *American Negro Poetry*, 1963), Margaret Danner examines this same complex of masking and confinement of women in aviary terms: "Our moulting days are in their twilight stage. / These lengthy dreaded suns of draggling plumes."

In *For My People* (1942), Margaret Walker chronicles the history of black women from slavery to freedom. The poem is grand and yet deeply personal; it deals with historical particulars and yet is all-encompassing in scope. For Walker, Africa is richly feminine—"sugar sands and Islands of Ferns"—as is Mississippi, with its golden grain and purple fruit." Through this imagery and story, Walker recreates a collective black and female reality that is whole and yet separate from the mainstream of American ideology. It is this perception of a unified, unique reality that makes the poetry of black American women more than the simple outpourings of oppressed voices.

"Molly Means" and "Kissie Lee" (see pp. 95–97) from *For My*

People celebrate a strong black indigenous female culture whose most famous practitioner is Marie Le Veau, the queen of hoodoo in New Orleans.* This is a culture of heroic women who are bigger than the slave history that gave them birth. Molly Means "was born with a veil on her face" and "could look through unnatural space." Her difference gives her power:

> Sometimes at night through the shadowy trees
> She rides along in a winter breeze
> You can hear her holler and whine and cry
> Her voice is thin and her moan is high,
> And her cackling laugh on her barking cold
> Bring terror to the young and old.

Molly Means and Kissie Lee are in the tradition of word conjurors, witches, and rebels. They wonderfully anticipate Toni Morrison's *Sula* (1973), who is an outcast orphan-woman and pariah and who enjoys untrammeled freedom to choose the uncommon. All three women are sisters to blues artists like Bessie Smith, whose real-life career in migratory farm work and "hollering"—due as much to a lack of opportunity as to her need for independence—they trace in their literary journeys.

Since the eighteenth century, black women have explored a personal landscape in their poetry through symbols of flowers and houses. The house represents the historic quest by black women for homes of their own—apart from the house of slavery, the common house of bondage, the house of the patriarchy. The house embodies women's search for place and belonging and for a whole and complete identity, as well as representing the historical house that was so difficult to get. In addition, the house is a symbol for place—heaven, haven, home, the heart, women's estate, the earthly tenement, the hearth—and for region—Africa, the West Indies, America, Asia, the North, and the South. In 1979, on a CBS "Ed Bradley Report," an elderly black Southern woman articulated her desire for "a house on the front." Her words remind me of Harper's Chloe in "Learning to Read" (see p. 29), who reports with satisfaction how:

> Then I got a little cabin,
>   A place to call my own—
> And I felt as independent
>   As the queen upon her throne.

---

*See Zora Neale Hurston, *Mules and Men* (Bloomington: Indiana University Press, 1978), pp. 200ff.

The old woman's desire draws us even farther back to Phillis Wheatley's poignant memories of her African home in "To the Right Honourable William, Earl of Dartmouth, His Majesty's Principal Secretary of State for North America, &c" (1773):

> Should you, my lord, while you peruse my song,
> Wonder from whence my love of *Freedom* sprung . . .
> I, young in life, by seeming cruel fate
> Was snatch'd from Afric's fancy'd happy seat:
> What pangs excruciating must molest,
> What sorrows labour in my parent's breast?
> Steel'd was that soul and by no misery mov'd
> That from a father seiz'd his babe belov'd:
> Such, such my case. And can I then but pray
> Others may never feel tyrannic sway?

The flower is an image of rootedness and, by contrast, rootlessness. Flowers symbolize the cultural diversity of women; like flowers, black women are rooted in the culture of which they are part. They join *with* and *become* their landscape. They must be transplanted to open soil and fresh air to breathe and extend their roots. Yet they bloom both within and outside captivity. Their seeds have been widely dispersed. The insistent metaphor of the flower has a personal significance in the poetry of Wheatley ("In trees, and plants, and all the flowery race"), in that of Spencer (daylilies, nasturtiums, flame torchers, and peonies), of Harper (dandelions, crocuses, verbena, lilies, daisies, roses, and marigolds), and of Alice Walker (purple petunias).

Black women poets have not benefited from a self-conscious tradition: all too often it seems that they have written in isolation without the inspiration of earlier sister poets or the help of contemporaries. Nevertheless, they have created the tradition of symbol and metaphor that I have briefly discussed here. For black women, the house is—and has been—more than a symbol for identity or family; historically, having a house of one's own has been an economically difficult, if not impossible, goal to achieve. For black women, masks are not something they can choose to wear; often they have had to don them for survival. All the images that black women poets have created and explored over the centuries share this characteristic: they are more resonant because a specific historical heritage lies behind them. The work of these poets is not outside the mainstream of the Western literary tradition—flowers, masks, houses, and heroines are not unique to their work—but the poetry of black American women does form a coherent and bright strand in that history. Establishing this heritage and recovering the poems of the women involved are only the first steps in scholarship. The job that must wait for another time and another place is that of writing a new literary history that takes this work into account.

EIGHTEENTH- AND
NINETEENTH-CENTURY POETS

The history of black women's poetry in the United States began when Lucy Terry (1730–1821) of Deerfield, Massachusetts, wrote "Bars Fight, August 28, 1746,"* long before Phillis Wheatley (ca. 1753–84), the most popular black poet of that century, was born. Terry is the first black poet to be recognized in America. "Bars Fight" (see p. 12) has color, tragedy, and adventure: it tells the story of an Indian raid in which the whites are the losers. Terry records the struggle of the valiant settlers ("Samuel Allen like a hero fout"), the not so valiant ("John Saddler fled across the water"), and the slightly ridiculous:

> Eunice Allen see the Indians comeing,
> And hoped to save herself by running,
> And had not her petticoats stopt her,
> The awful creatures had not cotched her.

Wheatley was about eight when she arrived in America on a slave ship from Africa and was bought by John Wheatley, a Boston merchant. The Wheatleys educated her. By the time she was ten she was translating Ovid's tales from Latin and by her early teens writing poetry in fluent English. In 1773 she was sent to England for her health, and it was there that *Poems on Various Subjects, Religious and Moral* was published. Dedicated to "The Right Honorable The Countess of Huntington," Wheatley's hostess in England, the volume was signed by the governor and the lieutenant governor of Boston, testifying to the fact that Wheatley had written the poems herself. An American edition did not appear until 1786.

Her charm and intelligence won Wheatley many friends in England and America, and for a brief time she was lionized. But after her return to Boston she lost her audience: patrons and acquaintances showed indifference to her work. She married, but her husband repeatedly left her, and two of their three children died. Finally, poverty and hard work broke her health, and both she and her last child died on December 5, 1784. After her death, her husband disappeared with what remained of her work, the crowning blow to a sad history.

Wheatley's poetry has none of the zest, sentiment, and spirit of Lucy Terry's. Wheatley relies heavily on the refined, neoclassical conventions of her day, such as iambic pentameter, couplets, personification, and epithets. Her poems open with the obligatory in-

---

*This poem was not published until 1895, when it appeared in *A History of Deerfield, Massachusetts* by George Sheldon (Deerfield: 1895). Terry has a remarkable story. Apparently she convinced the authorities at Williams College to admit her son; at another time she successfully argued her own case in a court land dispute. No full biography of Terry is available.

vocation to the muse: "Celestial muse! for sweetness fam'd inspire/ My wondrous theme with true poetic fire." They consider the "proper" poetic subjects, like "Imagination" and "On Recollection," and the images they contain, reminiscent of those of John Milton and Alexander Pope, are from Graeco-Roman mythology.

As a result, Wheatley has been placed all too comfortably in the tradition of Pope. But she is not the "servile" imitator current criticism would have us think. The strength of her poetics lies in the mastery, skill, perception, and black female consciousness that she fuses with these conventional models. Balance, decorum, and restraint mark Wheatley's work, as in these lines from "Liberty and Peace, A Poem," published in 1784 (see p. 13):

> *Britain*, whose Navies swept th' *Atlantic* o'er,
> And Thunder sent to every distant Shore:
> E'en thou, in Manners cruel as thou art,
> The Sword resign'd, resume the friendly Part!

"On Recollection" is an example of her unorthodox treatment of a standard poetic subject. What is unconventional is her injection of a personal element, her social identity: "Mneme begin. Inspire, ye sacred nine,/Your vent'rous Afric in her great design." Wheatley's sense of an African identity is also present in her patriotic poems such as "America" (1784): "Thy Power, O Liberty, makes strong the weak/ And wond'rous instinct Ethiopians speak."

As was customary in her day, Wheatley wrote for and dedicated her poems to prominent citizens like George Washington and leading business and religious leaders. As bard of the upper classes—including slaveholders and pro-slavery figures like the Reverend George Whitefield, addressed in the following extract from "America"—she sang their praises and she lamented their sorrows:

> Be your complaints on his kind bosom laid:
> Take him, ye Africans, he longs for you,
> Impartial Saviour is his title due.

Illness, death, and dying are the private truths of women's lives: as wives and mothers, women in the eighteenth century lived in close contact with them. Wheatley wrote many vivid poems on the deaths of women and children, and she paid particular attention to the suffering of mothers. These poems particularize the emotion of loss, and they imply the importance of women's experience, which was largely ignored in her time. Wheatley made the death of a woman in a hurricane or the death of an infant as significant as that of a public figure. Her poems teach women how to survive the loss of husbands, sisters, brothers, fathers, and especially children. Social conditioning taught women to acquiesce silently when their children died, and Wheatley's "To a Gentleman and Lady on the Death of the Lady's Brother and Sister, and a Child of the Name of Avis, Aged One Year" (see p. 14) illustrates this training. Children are born to die, and after a brief sojourn on earth they return sinless to heaven:

> Resign thy friends to that Almighty hand,
> Which gave them life, and bow to his command;
> Thine Avis give without a murm'ring heart,
> Though half thy soul be fated to depart.
> To shining guards consign thine infant care
> To waft triumphant through the seas of air:
> Her soul enlarg'd to heav'nly pleasure springs,
> She feeds on truths and uncreated things.

Wheatley is sympathetic to her white patrons—white women in particular—in these poems on death and illness. She was characteristically deferential, and she insisted on observing the proper social distance between herself and her masters. She accepted the world of masters and servants and acted according to the accepted code that demanded that she be "humble, modest, wise." But in her poetry she can give advice of a personal and religious nature that would otherwise be unfitting. The rhetoric of religion allowed Wheatley a directness in her poetry that she could never assume in life. In addition, the Christian creed of love was such a strong part of Wheatley's thinking that a transgression against it could lead her gently to rebuke even white Christians, as she does in "On Being Brought from Africa to America":

> Some view our sable race with scornful eye,
> "Their colour is a diabolic die."
> Remember, Christians, Negroes, black as Cain,
> May be refin'd, and join the angelic train.

Here, as in many of her other poems, Wheatley demonstrates her faith in the saving grace of Christianity for people of every color.

Frances E. W. Harper is a product of the shifting literary emphases of mid- to late-nineteenth-century America. Her Christian humanism, her preoccupation with the state of her soul and of her neighbor's, her social awareness in terms of temperance, suffrage, and club and charity work, her race loyalty, and her empathy with the sufferings of women are all reflected in her prose and her poetry. Her novel, *Iola*

Leroy, or Shadows Uplifted (1892), incorporates features of both the historical romance and the emerging "problem" novel of realism. Harper's poems include elements of oratory and history, dialect and humor. They combine the simplicity and didactic nature of narrative poetry—like ballads—with the more formal qualities of polish, wit, and satire found in classical verse. Her writings encompass many varieties of tone: the sentimental and the idealized, the mundane and the humorous, and the seriousness of high morality that emphasizes the American values of thrift, industry, temperance, and initiative.

Harper's brand of religion had the resonance of an artistic and political credo. In contrast to Wheatley and in keeping with the Christian teachings concerning humility, Harper directed much of her poetry to the less fortunate, claiming that her purpose was to "make songs for the people . . . for the old and young" (from "Songs for the People," *Atlanta Offering Poems*, 1895). In her poems, she attends to such simple things as "A Grain of Sand," "Mary at the Feet of Christ," "The Mother's Blessing," "The Dying Bondsman," "The Sparrow's Fall," "Dandelions," "The Hermit's Sacrifice," "To a Babe Smiling in Her Sleep," and "The Dying Mother."

Harper was uncompromising in her attacks on the institution of slavery, and she was vitriolic in her criticism of white Christians who fail to show love and charity toward blacks. Her poetry reveals an awareness of the contradiction between Christian charity and the institution of slavery, as in "Simon's Countrymen" (*Idylls of the Bible*, 1901):

> And yet within our favored land,
>   Where Christian churches rise,
> The dark-browed sons of Africa
>   Are hated and despised.

Harper earned her living first as a teacher and then as an antislavery lecturer. After her husband of four years died, she resumed lecturing on temperance and black education. While she lived outside the narrow confines of hearth and home—the static ideal of "woman's sphere"—Harper nevertheless accepted the popular notion that women are civilizing influences on men and that the womanly virtues of piety, domesticity, and sacrifice strengthened manners and morals and assured the sanctity of the home. This faith in womanhood meshed with her antislavery beliefs to make her critical of white women whose silence on the issue of slavery amounted to complicity. In "An Appeal to My Countrywomen" (see p. 31) Harper suggests that those who "mourn o'er the exile of Russia" ought to look to the South and the "sobs of anguish" there. She concludes bitterly:

> Weep not, oh, my well-sheltered sisters,
>   Weep not for the Negro alone,
> But weep for your sons who must gather
>   The crops which their fathers have sown.

Thus Harper connects the lack of sisterhood between black and white women in America to their mutual enslavement under the patriarchy and the slavocracy.

The compelling issue of race did not override Harper's understanding of the sex and class similarities between black and white women. On the other hand, she was not so naive as to believe that universal suffrage would be a complete antidote to slavery or to sexism. As early as 1859 she wrote in "Is Money the Answer" (*The Anglo-African* 1, May 1859):

> It is no honor to shake hands politically with men who whip women and steal babies. If this government has no call for our services, no aim for our children, we have the greater need for them to build up a sure manhood and womanhood for ourselves.

Like Wheatley, Harper believed that ultimately only the saving grace of Christian love and sacrifice could triumph over these moral dilemmas ("The Burden of All" from *Poems* (Philadelphia: Merrihew, 1871):

> How to solve life's saddest problems,
>   Its weariness, want and woe,
> Was answered by one who suffered
>   In Palestine long ago.

Religion provided Harper with the moral basis for her antislavery stance, but it also supplied her with images that conveyed hope for the future. By recasting and retelling biblical stories and infusing them with the spirit of black life, Harper found a language that was accessible to blacks, who may have been illiterate but who knew these tales well. For example, in the parable "Deliverance" (*Idylls of the Bible*, 1901) Harper developed the parallel between the children of Israel and the recently freed black slaves:

> Shall Israel thro' long varied years
>   These memories cherish yet,
> And we who lately redeemed
>   Our broken chains forget?

Folk history is used here to imply both the nationhood of black people and the possibility of change. In fact, the frequency of parables in her poetry along with her popularity as an orator enhanced Harper's image as a tireless proselytizer.

Harper's protest poetry focuses on the right of women to rebel against unjust laws promulgated by those in authority. Her thorough biblical knowledge strengthened this view, for the Bible was replete with the stories of rebellious women: Esther, Vashti, Sarah, Miriam, Deborah. Harper's "Vashti" (see p. 27) celebrates the queen in Esther I who refuses to obey the king's command to "unveil her lovely face" before his "lords and mighty men." Vashti is banished. The king and his men assume her exile and loss of status will prevent other women, "restive 'neath our rule," from learning to "scorn our name." But it is Vashti who triumphs, for she maintains her integrity. She remains "a woman who could bend to grief / But would not bend to shame."

In *Moses: A Story of the Nile* (1869) Harper paints a bold portrait of a woman in rebellion against the authority of another king. Princess Charmian saves Moses from the death her father decreed. Similarly, "The Jewish Grandfather's Story" (*Sketches of Southern Life*, 1872) tells the story of Deborah and illustrates Harper's twin themes of rebellion and deliverance:

> How Deborah, neath her spreading palms,
>   A judge in Israel rose,
> And wrested victory from the hands
>   Of Jacob's heathen foes.

The theme of the woman rebel was not the only image that caught Harper's imagination: the flower provided her with an alternative and equally rich metaphor for women. Harper wrote several poems on the subject of flowers, and many others contain floral references. But her works that best illustrate the link between women and flowers are "The Crocuses" and the prose poem "The Mission of the Flowers" (see pp. 34–36). In them the flower serves as both an artistic and a political metaphor. In "The Crocuses" black women are crocuses and "daughters of the sun," while white women are daffodils and daisies and "fairhaired dandelions." Harper delights in "a host of lovely flowers," but it is the crocuses whose "rich tints of beauty rare" she singles out for special praise. Her message is much more obvious in "The Mission of the Flowers," where the much favored rose is given her wish that "every flower could . . . be a rose." Through the devastation the arrogant rose brings to the garden Harper illustrates for her readers the necessity of respecting "the individuality of . . . sister flowers [who have] . . . their own missions."

Harper wrote odes, lyrics, and fashionable eulogies in addition to protest poetry. *Sketches of Southern Life* (1872) contains several dialect narrative poems. In them Harper uses humor to defuse the politically sensitive subjects of suffrage and slavery. "Aunt Chloe" is a long local-color poem in which Aunt Chloe has the last laugh at the expense of the "Mistus," who "prayed up in the parlor" while his slaves "were praying in the cabins / Wanting freedom to begin." Slavery was a serious matter for Harper. Nevertheless, she often brought to the subject a graceful humor, as in "Learning to Read" (see p. 29), also from *Sketches*. Slaves had been denied "book learning" by the "Rebs" for "twould make us all too wise." But the blacks persisted:

> I remember Uncle Caldwell,
>   Who took pot liquor fat
> And greased the pages of his book,
>   And hid it in his hat.
>
> And had his master ever seen
>   The leaves upon his head,
> He'd have thought them greasy papers,
>   But nothing to be read.

The literary history of black women poets in the eighteenth and nineteenth centuries had an auspicious beginning in the work of Terry, Wheatley, Harper, and their sister poets. Yet this history is neither completely documented nor widely appreciated. Many black women accepted their society's racist assumptions and made little effort to preserve their writings. What remains of their diaries, letters, and journals lies buried in archives and private holdings scattered throughout the country. Though they have not been valued as literary texts or as historical documents, the material contains details that historians and literary scholars should be aware of. For example, the journal of Charlotte Forten [Grimké] (1837–1914), one of the few of these documents that has been published, allows us to establish one link of literary history. Forten wrote on July 28, 1854:

> This evening read poems of Phillis Wheatley an African slave who lived in Boston at the time of the Revolution. She was a wonderfully gifted woman and many of her poems are very beautiful. Her character and genius afford a striking proof of the falseness of the assertion made by some that hers is an inferior race.*

The Journal of Charlotte L. Forten edited with an introduction by Ray Allen Billington (New York: Dryden Press, 1953). This is the earliest known journal kept by a black American woman and covers the years 1854 to 1864. It remained in manuscript for a century.

Other black women published their poetry anonymously or used a nom de plume. Poems against slavery by "Ada" appeared regularly in William Lloyd Garrison's *The Liberator* between 1836 and 1855. She called herself "a young woman of color" and was reportedly from Philadelphia. But that is all we know of her. Documentation is further complicated by the fact that these women published in a wide variety of religious journals, temperance and antislavery magazines, Afro-American newspapers, and popular journals and weeklies, many of which are now rare, including *A. M. E. Church Review, Anglo-African, Women's Era, Monthly Review, Atlantic Monthly, Golden Days, Ringwood's Magazine, Free Speech* (edited by Ida B. Wells), *St. Martin's Lyceum, Woman's Light and Love, Waverly Magazine,* the *Boston Herald,* and the *Philadelphia Press.*

Not only were many records not preserved and much of the poetry lost in ephemeral journals, but publishers also seemed loath to produce books of poetry by black women. Aside from the single volume by Wheatley and a few others by Harper, there was no book-length collection of poems by a black woman published in the United States before 1890. Some women had their work published in England. Maria and Harriet Falconar arranged to have their *Poems on Slavery* published in London in 1788. Even the popular Wheatley was bullied by the literary establishment. Editors who were not always sympathetic poured over and selected from her corpus. Her poetry was censored in the United States and some poems were published only in England.

But there was no lack of intellect, imagination, and energy among black women. In 1774 "Happy" Kate Ferguson opened New York's first Sabbath School and became known as "the dusky hand that broke the alabaster box." Though she had been born a slave, Ferguson eventually educated as many as twenty-five black and white students at a time in her school. Eight years later Deborah Bannett enlisted in the Revolutionary Army as Robert Shurtliffe. She served from May 1782 through October 1783, when she retired with a pension. Elizabeth Freeman, better known as "Mum Bett," and Jenny Slew of Ipswich, Massachusetts, sued for and won their liberty under the Bill of Rights in 1791. Harriet Tubman—a scout, spy, and nurse for the Union Army, and a fugitive herself—returned to the South at least nineteen times to help more than four hundred slaves escape. Sojourner Truth was also a fugitive who worked in the antislavery, suffrage, and temperance movements. Harper managed to support a family on her writing and lecturing after she was widowed. The point of this list is to demonstrate that the talent—in every sphere of life from art to war—*was there.* To explain why almost none of the black women of the period were taken seriously enough as poets to be published in book form, we have to look at the publishing industry and the social bias that that industry reflected.

Facing racial and sexual oppression, further crippled by poverty, black women did not have control of the institutions that enable writers to get their thoughts and visions into print. Even if all the preparatory routes to publication were not filled with obstacles, their way was still blocked by the business interests of the publishing industry. Books by black women were not profitable and were thought to have "limited appeal." Decisions not to print, distribute, and promote the works guaranteed, of course, that their appeal would remain limited. A glance at the bibliography of *Black Sister* (see pp. 295–312) shows how little this has changed. It has only been within the last decade or so that there has been any substantial increase in the number of works published and this increase can be attributed in part to the rise of black controlled firms like Broadside Press and Lotus Press in Detroit.

Kristen Hunter is speaking of the modern blues singer in her poem "Sepia Nightingale," (*The Landlord*, 1966) yet she sums up the position of the black woman poet in the eighteenth and nineteenth centuries as well:

> She's only the Sepia Nightingale . . . the
> Queen of the Blues. The Tragic Voice of the
> Twenties and Thirties. She started out
> in New Orleans. When she came to Harlem,
> the lines stretched for five blocks out-
> side Small's Paradise. The cover charge
> went to ten dollars, and *still* they
> stretched. She had rooms full of orchids.
> Cars a block long. Proposals from Euro-
> pean royalty. She only made a few records.
> And then she disappeared. . . . *Where is She?*

LUCY TERRY
(1730–1821)

BARS FIGHT, AUGUST 28, 1746

August 'twas, the twenty-fifth,
Seventeen hundred forty-six,
The Indians did in ambush lay,
Some very valient men to slay,
The names of whom I'll not leave out:
Samuel Allen like a hero fout,
And though he was so brave and bold,
His face no more shall we behold;
Eleazer Hawks was killed outright,
Before he had time to fight,
Before he did the Indians see,
Was shot and killed immediately;
Oliver Amsden, he was slain,
Which caused his friends much grief and pain;
Simeon Amsden they found dead,
Not many rods off from his head;
Adonijah Gillet, we do hear,
Did lose his life, which was so dear;
John Saddler fled across the water,
And so escaped the dreadful slaughter;
Eunice Allen see the Indians comeing,
And hoped to save herself by running,
And had not her petticoats stopt her,
The awful creatures had not cotched her,
And tommyhawked her on the head,
And left her on the ground for dead;
Young Samuel Allen, oh! lack-a-day,
Was taken and carried to Canada.

    Written in 1746; published in *A History of Deerfield, Massachusetts* by George Sheldon (Deerfield: 1895).

PHILLIS WHEATLEY
(ca. 1753–1784)

Selection from
LIBERTY AND PEACE, A POEM

Lo! Freedom comes. Th' prescient Muse foretold,
    All Eyes the' accomplish'd Prophecy behold:
Her Port describ'd, "*She moves divinely fair,*
Olive and Laurel bind her golden Hair."
She, the bright Progeny of Heaven, descends,
And every Grace her sovereign Step attends;
For now kind Heaven, indulgent to our Prayer,
In smiling *Peace* resolves the Din of *War.*
Fix'd in *Columbia* her illustrious Line,
And bids in thee her future Councils shine.
To every Realm her Portals open'd wide,
Receives from each the full commercial Tide.
Each Art and Science now with rising Charms,
Th' expanding Heart with Emulation warms.
E'en great *Britannia* sees with dread Surprize,
And from the dazzling Splendor turns her Eyes!
Britain, whose Navies swept the' *Atlantic* o'er,
And Thunder sent to every distant Shore;
E'en thou, in Manners cruel as thou art,
The Sword resign'd, resume the friendly Part.

According to Julian D. Mason, editor of *The Poems of Phillis Wheatley* (Chapel Hill: University of North Carolina Press, 1966), the poem from which this selection was taken was first published in 1784 as a four page pamphlet by Warden and Russell, Marlborough Street, Boston. It is also one of the two poems that Wheatley published under her married name, Phillis Peters. In lines 3 and 4 Wheatley quotes from an earlier poem of hers, "His Excellency, General Washington," written in 1776.

TO A GENTLEMAN AND LADY ON THE DEATH OF THE LADY'S BROTHER AND SISTER, AND A CHILD OF THE NAME AVIS, AGED ONE YEAR

On *Death's* domain intent I fix my eyes,
Where human nature in vast ruin lies:
With pensive mind I search the drear abode,
Where the great conqu'ror has his spoils, bestow'd;
There, there the offspring of six thousand years
In endless numbers to my view appears;
Whole kingdoms in his gloomy den are thrust,
And nations mix with their primeval dust:
Insatiate still he gluts the ample tomb;
His is the present, his the age to come.
See here a brother, here a sister spread,
And a sweet daughter mingled with the dead.

But, *Madam,* let your grief be laid aside,
And let the fountain of your tears be dry'd;
In vain they flow to wet the dusty plain,
Your sighs are wafted to the skies in vain,
Your pains they witness, but they can no more,
While *Death* reigns tyrant o'er this mortal shore.

The glowing stars and silver queen of light
At last must perish in the gloom of night:
Resign thy friends to that Almighty hand,
Which gave them life, and bow to his command;
Thine *Avis* give without a murm'ring heart,
Though half thy soul be fated to depart.
To shining guards consign thine infant care
To waft triumphant through the seas of air:
Her soul enlarg'd to heav'nly pleasure springs,
She feeds on truth and uncreated things.
Methinks I hear her in the realms above,
And leaning forward with a filial love,

The poems by Phillis Wheatley are from her collection *Poems on Various Subjects, Religious and Moral* (London: A. Bell, Bookseller, Aldgate and sold by Messrs. Cox and Berry, King Street, Boston, 1773).

Invite you there to share immortal bliss
Unknown, untasted in a state like this.
With tow'ring hopes, and growing grace arise,
And seek beautitude beyond the skies.

TO S.M. A YOUNG AFRICAN PAINTER,
ON SEEING HIS WORK

To show the lab'ring bosom's deep intent,
And thought in living characters to paint,
When first thy pencil did those beauties give,
And breathing figures learned from thee to live,
How did those prospects give my soul delight,
A new creation rushing on my sight?
Still, wond'rous youth, each noble path pursue,
On deathless glories fix thine ardent view:
Still may the painter's and the poet's fire
To aid thy pencil, and thy verse conspire!
And may the charms of each seraphic theme
Conduct thy footsteps to immortal fame!
High to the blissful wonders of the skies
Elate thy soul, and raise thy wishful eyes.
Thrice happy, when exalted to survey
That splendid city, crowned with endless day,
Whose twice six gates on radiant hinges ring:
Celestial Salem blooms in endless spring.
Calm and serene thy moments glide along,
And may the muse inspire each future song!
Still, with the sweets of contemplation blessed,
May peace with balmy wings your soul invest.
But when these shades of time are chased away,
And darkness ends in everlasting day,
On what seraphic pinions shall we move,
And view the landscapes in the realm above?
There shall thy tongue in heav'nly murmurs flow,
And there my muse with heav'nly transport glow:

According to William H. Robinson, editor of *Early Black American Poets* (1969)
S.M. was "Scipio Moorhead, a Negro artist, servant to Rev. John Moorhead of Boston."

No more to tell of Damon's tender sighs,
Or rising radiance of Aurora's eyes,
For nobler themes demand a nobler strain,
And purer language on th' ethereal plain.
Cease, gentle muse! the solemn gloom of night
Now seals the fair creation from my sight.

ON IMAGINATION

Thy various works, imperial queen, we see,
How bright their forms! how decked with pomp by thee!
Thy wond'rous acts in beauteous order stand,
And all attest how potent is thine hand.
From *Helicon's* refulgent heights attend
Ye sacred choir, and my attempts befriend:
To tell her glories with a faithful tongue,
Ye blooming graces, triumph in my song.
Now here, now there, the roving *Fancy* flies,
Till some lov'd object strikes her wand'ring eyes,
Whose silken fetters all the senses bind,
And soft captivity involves the mind.
Imagination! who can sing thy force?
Or who describe the swiftness of thy course?
Soaring through air to find the bright abode,
Th' empyreal palace of the thund'ring God,
We on thy pinions can surpass the wind,
And leave the rolling universe behind:
From star to star the mental optics rove,
Measure the skies, and range the realms above.
There in one view we grasp the mighty whole,
Or with new worlds amaze th' unbounded soul.
Through Winter's frowns to Fancy's raptur'd eyes
The fields may flourish, and gay scenes arise;
The frozen deeps may break their iron bands,
And bid their waters murmur o'er the sands.
Fair *Flora* may resume her fragrant reign,
And with her flow'ry riches deck the plain;
Sylvanus may diffuse his honors round,
And all the forest may with leaves be crown'd:

Show'rs may descend, and dews their gems disclose,
And nectar sparkle on the blooming rose.
Such is thy pow'r, nor are thine orders vain,
O thou the leader of the mental train:
In full perfection all thy works are wrought,
And thine the sceptre o'er the realms of thought.
Before thy throne the subject-passions bow,
Of subject-passions sov'reign ruler thou:
At thy command joy rushes on the heart,
And through the glowing veins the spirits dart.
Fancy might now her silken pinions try
To rise from earth, and sweep th' expanse on high;
From *Tithon's* bed now might *Aurora* rise,
Her cheeks all glowing with celestial dyes,
While a pure stream of light o'erflows the skies.
The monarch of the day I might behold,
And all the mountains tip't with radiant gold,
But I reluctant leave the pleasing views,
Which *Fancy* dresses to delight the *Muse*;
Winter austere forbids me to aspire,
And northern tempests damp the rising fire;
They chill the tides of *Fancy's* flowing sea,
Cease then, my song, cease the unequal lay.

ADA

LINES

Suggested on Reading 'An Appeal to Christian Women of the
South,' by A.E. Grimké.

My spirit leans in joyousness tow'rd thine,
My gifted sister, as with gladdened heart
My vision flies along thy 'speaking pages.'
Well hast thou toiled in Mercy's sacred course;

Published in *The Liberator* 6 (October 29, 1836).

And thus another strong and lasting thread
Is added to the woof our sex is weaving,
With skill and industry, for Freedom's garb.
Precious the privilege to labor here,
Worthy the lofty mind and handy-work
Of Chapman, Chandler, Child and Grimke too.
There is much in woman's influence, ay much,
To swell the rolling tide of sympathy,
And are those champions of a fettered race,   »
Now laboring arduous in the moral field.
One may not 'cry aloud' as they are bid,
And lift our voices in the *public* ear;
Nor yet be mute. The pen is ours to wield,
The heart to will, and hands to execute.
And more the gracious promise gives to all
Ask, says the saviour, and ye shall receive.
In concert then, Father of love, we join,
To wrestle with thy presence, as of old
Did Israel, and will not let thee go
Until them bless. The cause is thine—for tis
Thy guiltless poor who are oppressed, on whom
The sun of Freedom may not cast his beams,
Nor dew of heavenly knowledge e'er descend.
And for their fearless advocates we ask
The wisdom of the serpent—above all,
Our heavenly Father, clothe, oh clothe them with
The dove-like spirit of thine own dear Son.
Then are they safe; tho' persecution's waves
Dash o'er their backs, and furious winds assail—
Still they are safe.
                  Yes, this is woman's work,
Her own appropriate sphere; and nought should drive
Her from the mercy seat, til mercy's work be finished.
                  Whose is that wail, piercing the ear
Of night, with agony too deep for words
To give birth? 'Tis woman's—she of Ramab—
Another Rachel, weeping for her babes,
And will not be consoled, for they are not.
Oh! slavery, with all its withering power,
Can never wholly quench the flame of love,
Nor dry the stream of tenderness that flows

In breasts maternal. *A mother's love!* deep grows
That plant of Heaven, fast by the well of life,
And nought can pluck it thence till woman cease
To be. Then, long as mothers' hearts are breaking
Beneath the hammer of the auctioneer,
And ruthless Avarice tears asunder bonds,
That the fiat of the Almighty joined,
So long should woman's melting voice be heard,
In intercession strong and deep, that this
Accused thing, this Achan in our camp,
May be removed.

[UNTITLED]

'Call it not an idle fancy to wish that trees should wave, and birds sing, over this wasted form; for nature has been so lovely to me, that I have a kind of gratitude to her, and it is sweet to think that I shall repose among those objects which God has given me sensibility to enjoy.'—C. Gilman.

Oh, when this earthly tenement
    Shall join its kindred clay,
And when this feverish being, frail,
    Shall sink to earth away;
No costly marble shall be reared,
    No Mausoleum's pride—
Nor chiselled stone be raised, to tell
    That I have lived and died.

For I would seek a resting place
    Among my favorite bowers,
'Mid warbling birds, and waving trees,
    And amaranthine flowers.
Delightful thought! that when the toils
    And cares of life shall close,
Amid the scenes I love so well,
    Shall be my last repose.

But, anxious, thus, for that which dies,
    Forget not, oh, my soul,

Thy own immortal destiny,
    The spirit's higher goal;
So live, that when thy summons comes,
    To join the train gone by,
Thou may attain a brighter home,
    A home beyond the sky.

LINES

On the suppression, by a portion of our public journals, of the intelligence of the Abolition of Slavery in the British West Indies.

From fair Jamaica's fertile plains,
    Where joyous summer smiles,
To where eternal winter reigns,
    On Greenland's naked isles;
Or, from Barbadoes, eastward borne,
    Upon the fresh'ning breeze,
To every sunny isle that decks
    The Asiatic seas;

Wherever mild Religion's light
    Has shed its cheering ray,
Or where the gloom of heathen night
    Excludes the Gospel day—
Where e'er the poor down-trodden slave
    In weary bondage pines,
From proud Columbia's fair domain,
    'To Sibir's dreary mines'—

Truth shall prevail, and Freedom's light
    Shall speed its onward course,
Impeded by no human might,
    Quelled by no human force.
Vain, then, the endeavor to suppress,
    In this enlightened land,
Those tidings which create such joy
    Upon West Indies' strand.

Published in The Liberator 8 (September 28, 1839).

No sword was drawn, no blood was spilt
    Upon the verdant sod,
Yet man, enfranchised, stands erect,
    The image of his God.
Then let the joyful news be given
    To every human ear,
Which e'en the Angels, high in Heaven,
    Might lean to earth to hear.

TO THE MEMORY OF J. HORACE KIMBALL,

Late Editor of the Herald of Freedom

Another youthful advocate of truth and right has gone;
Called from the moral battle-field ere victory was won.
Bright spirit, though, we humbly trust, to thee henceforth is given
A crown of life and golden harp within the courts of Heaven,
We mourn the aching void thus left in many a Christian heart,
And from the founts of sympathy, the gathering teardrops start.
Nor 'midst New England's bills alone, shall gushing tears be shed
For thee, the loved and early lost, now numbered with the dead;
But in those islands, once in bonds, where Freedom's light now
    shines,
Or where, in weary vassalage, the sad apprentice pines,
Those 'thoughts that breathe, those words that burn,'* thy monument
    shall stand,
And, as we trace each graphic sketch, drawn by a master hand,
We mourn the buds of promise crushed in manhood's opening years,
And every page on which we dwell is moistened with our tears.

How often when the soul recedes from earth and earthly schemes,
The Heaven-born fires of intellect send forth their brightest gleams;
The spirit, freed from cares of time, exulting, walks abroad,
And, in 'communion large and high,' holds converse with her God.
Thus, though Consumption's vampyre grasp had seized thy mortal
    frame,

Published in *The Liberator* 8 (May 18, 1838).
    *The editors of *The Liberator* tell us that this line alludes to "the interesting volume just published, entitled Emancipation in the West Indies. A six month tour in Antigua, Barbadoes and Jamaica, in the year 1837: By James A. Thome, and J. Horace Kimball."

Thy ardent and aspiring mind, untouched, remained the same;
And, as on Pisgah's lofty mount the Prophet took his stand,
And, from its cloud-capt heights, afar, beheld the promised land,
So, from the realms of Hope and Faith, thy spirit's wings, unfurled,
Soared high to view a brighter scene, the wide, enfranchised world.
'Mid contemplation, such as these, the King of Terrors came,
Devoid of dread to those who love their blest Redeemer's name.
'If spirits ever earthward flee,' thine well might linger near,
For, e'en though dead, thou speakest still, by thy example here,
Green be the turf upon thy tomb, thy Memory hallowed be,
When slavery's galling chains are loosed, and all the oppressed are
    free.

CHARLOTTE FORTEN [GRIMKÉ]
(1839–1914)

A PARTING HYMN

When Winter's royal robes of white
From hill and vale are gone
And the glad voices of the spring
Upon the air are borne,
Friends who have met with us before,
Within these walls shall meet no more.

Forth to a noble work they go:
O, may their hearts keep pure,
And hopeful zeal and strength be theirs
To labor and endure,
That they an earnest faith may prove
By words of truth and deeds of love.

May those, whose holy task it is,
To guide impulsive youth,
Fail not to cherish in their souls
A reverence for truth;
For teachings which the lips impart
Must have their source within the heart.

From *The Black Man* by William Wells Brown (New York, 1863), p. 191.

May all who suffer share their love—
The poor and the oppressed;
So shall the blessing of our God
Upon their labors rest.
And may we meet again where all
Are blest and freed from every thrall.

POEM

In the earnest path of duty,
    With the high hopes and hearts sincere,
We, to useful lives aspiring,
    Daily meet to labor here.

No vain dreams of earthly glory
    Urge us onward to explore
Far-extending realms of knowledge,
    With their rich and varied store;

But, with hope of aiding others,
    Gladly we perform our part;
Nor forget, the mind, while storing,
    We must educate the heart,—

Teach it hatred of oppression,
    Truest love of God and man;
Thus our high and holy calling
    May accomplish His great plan.

Not the great and gifted only
    He appoints to do his will,
But each one, however lowly,
    Has a mission to fulfill.

Knowing this, toil we unwearied,
    With true hearts and purpose high;—
We would win a wreath immortal
    Whose bright flowers ne'er fade and die.

Published in The Liberator 23 (August 24, 1856).

TO W.L.G.* ON READING HIS 'CHOSEN QUEEN'

A loyal subject, thou, to that bright Queen,
To whom the homage of thy soul is paid;
Long to her cause devoted hast thou been,
And many a sacrifice for her hast made.
Thy chosen Queen, O champion of Truth,
Should be th' acknowledged sovereign of all;
Her first commands should fire the heart of youth
And graver age list heedful to her call.
Thou, who so bravely dost her battles fight,
With truer weapons than the blood-stained sword,
And teachest us that greater is the might
Of *moral* warfare, noble thought and word,
On thee shall rest the blessing of mankind,
As one who nobly dost the Right defend;
Than thee, thy chosen Queen shall never find
A truer subject nor a firmer friend.

SOJOURNER TRUTH
(1797–1883)

AIN'T I A WOMAN?†

That man over there say
    a woman needs to be helped into carriages
and lifted over ditches
    and to have the best place everywhere.
Nobody ever helped me into carriages
    or over mud puddles
        or gives me a best place . . .

Published in *The Liberator* 22 (March 16, 1855).
*W.L.G. is William Lloyd Garrison, abolitionist and editor of *The Liberator*.

†There is no exact copy of this speech given at the Women's Rights Convention in Akron, Ohio in 1852. The speech has been adapted to the poetic format by Erlene Stetson from the copy found in *Sojourner, God's Faithful Pilgrim* by Arthur Huff Fauset (Chapel Hill: University of North Carolina Press, 1938.)

And ain't I a woman?
    Look at me
Look at my arm!
    I have plowed and planted
and gathered into barns
    and no man could head me . . .
And ain't I a woman?
    I could work as much
and eat as much as a man—
    when I could get to it—
and bear the lash as well
    and ain't I a woman?
I have born 13 children
    and seen most all sold into slavery
and when I cried out a mother's grief
    none but Jesus heard me . . .
and ain't I a woman?
    that little man in black there say
a woman can't have as much rights as a man
   cause Christ wasn't a woman
Where did your Christ come from?
    From God and a woman!
Man had nothing to do with him!
    If the first woman God ever made
was strong enough to turn the world
    upside down, all alone
together women ought to be able to turn it
    rightside up again.

FRANCES E[LLEN] W[ATKINS] HARPER
(1825–1911)

A DOUBLE STANDARD

Do you blame me that I loved him?
    If when standing all alone
I cried for bread, a careless world
    Pressed to my lips a stone?

Do you blame me that I loved him,
    That my heart beat glad and free,
When he told me in the sweetest tones
    He loved but only me?

Can you blame me that I did not see,
    Beneath his burning kiss,
The serpent's wiles, nor even less hear
    The deadly adder hiss?

Can you blame me that my heart grew cold,
    That the tempted, tempter turned—
When he was feted and caressed
    And I was coldly spurned?

Would you blame him, when you drew from me
    Your dainty robes aside,
If he with gilded baits should claim
    Your fairest as his bride?

Would you blame the world if it should press
    On him a civic crown;
And see me struggling in the depth,
    Then harshly press me down?

Crime has no sex and yet today
    I wear the brand of shame;
Whilst he amid the gay and proud
    Still bears an honored name.

From *Poems* by Frances E. W. Harper (Philadelphia: George S. Ferguson, 1895).

Can you blame me if I've learned to think
    Your hate of vice a sham,
When you so coldly crushed me down,
    And then excused the man?

Yes, blame me for my downward course,
    But oh! remember well,
Within your homes you press the hand
    That led me down to hell!

I'm glad God's ways are not your ways,
    He does not see as man;
Within his love I know there's room
    For those whom others ban.

I think before His great white throne,
    His theme of spotless light,
That whited sepulchres shall wear
    The hue of endless night.

That I who fell, and he who sinned,
    Shall reap as we have sown;
That each the burden of his loss
    Must bear and bear alone.

No golden weights can turn the scale
    Of justice in His sight;
And what is wrong in woman's life
    In man's cannot be right.

VASHTI

She leaned her head upon her hand
    And heard the King's decree—
"My lords are feasting in my halls;
    Bid Vashti* come to me.

"I've shown the treasures of my house,
    My costly jewels rare,

From *Atlanta Offering Poems* by Frances E. W. Harper (Philadelphia: George S. Ferguson, 1895).

*For the story of Vashti, see the Bible, Esther I.

But with the glory of her eyes
    No rubies can compare.

"Adorned and crowned, I'd have her come,
    With all her queenly grace,
And mid my lords and mighty men
    Unveil her lovely face.

"Each gem that sparkles in my crown,
    Or glitters on my throne,
Grows poor and pale when she appears,
    My beautiful, my own!"

All waiting stood the chamberlains
    To hear the Queen's reply.
They saw her cheek grow deathly pale,
    But light flashed to her eye:

"Go, tell the King," she proudly said,
    "That I am Persia's Queen,
And by his crowd of merry men
    I never will be seen.

"I'll take the crown from off my head,
    And tread it 'neath my feet,
Before their rude and careless gaze
    My shrinking eyes shall meet.

"A Queen unveiled before the crowd!
    Upon each lip my name!—
Why, Persia's women all would blush
    And weep for Vashti's shame.

"Go back!" she cried, and waved her hand,
    And grief was in her eye:
"Go tell the King," she sadly said,
    "That I would rather die."

They brought her message to the King;
    Dark flashed his angry eye;
'Twas as the lightning ere the storm
    Hath swept in fury by.

Then bitterly outspoke the King,
    Through purple lips of wrath—
"What shall be done to her who dares
    To cross your monarch's path?"

Then spake his wily counsellors—
    "O, King of this fair land,
From distant Ind to Ethiop,
    All bow to thy command.

But if, before thy servants' eyes,
    This thing they plainly see,
That Vashti doth not heed thy will
    Nor yield herself to thee,

The women, restive 'neath our rule,
    Would learn to scorn our name,
And from her deed to us would come
    Reproach and burning shame.

Then, gracious King, sign with thy hand
    This stern but just decree,
That Vashti lay aside her crown,
    Thy Queen no more to be."

She heard again the King's command,
    And left her high estate;
Strong in her earnest womanhood,
    She calmly met her fate,   — *dignified / virtuous to the end*

And left the palace of the King,
    Proud of her spotless name—
A woman who could bend to grief
    But would not bend to shame.

LEARNING TO READ

Very soon the Yankee teachers
    Came down and set up school;
But, oh! how the Rebs did hate it,—
    It was agin' their rule.

Our masters always tried to hide
    Book learning from our eyes;

From *Sketches of Southern Life* by Frances E. W. Harper (Philadelphia: Merrihew, 1872).

Knowledge didn't agree with slavery—
 'Twould make us all too wise.

But some of us would try to steal
 A little from the book,
And put the words together,
 And learn by hook or crook.

I remember Uncle Caldwell,
 Who took pot liquor fat
And greased the pages of his book,
 And hid it in his hat.

And had his master ever seen
 The leaves upon his head,
He'd have thought them greasy papers,
 But nothing to be read.

And there was Mrs. Turner's Ben,
 Who heard the children spell,
And picked the words right up by heart,
 And learned to read 'em well.

Well, the Northern folks kept sending
 The Yankee teachers down;
And they stood right up and helped us,
 Though the Rebs did sneer and frown.

And I longed to read my Bible,
 For precious words it said;
But when I begun to learn it,
 Folks just shook their heads.

And said there is no use trying,
 Oh! Chloe, you're too late;
But I was rising sixty,
 I had no time to wait.

So I got a pair of glasses,
 And straight to work I went,
And never stopped till I could read
 The hymns and Testament.

Then I got a little cabin,
 A place to call my own—
And I felt as independent
 As the queen upon her throne.

AN APPEAL TO MY COUNTRYWOMEN

You can sigh o'er the sad-eyed Armenian
    Who weeps in her desolate home.
You can mourn o'er the exile of Russia
    From kindred and friends doomed to roam.

You can pity the men who have woven
    From passion and appetite chains
To coil with a terrible tension
    Around their heartstrings and brains.

You can sorrow o'er little children
    Disinherited from their birth,
The wee waifs and toddlers neglected,
    Robbed of sunshine, music and mirth.

For beasts you have gentle compassion;
    Your mercy and pity they share.
For the wretched, outcast and fallen
    You have tenderness, love and care.

But hark! from our Southland are floating
    Sobs of anguish, murmurs of pain,
And women heart-stricken are weeping
    Over their tortured and their slain.

On their brows the sun has left traces;
    Shrink not from their sorrow in scorn.
When they entered the threshold of being
    The children of a King were born.

Each comes as a guest to the table
    The hand of our God has outspread,
To fountains that ever leap upward,
    To share in the soil we all tread.

When ye plead for the wrecked and fallen,
    The exile from far-distant shores,
Remember that men are still wasting
    Life's crimson around your own doors.

Have ye not, oh, my favored sisters,
    Just a plea, a prayer or a tear,

From *Poems* by Frances E. W. Harper (Philadelphia: George S. Ferguson, 1895).

For mothers who dwell 'neath the shadows
    Of agony, hatred and fear?

Men may tread down the poor and lowly,
    May crush them in anger and hate,
But surely the mills of God's justice
    Will grind out the grist of their fate.

Oh, people sin-laden and guilty,
    So lusty and proud in your prime,
The sharp sickles of God's retribution
    Will gather your harvest of crime.

Weep not, oh my well-sheltered sisters,
    Weep not for the Negro alone,
But weep for your sons who must gather
    The crops which their fathers have sown.

Go read on the tombstones of nations
    Of chieftains who masterful trod,
The sentence which time has engraven,
    That they had forgotten their God.

'Tis the judgment of God that men reap
    The tares which in madness they sow,
Sorrow follows the footsteps of crime,
    And Sin is the consort of Woe.

SHE'S FREE!

How say that by law we may torture and chase
A woman whose crime is the hue of her face?—
With her step on the ice, and her arm on her child,
The danger was fearful, the pathway was wild. . . .
But she's free! yes, free from the land where the slave,
From the hand of oppression, must rest in the grave;
Where bondage and blood, where scourges and chains,
Have placed on our banner indelible stains. . . .

From *Poems on Miscellaneous Subjects* by Frances E. W. Harper (Philadelphia: J. B. Ferrington & Son, 1854).

The bloodhounds have miss'd the scent of her way,
The hunter is rifled and foiled of his prey,
The cursing of men and clanking of chains
Make sounds of strange discord on Liberty's plains. . . .
Oh! poverty, danger and death she can brave,
For the child of her love is no longer a slave.

THE CROCUSES

They heard the South wind sighing
    A murmur of the rain;
And they knew that Earth was longing
    To see them all again.

While the snow-drops still were sleeping
    Beneath the silent sod;
They felt their new life pulsing
    Within the dark, cold clod.

Not a daffodil nor daisy
    Had dared to raise its head;
Not a fairhaired dandelion
    Peeped timid from its bed;

Though a tremor of the winter
    Did shivering through them run;
Yet they lifted up their foreheads
    To greet the vernal sun.

And the sunbeams gave them welcome.
    As did the morning air—
And scattered o'er their simple robes
    Rich tints of beauty rare.

Soon a host of lovely flowers
    From vales and woodland burst;
But in all that fair procession
    The crocuses were first.

From *Atlanta Offering Poems* by Frances E. W. Harper (Philadelphia: George S. Ferguson, 1895).

First to weave for Earth a chaplet
To crown her dear old head;
And to beautify the pathway
Where winter still did tread.

And their loved and white haired mother
Smiled sweetly 'neath the touch,
When she knew her faithful children
Were loving her so much.

THE MISSION OF THE FLOWERS

In a lovely garden, filled with fair and blooming flowers, stood a beautiful rose tree. It was the centre of attraction, and won the admiration of every eye; its beauteous flowers were sought to adorn the bridal wreath and deck the funeral bier. It was a thing of joy and beauty, and its earth mission was a blessing. Kind hands plucked its flowers to gladden the chamber of sickness and adorn the prisoner's lonely cell. Young girls wore them 'mid their clustering curls, and grave brows relaxed when they gazed upon their wondrous beauty. Now the rose was very kind and generous hearted, and, seeing how much joy she dispensed, wished that every flower could only be a rose, and like herself have the privilege of giving joy to the children of men; and while she thus mused, a bright and lovely spirit approached her and said, "I know thy wishes and will grant thy desires. Thou shalt have power to change every flower in the garden to thine own likeness. When the soft winds come wooing thy fairest buds and flowers, thou shalt breathe gently of thy sister plants, and beneath thy influence they shall change to beautiful roses." The rose tree bowed her head in silent gratitude to the gentle being who had granted her this wondrous power. All night the stars bent over her from their holy homes above, but she scarcely heeded their vigils. The gentle dews nestled in her arms and kissed the cheeks of her daughters; but she hardly noticed them;—she was waiting for the soft airs to

From *Idylls of the Bible* by Frances E. W. Harper (Philadelphia: George S. Ferguson, 1901).

awaken and seek her charming abode. At length the gentle airs greeted her, and she hailed them with a joyous welcome, and then commenced her work of change. The first object that met her vision was a tulip superbly arrayed in scarlet and gold. When she was aware of the intention of her neighbor, her cheeks flamed with anger, her eyes flashed indignantly, and she haughtily refused to change her proud robes for the garb the rose tree had prepared for her; but she could not resist the spell that was upon her, and she passively permitted the garments of the rose to enfold her yielding limbs. The verbenas saw the change that had fallen upon the tulip and dreading that a similar fate awaited them, crept closely to the ground, and, while tears gathered in their eyes, they felt a change pass through their sensitive frames, and instead of gentle verbenas they were blushing roses. She breathed upon the sleepy poppies; a deeper slumber fell upon their senses, and when they awoke, they too had changed to bright and beautiful roses. The heliotrope read her fate in the lot of her sisters, and bowing her fair head in silent sorrow, gracefully submitted to her unwelcome destiny. The violets, whose mission was to herald the approach of spring, were averse to losing their identity. "Surely," said they, "we have a mission as well as the rose;" but with heavy hearts they saw themselves changed like their sister plants. The snow drop drew around her robes of virgin white; she would not willingly exchange them for the most brilliant attire that ever decked a flower's form; to her they were the emblems of purity and innocence; but the rose tree breathed upon her, and with a bitter sob she reluctantly consented to the change. The dahlias lifted their heads proudly and defiantly; they dreaded the change, but scorned submission; they loved the fading year, and wished to spread around his dying couch their brightest, fairest flowers; but vainly they struggled, the doom was upon them, and they could not escape. A modest lily that grew near the rose tree shrank instinctively from her; but it was in vain, and with tearful eyes and trembling limbs she yielded, while a quiver of agony convulsed her frame. The marygolds sighed submissively and made no remonstrance. The garden pinks grew careless, and submitted without a murmur, while other flowers, less fragrant or less fair, paled with sorrow or reddened with anger; but the spell of the rose tree was upon them, and every flower was changed by her power, and that once beautiful garden was overran with roses; it had become a perfect wilderness of roses; the garden had changed, but that variety which had lent it so much beauty was gone, and men grew tired of roses, for they were everywhere. The smallest violet peeping faintly from its bed would have been welcome, the humblest primrose would have been hailed with delight,—even a dandelion would have been a harbinger of joy; and when the rose saw that the children of men were dissatisfied with the change she had made, her heart grew sad within her, and she wished the power had never been given her to change her sister plants to roses, and tears came into her eyes as she mused, when suddenly a rough wind shook her drooping form, and she opened her eyes and found that she had only been dreaming. But an important lesson had been taught; she had learned to respect the individuality of her sister flowers, and began to see that they, as well as herself, had their own missions,—some to gladden the eye with their loveliness and thrill the soul with delight; some to transmit fragrance to the air; others to breathe a refining influence upon the world; some had power to lull the aching brow and soothe the weary heart and brain into forgetfulness; and of those whose mission she did not understand, she wisely concluded there must be some object in their creation, and resolved to be true to her own earth-mission, and lay her fairest buds and flowers upon the altars of love and truth.

HENRIETTA CORDELIA RAY
(1861?–1916)

ROBERT G. SHAW*

When War's red banner trailed along the sky,
And many a manly heart grew all aflame
With patriotic love and purest aim,
There rose a noble soul who dared to die,
If only Right could win. He heard the cry
Of struggling bondmen and he quickly came,
Leaving the haunts where Learning tenders fame
Unto her honored sons; for it was ay
A loftier cause that lured him on to death.
Brave men who saw their brothers held in chains,
Beneath his standard battled ardently.
O friend! O hero! thou who yielded breath
That others might share Freedom's priceless gains,
In rev'rent love we guard thy memory.

IDYL:

Sunrise

Down in the dell,
A rose-gleam fell
From azure aisles of space;
There with light tread
A maiden sped,
Sweet yearning in her face.

The poems of Henrietta Cordelia Ray are from her collection, *Poems* (New York: The Grafton Press, 1910).

*Ray tells us that "Robert Gould Shaw (1837–1863) was the Boston born colonel of the 54th Massachusetts volunteers, the first regiment of Negro troops from a free state mustered into United States service. He was killed leading his troops on an assault on Fort Wagner, South Carolina.

"Idyl" is a series of four poems, "Sunrise," "Noontide," "Sunset" (see the following page) and "Midnight."

Amid the sheen,
The lark, I ween,
Thrilled love-lays to his mate;
The maiden sang,
Her joy notes rang;
"He cometh, so I wait."

IDYL:

Sunset

In western skies
Rare radiance lies
Aslant from jeweled seas.
The nightingale
Tells not a tale
More tender to the breeze

Than he to her;
No thought could stir
The calm within her soul:
When life's a dream
Does it not seem
That love can all control?

TO MY FATHER

A leaf from Freedom's golden chaplet fair,
We bring to thee, dear father. Near her shrine
None came with holier purpose, nor was thine
Alone the soul's mute sanction; every prayer
Thy captive brother uttered found a share
In thy wide sympathy; to every sigh
That told the bondman's need thou didst incline.
No thought of guerdon hadst thou but to bear
A long part in Freedom's strife. To see
Sad lives illumined, fetters rent in twain,

Tears dried in eyes that wept for length of days—
Ah! was not that a recompense for thee?
And now where all life's mystery is plain,
Divine approval is thy sweetest praise.

MILTON

O, poet gifted with the sight divine!
To thee 'twas given Eden's groves to pace
With that first pair in whom the human race
Their kinship claim: and angels did incline—
Great Michael, holy Gabriel—to twine
Their heavenly logic, through which thou couldst trace
The rich outpourings of celestial grace
Mingled with argument, around the shrine
Where thou didst linger, vision-rapt, intent
To catch the sacred mystery of Heaven.
Nor was thy longing vain; a soul resolved
To ponder truth supreme to thee was lent;
For thy not *sightless* eyes the veil was riv'n,
Redemption's problem unto thee well solved.

THE DAWN OF LOVE

Within my casement came one night
The fairy Moon, so pure and white.
    Around my brow a coronet
    Of shining silver quaintly set
With rainbow gems, she there did place;
But where I turned my wistful face,
Lo! she had vanished, and my gaze
Saw naught save shadows 'mid the haze.

I felt a throb within my heart,
In which sad sorrow had no part;

Within my soul a yearning grew;
So sweet, it thrilled me through and through.
A flute's soft warble echoed nigh,
As if an angel fluttered by;
And on my lips there fell a kiss;—
Speak! fairy Moon, interpret this!

ANTIGONE AND OEDIPUS

Slow wand'ring came the sightless sire and she,
Great-souled Antigone, the Grecian maid,
Leading with pace majestic his sad steps,
On whose bowed head grim Destiny had laid
A hand relentless; oft the summer breeze
Raised the gold tresses from her veined cheek,
As with a dainty touch, so much she seemed
A being marvelous, regal, yet meek.

Thus spake sad Oedipus; "Ah! whither now,
O daughter of an aged sire blind,
Afar from Thebes' pure, crested colonnades,
Shall we, sad exiles, rest and welcome find?
Who will look on us with a pitying eye?
But unto me sweet resignation's balm
Suff'ring and courage bring; yet moments come
When naught restored my spirit's wounded calm.

"O rare dim vales and glitt'ring sunlit caves!
O vine-clad hills soft with the flush of dawn!
O silver cataract dancing off the sea,
And shad'wy pines and silent dewy lawn!
I ne'er can see you more. Alas, alas.
But whither go we? Speak! O daughter fair;
Thou must indeed be sight unto thy sire.
Does here a temple consecrate the air?"

"My father! grieve not for our distant land."
Thus made Antigone reply: "I see
Amid the forest's music-echoing aisles,
A spot of peace and blessed repose for thee.

In solemn loftiness the towers rear
Their stately pinnacles; my eyes behold
The holy laurel decked in festive robes,
The olive pale, waving in sunset gold.

"In the green leafage, tender nightingales
Are chanting dulcet harmonies meanwhile,
In the clear river's liquid radiance
The early stars, of sheen resplendent smile.
It is a sacred spot; here we may shun
Dangers that threaten, and in sweet content
Ere we need wander more, a few short days
May in these hallowed shades be calmly spent.

"My father! sorrow not because of Fate!
Perchance the gods may kindly deign to look
With glance benignant on our mournful doom.
Together thou and I, can we not brook
Th' assaults of stern-browed Destiny? May not
The fatal mesh contain some golden thread,
Ere it be spun complete with all thy woe?
Father! my father, raise thy drooping head."

"Immortal asphodels ne'er crowned a brow
More greenlike than is thine, my peerless child,
Calm-browed Antigone. Ah, woe, sad fate!"
Then spake Antigone with aspect mild:
"My father, cease thy sadness. Wherefore grieve?
Oh, let us dream that from the azure sky,
The Gods gaze on us with pitying glance.
O, let us hope a little ere we die."

CLARA ANN THOMPSON

HIS ANSWER

He prayed for patience; Care and Sorrow came,
    And dwelt with him, grim and unwelcome guests;
He felt their galling presence night and day;
And wondered if the Lord had heard him pray,
    And why his life was filled with weariness.

He prayed again; and now he prayed for light;
    The darkness parted, and the light shone in;
And lo! he saw the answer to his prayer—
His heart had learned, through weariness and care,
    The patience, that he deemed he'd sought in vain.

MRS. JOHNSON OBJECTS

Come right in this house, Will Johnson!
    Kin I teach you dignity?
Chasin' aft' them po' white children,
    Jest because you wan' to play.

Whut does po' white trash keer fah you?
    Want you keep away fum them,
Next, they'll be a-doing' meanness,
    An' a-givin' you the blame.

Don't come mumblin' 'bout their playthings,
    Yourn is good enough fah you;
'Twas the best that I could git you,
    An' you've got to make them do.

Go'n' to break you fum that habit,
    Yes, I am! An' mighty soon,

The poems by Clara Ann Thompson are from her collection, *Songs from Wayside* (Rossmoyne, Ohio: By the author, 1908).

Incomprehensible

Incomprehensible

Next, you'll grow up like the white-folks,
    All time whinin' fah the moon.

Runnin' with them po' white children—
    Go'n' to break it up, I say!—
Pickin' up their triflin' habits,
    Soon, you'll be as spilte as they.

Come on here, an' take the baby—
    Mind now! Don't you let her fall—
'Fo' I'll have you runnin' with them,
    I won't let you play at all.

Jest set there, an' mind the baby
    Till I tell you—You may go;
An' jest let me ketch you chasin'
    Aft' them white trash any mo'.

ANN PLATO

THE NATIVES OF AMERICA

"Tell me a story, father, please,"
And then I sat upon his knees.
Then answered he, "What speech make known,
Or tell the words of native tone,
Of how my Indian fathers dwelt,
And of sore oppression felt;
And how they mourned a land serene—
It was an ever mournful theme."

"Yes," I replied,—"I like to hear,
And bring my father's spirit near;
Of every pain they did forego,
Oh, please to tell me all you know.
In history often do I read
Of pain which none but they did heed."

The poems by Ann Plato are from her collection *Essays, Including Biographies and Miscellaneous Pieces in Prose and Poetry*. With an introduction by the Rev. James W. C. Pennington (Hartford, Conn.: 1841).

He thus began. "We were a happy race,
When we no tongue but ours did trace;
We were in ever peace,
We sold, we did release—
Our brethren, far remote and far unknown.
And spoke to them in silent, tender tone.
We all were then as in one band;
We joined and took each other's hand.
Our dress was suited to the clime;
Our food was such as roamed that time,
Our houses were of sticks composed—
No matter, for they us enclosed.

But then discovered was this land indeed
By European men, who then had need
Of this far country. Columbus came afar,
And this before we could say, 'Ah,
What meaneth this?'—We fell in cruel hands.
Though some were kind, yet others then held bands
Of cruel oppression. Then, too, foretold our chief—
'Beggars you will become—is my belief.'
We sold, then bought some lands,
We altogether moved in foreign lands.

War ensued. They knew the handling of firearms.
Mothers spoke—no fear this breast alarms,
'They will not cruelly us oppress,
Or this our lands possess.'
Alas, it was a cruel day. We were crushed.
Into the dark, dark woods we rushed
To seek refuge.
My daughter, we are now diminished, unknown,
Unfelt. Alas, no tender tone
To cheer us when the hunt is done;
Fathers asleep—were silent, every one.

Oh, silent the honor, and fierce the fight,
When my brothers were shrouded in night;
Strangers did us invade—strangers destroyed
The fields, which were by us enjoyed.

Our country is cultured, and looks all sublime,
Our fathers are sleeping who lived in the time
That I tell. Oh, could I tell them my grief
In its flow, that in roaming we find no relief.

I love my country, and shall until death
Shall cease my breath.
Now, daughter dear, I've done.
Seal this upon thy memory; until the morrow's sun
Shall sink, to rise no more;
And if my years should score,
Remember this, though I tell no more."

TO THE FIRST OF AUGUST

Britannia's isles proclaim
    That freedom is their theme;
And we do view those honored lands
    with soul-delighting mien.

And unto those they held in gloom,
    Gave ev'ry one their right;
They did disdain fell slavery's shade,
And trust in freedom's light.

Then unto ev'ry British blood,
    Their noble worth revere,
And think them ever noble men,
And like them hence appear.

And when on Britain's isles remote
    We're then in freedom's bounds,
And while we stand on British ground,
    "You're free—you're free!" resounds.

Lift ye that country's banner high,
    And may it nobly wave,
Until beneath the azure sky,
    Man shall be no more a slave.

And, oh, when youth's ecstatic hour,
    When winds and torrents foam,

And passion's glowing noon are past
    To bless that free born home;

Then let us celebrate the day
    And lay the thought to heart,
And teach the rising race the way
    That they may not depart.

REFLECTIONS, WRITTEN ON VISITING THE GRAVE OF A VENERATED FRIEND

Deep in this grave her bones remain,
She's sleeping on, bereft of pain;
Her tongue in silence now does sleep,
And she no more time's call can greet.

She lived as all God's saints should do,
Resigned to death and suffering too;
She feels not pain or sin oppress,
Nor does of worldly cares possess.

White were the locks that thinly shed
Their snows around her honored head,
And furrows not to be effaced
Had age amid her features traced.

I said, "My sister, do tread light,
Faint as the stars that gleam at night,
Nor pluck the tender leaves that wave
In sweetness over this sainted grave."

The rose I've planted by her side,
It tells me of that fate decried;
And bids us all prepare to die,
For that our doom is hast'ning nigh.
Oh, that the gale that sweeps the heath
Too roughly o'er your leaves should breathe,
Then sigh for her—and when you bloom,
Scatter your fragrance o'er her tomb.

Alone I've wandered through the gloom,
To pour my lays upon her tomb;
And I have mourned to see her bed
With brambles and with thorns o'erspread.

O, surely, round her place of rest
I will not let the weed be blest;
It is not meet that she should be
Forgotten or unblest by me.

My sister said, "Tell of this grave!"
Go ask, said I, the thoughtless wave;
And spend one hour in anxious care—
In duty, penitence, and prayer.

Farewell! let memory bestow,
That all may soon be laid as low,
For out of dust, God did compose:
We turn to dust, to sleep, repose.

TWENTIETH-CENTURY POETS

Black women poets in this century, while rooted in the historical experience that links them with earlier poets, have pushed on to explore new relationships. Their poetry is linked with black women's lyric expression in the blues and other popular music on the one hand, and with bold public and political action on the other. Nikki Giovanni (1943), the "Princess of Black Poetry," enjoys special prominence. Her writings have been prolific and varied: she has written several volumes of poetry and an autobiography of her first twenty-five years, edited a volume of poetry, and recorded her poetry to musical accompaniment. Her "raps" with Margaret Walker and James Baldwin have been published as books. Like her sister poets, Giovanni writes as a member of the black community, incorporating the thematic concerns of that world, and yet she has stamped her work with a distinctive perspective.

Polarity is characteristic of Giovanni's poetic message; she writes about clarity and confusion, love and hate, complexity and simplicity, unity and diversity, permanence and change, and tradition and innovation. Her themes of black unity, love, communal spirit, self-determination, personhood, awareness of the oppressors' stratagems, redefinition of black images, and a recognition of a Southern and African heritage all reflect a poet interested not only in the aesthetic significance of her art, but also its cultural and political import. Speaking primarily to black audiences, she raises their level of consciousness in order to promote positive change and unity within an embattled black community.

Like many contemporary black poets, Giovanni has often been perceived narrowly as a "revolutionary" poet, an advocate of violence who spares no "motherfuckas." Passages like the following from "For Saundra" (*Black Judgement*, 1968) surely gained her notoriety:

> it occurred to me
> maybe i shouldn't write
> at all
> but clean my gun
> and check my kerosene supply

In her poems on womanhood, notably "Revolutionary Dreams" (*Re: Creation*, 1970), her tone is controlled and soft, but no less powerful:

> if i dreamed natural
> dreams of being natural
> women doing what a woman
> does when she's natural
> i would have a revolution

Race is not the only controversial issue that Giovanni is concerned with, as "Homosexuality" (*My House*, 1972) shows:

> homosexuality . . .
> is two people
> of similar sex
> DOING IT
> that's all

Yet this radical stance forms only a small part of her poetic mosaic. She can be nostalgic about a Southern childhood, where you could "go to the mountains with / Your grandmother / And go barefooted / And be warm / All the time ("Knoxville, Tennessee," see p. 237). Natures images convey many of her softer messages, as in "Autumn Poems" that speaks about both autumn and love (*Re: Creation*, 1970):

> the heat you left with me
> last night
> still smolders
> the wind catches your scent

Giovanni's poetry incorporates stylistic innovations based on black idioms. Rather than rejecting the adopted, though alien, tongue and the massive influence of Anglo-American thought and style, Giovanni fuses English with black elements. Her poetry relies heavily on distinctively black ideas, jazz, the blues, African drumming rhythms, chants, and symbols and images from black culture and ritual. At the same time it ignores traditional rules of versification, punctuation, grammar, and even spelling. Chanting rhythms give an aura of ritual to her work. By capturing these patterns of black speech and music, Giovanni has found a supple language that is intelligible to her black audience. Her poetry expresses her aesthetic appreciation of black speech and her respect for the oral traditions of African and Afro-American cultures—traditions which her free verse is especially suited to convey.

The theme of much of Giovanni's poetry is black love. It is not anti-white but pro-black, just as surely as was Mamie Smith's "That Thing Called Love," first electronically recorded in 1919. Giovanni's poetry shares the immediacy, brashness, emotional appeal, and unadorned style of the blues. But Giovanni is not the only black poet who has responded to the coercive pull of black music. The indigenous black musical forms like the blues, spirituals, chants, and hollers have provided the themes and stylistic features of rhythm, improvisation, and repetition characteristic of black women's poetry in this century.

Georgia Douglas Johnson's three volumes of poetry modeled on the sonata form set the stage early in the century for this interchange between music and poetry. The first volume, *The Heart of a Woman* (1918), is an intensely personal statement echoing the springtime of young womanhood. It was followed by *Bronze* (1922), which explores the pain and joy of motherhood. *An Autumn Love Cycle* (1928) summons up the mood of the older woman when "love's triumphant day is done." Each volume represents a division of the sonata form, serving respectively as exposition, development, and recapitulation. In these volumes Johnson frequently refers to stringed instruments like the lute, viol, dulcet, and especially the dulciana, which has a labial pipe-organ stop that produces a soft, sweet sound.

Gwendolyn Brooks in "De Witt Williams on His Way to Lincoln Cemetery" (*A Street in Bronzeville*, 1945) uses the repetitive elements of a well-known spiritual to emphasize the message of her funeral dirge: "Swing low, swing low sweet chariot / Nothing but a plain black boy." Later Mari Evans in "And the Old Women Gathered" (see p. 146) reminds us that the rhythmic chant of the spiritual can move even those for whom it is not a natural expression:

It was fierce and
Melodic and
Although we ran
The sound of it
Stayed in our ears.

The blues have provided these poets with more than just rhythms and stylistic devices. The lives as well as the songs of such great blues singers as Bessie Smith, Ma Rainey, Mamie Smith, and Billie Holliday have inspired them. In "So Many Feathers" (see pp. 155–57) Jayne Cortez celebrated Josephine Baker, who shimmied, snake-hipped, charlestoned, lindy-hopped, geechie-walked, barrel-housed, and jigged her way through Africa, Europe, and the United States. Sherley Williams honored Bessie Smith, the Queen of the Blues, in "The Empress Brand Trim: Ruby Reminisces" (see p. 253). Giovanni's poem on the blues- and soul-singer Aretha Franklin, "Poem for Aretha" (*The Women and the Men*, 1975), traces the tradition of black women's blues: "aretha doesn't have to relive billie holidays life doesn't / have / to relive dinah washington's death but who will / stop the pattern.

Margaret Walker's *For My People* (1942) is a blues lyric with flowing, liquid rhythms; it beats out the joys, frustrations, hopes, fears, weaknesses, and strengths of black people. Her ballads recall the black-hand arts of the goopher man and the conjure visions of a black culture steeped in superstition. Her civil rights poems, like those in

Prophets for a New Day (1970), use the symbolic language of the blues, particularly roads, railroad tracks, and trains to symbolize survival, movement, and change. *Prophets for a New Day* chronicles the demonstrations, arrests, and martyrdoms that won the fight for human dignity and justice. Like the blues, this volume, along with *For My People*, articulates the joy and despair of a displaced peasantry and a disaffected black populace.

The culmination of this historical progression is Ntozake Shange's choreopoem, *For Colored Girls Who Have Considered Suicide When the Rainbow is Enuf* (1975). This is a group of twenty poems to be performed as a single piece combining dance (modern, jazz, and popular), theater, and poetry to portray the experience of seven black women. In 1976 it successfully ran on Broadway. By using this variety of artistic forms, Shange has shaped a powerful illustration of the creative breadth of black American women.

This modern poetry as a whole can be called a blues song: though deeply personal, it is not merely concerned with present conditions nor does it allow its audience to receive it passively and then rest content. It challenges the poet and her audience. It is an active dialogue, and sometimes even an argument, among the poets and between the poets and their readers, about what action modern problems require. (Compare, for example, Giovanni and Kunjufu on lesbianism.) Whether they come from the rural South, the northern ghettos, or the fragile security of academe and the professions, black women poets have created an oral-aural poetry that demands involvement and participation.

ROSALIE JONAS

BALLADE DES BELLES MILATRAISSES

The Octoroon Ball
New Orleans, 1840–1850

These celebrated "Octoroon Balls" took place in a handsome
building in the Creole quarter of New Orleans. In later days
this same building has been turned into a Catholic convent.
"Milatraisses" was the generic term for all that class—the
octoroon, or quadroon woman. "Cocodrie" (meaning in
Spanish *Cocodrilla*, the crocodile) was the nickname for the
unmixed black man, who lighted "les belles milatraisses"
through the dark Spanish streets by the ray of his hand
lantern, but could go no further than the door of the hall, on
the pain of death. "Trouloulou" (the Turtle) was the nick-
name applied to the male octoroon, the one man of "color"
admitted, who could find admittance to these orgies only in
the capacity (in those days distinctly menial) of musician—
"fiddler."

"Tis the Octoroon ball! And the halls are alight!
The music is playing an old-time "Galop"
The women are "fair," and the cavaliers white,
(Play on! fiddler-man, keep your eyes on your bow!)
Cocodrie! Cocodrie! what strange shadows you throw
Along the dark streets, by your hand-lantern's ray!
Light "les belles milatraisses" to the portal, that they
May pass; but is doubly barred, black slave! to you:
And the lilt of the old Creole song goes this way:
"Trouloulou! Trouloulou! c'est pas zaffaire a tou!"

The music grows madder! the ball's at its height!
For beauty and kisses, it's Hey! and it's Ho!
These women are fair—for an hour a night—
(Play on! fiddler-man, keep your eyes on your bow!)
And for all dull to-morrows, to-night who'd forego!

Published in *The Crisis* 1 (March 1911).

The music grows madder! "Play! Trouloulou! play!"
Your women are frail, and your masters are gay!
Cocodrie in the dark marks them flee and pursue!
And the lilt of the old Creole song goes this way:
"Trouloulou! Trouloulou! c'est pas zaffaire a tou!"

They are ready and willing to love or to fight!
Hot blood is aflame! and the red wine aflow!
These women are theirs! who dare question their right!
(Play on! fiddler-man, keep your eyes on your bow!)
Who is it that prowls in the dark to and fro,
To and fro—there! Outside!—The door bursts! and at bay!
Cocodrie! in the entrance! not easy to slay!
(Hands off! you mad fiddler! or die with him, too!)
And the lilt of the old Creole song goes this way:
"Trouloulou! Trouloulou! c'est pas zaffaire a tou!"

Envoy—The Convent
New Orleans 1840–1850

They are gone, those light gallants of times long ago!
(Fiddler-man of the past! is this dirge from your bow?)
Are these black-hooded ghosts of the dancers we knew
On their knees at the last? "C'est pas zaffaire a tou!"

BROTHER BAPTIS' ON WOMAN SUFFRAGE

When hit come ter de question er de female vote,
De ladies an' de cullud folks is in de same boat.
Ef de Boss feelin' good, an' we eats out his han',
We kin shout fur freedom, an' foller de ban'.
We kin play at freedom, so long's we play.
But ef we gits thinkin', an' comes out an' say:
Case one's borned a female, an' one's borned black,
Is dat any reason fur sottin' way back?
Is dat any reason fur sottin' da-put?
You kin betcher bottom dollar dat de Boss's fut
Gwine ter sprout big claws, till dey comes clar thoo,
An' he climps hit heavy on bofe us two.
Case de tears er de mudder, nur de sign, er de cross,
Ain't shame all de debbil yit, outen de Boss!

Published in *The Crisis* 4 (September 1912).

LUCY ARIEL WILLIAMS
(1905)

NORTHBOUN'

O' de wurl' ain't flat
An' de wurl' ain't roun',
Hit's one long strip
Hanging' up an' down—
Jes' Souf an' Norf;
Jes' Norf an' Souf.

Talkin' 'bout sailin' 'roun' de wurl'—
Huh! I'd be so dizzy my head 'ud twurl
If dis heah earf wuz jes' a ball
You know the people all 'ud fall.

O' de wurl' ain't flat,
An' de wurl' ain't roun'.
Hit's one long strip
Hanging' up an' down—
Jes' Souf an' Norf;
Jes' Norf an' Souf.

Talkin' 'bout the City whut Saint John saw—
Chile, you oughta go to Saginaw;
A nigger's chance is "finest kind,"
An' pretty gals ain't hard to find.

Huh! de wurl' ain't flat,
An' de wurl' ain't roun',
Jes' one long strip
Hangin' up an' down.
Since Norf is up,
An' Souf is down,
An' Hebben is up,
I'm upward boun'.

Published in *Opportunity* 4 (October 1926). Later reprinted in *Caroling Dusk* edited by Countee Cullen (New York: Harper & Brothers, 1927).

GEORGIA DOUGLAS JOHNSON
(1886–1966)

I WANT TO DIE WHILE YOU LOVE ME

I want to die while you love me,
   While yet you hold me fair,
While laughter lies upon my lips
   And lights are in my hair.

I want to die while you love me
   And bear to that still bed
Your kisses turbulent, unspent
   To warm me when I'm dead.

I want to die while you love me
   Oh, who would care to live
Till love has nothing more to ask
   And nothing more to give?

I want to die while you love me
   And never, never see
The glory of this perfect day
   Grow dim or cease to be!

THE HEART OF A WOMAN

The heart of a woman goes forth with the dawn,
As a lone bird, soft winging, so restlessly on,
Afar o'er life's turrets and vales does it roam
In the wake of those echoes the heart calls home.

The heart of a woman falls back with the night,
And enters some alien cage in its plight,
And tries to forget it has dreamed of the stars
While it breaks, breaks, breaks on the sheltering bars.

From *An Autumn Love Cycle* by Georgia Douglas Johnson (Boston: Cornhill Publishing Company, 1928).

From *The Heart of a Woman and Other Poems* by Georgia Douglas Johnson (Boston: Cornhill Publishing Company, 1918).

MY LITTLE DREAMS

I'm folding up my little dreams
    Within my heart tonight,
And praying I may soon forget
    The torture of their sight.

For time's deft fingers scroll my brow
    With fell relentless art—
I'm folding up my little dreams
    Tonight, within my heart.

SMOTHERED FIRES

A woman with a burning flame
    Deep covered through the years
With ashes—ah! she hid it deep,
    And smothered it with tears.

Sometimes a baleful light would rise
    From out the dusky bed,
And then the woman hushed it quick
    To slumber on, as dead.

At last the weary war was done,
    The tapers were alight,
And with a sigh of victory
    She breathed a soft—goodnight!

From *The Heart of a Woman and Other Poems* by Georgia Douglas Johnson (Boston: Cornhill Publishing Company, 1918).

From *The Heart of a Woman and Other Poems* by Georgia Douglas Johnson (Boston: Cornhill Publishing Company, 1918).

ANGELINA WELD GRIMKÉ
(1880–1958)

A MONA LISA

1.

I should like to creep
Through the long brown grasses
   That are your lashes;
I should like to poise
   On the very brink
Of the leaf-brown pools
   That are your shadowed eyes;
I should like to cleave
   Without sound,
Their glimmering waters,
   Their unrippled waters,
I should like to sink down
   And down
     And down. . . .
      And deeply drown.

2.

Would I be more than a bubble breaking?
   Or an ever-widening circle
   Ceasing at the marge?
Would my white bones
   Be the only white bones
Wavering back and forth, back and forth
   In their depths?

From *Caroling Dusk* edited by Countee Cullen (New York: Harper & Brothers, 1927). The bulk of Grimké's poetry has not been published, though it is available in the Manuscript Collection of the Moorland-Spingarn Research Center, Washington, D.C. Gloria C. Hull, in her essay "Under the Days" in *Conditions* 5 (August 1979), maintains that Grimké's work was not published because of the open lesbianism she expressed in it. I have ascertained from Grimké's correspondence that the woman addressed in the above poem was Miss Mary P. Burrill, dramatics teacher at the Dunbar High School, Washington, D.C.

AT APRIL

Toss your gay heads,
     Brown girl trees;
Toss your gay lovely heads;
Shake your downy russet curls
All about your brown faces;
Stretch your brown slim bodies;
Stretch your brown slim arms;
Stretch your brown slim toes.
Who knows better than we,
With the dark, dark bodies,
What it means
When April comes a-laughing and a-weeping
Once again
At our hearts?

TO KEEP THE MEMORY OF CHARLOTTE FORTEN GRIMKÉ

Still are there wonders of the dark and day;
The muted shrilling of shy things at night,
So small beneath the stars and moon;
The peace, dream-frail, but perfect while the light
Lies softly on the leaves at noon.
These are, and these will be
Until Eternity;
But she who loved them well has gone away.

Each dawn, while yet the east is veiled gray,
The birds about her window wake and sing;
And far away each day some lark
I know is singing where the grasses swing;
Some robin calls and calls at dark.
These are, and these will be
Until Eternity;
But she who loved them well has gone away.

Published in *Opportunity* 3 (March 1925).

Published in *The Crisis* 9 (January 1915). Later reprinted in *Negro Poets and Their Poems* edited by Robert T. Kerlin (Associated Publishers: Washington, D.C., 1923).

The wild flowers that she loved down green ways stray;
Her roses lift their wistful buds at dawn,
But not for eyes that loved them best;
Only her little pansies are all gone,
Some lying softly on her breast.
And flowers will bud and be
Until Eternity;
But she who loved them well has gone away.

Where has she gone? And who is there to say?
But this we know: her gentle spirit moves
And is where beauty never wanes,
Perchance by other streams, 'mid other groves;
And to us here, ah! she remains
A lovely memory
Until Eternity.
She came, she loved, and then she went away.

The subject of these beautiful memorial verses was not simply in feeling but in expression also a poet herself. From "A June Song" written by her I will take a stanza in evidence:

How shall we crown her bright young head?
Crown it with roses, rare and red;
Crown it with roses, creamy white,
As the lotus bloom that sweetens the night.
Crown it with roses as pink as shell
In which the voices of ocean dwell.
And a fairer queen
Shall ne'er be seen
Than our lovely, laughing June.

FOR THE CANDLE LIGHT

The sky was blue, so blue that day
    And each daisy white, so white,
Oh, I knew that no more could rains fall gray—
    And night again be night.

I knew, I knew. Well, if night is night,
    And the gray skies grayly cry,
I have in a book for the candle light
    A daisy dead and dry.

JESSIE REDMON FAUSET
(1888–1961)

TOUCHÉ

Dear, when we sit in that high, placid room,
"Loving" and "doving" as all lovers do,
Laughing and leaning so close in the gloom,—

What is the change that creeps sharp over you?
Just as you raise your fine hand to my hair,
Bringing that glance of mixed wonder and rue?

"Black hair," you murmur, "so lustrous and rare,
Beautiful too, like a raven's smooth wing;
Surely no gold locks were ever more fair."

Why do you say every night that same thing?
Turning your mind to some old constant theme,
Half meditating and half murmuring?

Tell me, that girl of your young manhood's dream,
Her you loved first in that dim long ago—
Had *she* blue eyes? Did *her* hair goldly gleam?

Published in *Opportunity* 3 (September 1925). Later reprinted in *Caroling Dusk* edited by Countee Cullen (New York: Harper & Brothers, 1927).

From *Caroling Dusk* edited by Countee Cullen (New York: Harper & Brothers, 1927).

Does *she* come back to you softly and slow,
Stepping wraith-wise from the depths of the past?
Quickened and fired by the warmth of our glow?

There I've divined it! My wit holds you fast.
Nay, no excuses; 'tis little I care.
I knew a lad in my own girlhood's past,—
Blue eyes he had and such waving gold hair!

ORIFLAMME

"I can remember when I was a little, young girl, how my old
mammy would sit out of doors in the evenings and look up at the
stars and groan, and I would say, 'Mammy, what makes you groan
so?' And she would say, 'I am groaning to think of my poor chil-
dren; they do not know where I be and I don't know where they be. I
look up at the stars and they look up at the stars!'"—Sojourner
Truth.

I think I see her sitting bowed and black,
    Stricken and seared with slavery's mortal scars,
Reft of her children, lonely, anguished, yet
    Still looking at the stars.

Symbolic mother, we thy myriad sons,
    Pounding our stubborn hearts on Freedom's bars,
Clutching our birthright, fight with faces set,
    Still visioning the stars!

Published in *The Crisis* 19 (January 1920). Later reprinted in *The Book of Negro Poetry* edited by James Weldon Johnson (New York: Harcourt, Brace and Company, 1922).

ALICE DUNBAR-NELSON
(1875–1935)

SONNET

I had no thought of violets of late,
The wild, shy kind that spring beneath your feet
In wistful April days, when lovers mate
And wander through the fields in raptures sweet.
The thought of violets meant florists' shops,
And bows and pins, and perfumed papers fine;
And garish lights, and mincing little fops
And cabarets and songs, and deadening wine.
So far from sweet real things my thoughts had strayed,
I had forgot wide fields, and clear brown streams;
The perfect loveliness that God has made,—
Wild violets shy and Heaven-mounting dreams.
And now—unwittingly, you've made me dream
Of violets, and my soul's forgotten gleam.

I SIT AND SEW

I sit and sew—a useless task it seems,
My hands grown tired, my head weighed down with dreams—
The panoply of war, the martial tread of men,
Grim-faced, stern-eyed, gazing beyond the ken
Of lesser souls, whose eyes have not seen Death
Nor learned to hold their lives but as a breath—
But—I must sit and sew.

I sit and sew—my heart aches with desire—
That pageant terrible, that fiercely pouring fire

Published in *The Crisis* 18 (August 1919).

From *The Dunbar Speaker* edited by Alice Dunbar-Nelson (Naperville, Ill.: J. L. Nichols & Company, 1920).

On wasted fields, and writhing grotesque things
Once men. My soul in pity flings
Appealing cries, yearning only to go
There in that holocaust of hell, those fields of woe—
But—I must sit and sew.

The little useless seam, the idle patch;
Why dream I here beneath my homely thatch,
When there they lie in sodden mud and rain,
Pitifully calling me, the quick ones and the slain?
You need me, Christ! It is no roseate dream
That beckons me—this pretty futile seam,
It stifles me—God, must I sit and sew?

SNOW IN OCTOBER

Today I saw a thing of arresting poignant beauty:
A strong young tree, brave in its Autumn finery
Of scarlet and burnt umber and flame yellow,
Bending beneath a weight of early snow,
Which sheathed the north side of its slender trunk,
And spread a heavy white chilly afghan
Over its crested leaves.

Yet they thrust through, defiant, glowing,
Claiming the right to live another fortnight,
Clamoring that Indian Summer had not come,
Crying "Cheat! Cheat!" because Winter had stretched
Long chill fingers into the brown, streaming hair
Of fleeing October.

The film of snow shrouded the proud redness of the tree,
As premature grief grays the strong head
Of a virile, red-haired man.

From *Caroling Dusk* edited by Countee Cullen (New York: Harper & Brothers, 1927).

MUSIC

Music! Lilting, soft and languorous,
Crashing, splendid, thunderous,
Blare of trumpets, sob of violins,
Tinkle of lutes and mandolins;
Poetry of harps, rattle of castanets,
Heart-break of cellos, wood-winds in tender frets;
Orchestra, symphony, bird-song, flute;
Coronach of contraltos, shrill strings a-mute.
Sakuntala* sobbing in the forest drear,
Melisande moaning in crescendic fear;
Splendor and tumult of the organs roll,
Heraldic trumpets pierce the inner soul;
Syphonic syncopation that Dvořák wove,
Valkyric crashes when the Norse gods strove;
Salome's triumph in grunt obscene,
Tschaikowsky peering through forest green;
Verdi's high treble of saccharine sound,
Celeste! Miserere! Lost lovers found.
Music! With you, touching my finger-tips!
Music! With you, soul on your parted lips!
Music—is you!

Published in *Opportunity* 3 (July 1925).
    *Sakuntala is the heroine of a play by the fifth-century Hindu poet and dramatist,
Kalidasa.

ANNE SPENCER
(1882–1975)

AT THE CARNIVAL

Gay little Girl-of-the-Diving-Tank,
I desire a name for you,
Nice, as a right glove fits;
For you—who amid the malodorous
Mechanics of this unlovely thing,
Are darling of spirit and form.
I know you—a glance, and what you are
Sits-by-the-fire in my heart.
My Limousine-Lady knows you, or
Why does the slant-envy of her eyes mark
Your straight air and radiant inclusive smile?
Guilt pins a fig-leaf; Innocence is its own adorning.
The bull-necked man knows you—this first time
His itching flesh sees from divine and vibrant health,
And thinks not of his avocation.
I came incuriously—
Set on no diversion save that my mind
Might safely nurse its brood of misdeeds
In the presence of a blind crowd.
The color of life was gray.
Everywhere the setting seemed right
For my mood!

Here the sausage and garlic booth
Sent unholy incense skyward;
There a quivering female-thing
Gestured assignations, and lied
To call it dancing;
There, too, were games of chance
With chances for none;
But oh! the Girl-of-the-Tank, at last!

From *The Book of American Negro Poetry* edited by James Weldon Johnson (New York: Harcourt, Brace and Company, 1922).

Gleaming Girl, how intimately pure and free
The gaze you send the crowd,
As though you know the dearth of beauty
In its sordid life.
We need you—my Limousine-Lady,
The bull-necked man, and I.
Seeing you here brave and water-clean,
Leaven for the heavy ones of earth,
I am swift to feel that what makes
The plodder glad is good; and
Whatever is good is God.
The wonder is that you are here;
I have seen the queer in queer places,
But never before a heaven-fed
Naiad of the Carnival-Tank!
Little Diver, Destiny for you,
Like as for me, is shod in silence;
Years may seep into your soul
The bacilli of the usual and the expedient;
I implore Neptune to claim his child to-day!

BEFORE THE FEAST OF SHUSHAN

Garden of Shushan!
After Eden, all terrace, pool, and flower recollect thee:
Ye weavers in saffron and haze and Tyrian purple,
Tell yet what range in color wakes the eye;
Sorcerer, release the dreams born here when
Drowsy, shifting palm-shade enspells the brain;
And sound! ye with harp and flute ne'er essay
Before these star-noted birds escaped from paradise awhile to
Stir all dark, and dear, and passionate desire, till mine
Arms go out to be mocked by the softly kissing body of the wind—
Slave, send Vashti to her King!

The fiery wattles of the sun startle into flame
The marbled towers of Shushan:

Published in *The Crisis* 19 (February 1920). Later reprinted in *The Book of American Negro Poetry* edited by James Weldon Johnson (New York: Harcourt, Brace & Company, 1922).

So at each day's wane, two peers—the one in
Heaven, the other on earth—welcome with their
Splendor the peerless beauty of the Queen.

Cushioned at the Queen's feet and upon her knee
Finding glory for mine head,—still, nearly shamed
Am I, the King, to bend and kiss with sharp
Breath the olive-pink of sandaled toes between;
Or lift me high to the magnet of a gaze, dusky,
Like the pool when but the moon-ray strikes to its depth;
Or closer press to crush a grape 'gainst lips redder
Than the grape, a rose in the night of her hair;
Then—Sharon's rose in my arms.

And I am hard to force the petals wide;
And you are fast to suffer and be sad.
Is any prophet come to teach a new thing
Now in a more apt time?
Have him 'maze how you say love is sacrament;
How says Vashti, love is both bread and wine;
How to the altar may not come to break and drink,
Hulky flesh nor fleshly spirit!

I, thy lord, like not manna for meat as a Judahn;
I, thy master, drink, and red wine, plenty, and when
I thirst. Eat meat, and full, when I hunger.
I, thy King, teach you and leave you, when I list.
No woman in all Persia sets out strange action
To confuse Persia's lord—
Love is but desire and thy purpose fulfillment;
I, thy King, so say!

LETTER TO MY SISTER

It is dangerous for a woman to defy the gods;
To taunt them with the tongue's thin tip,
Or strut in the weakness of mere humanity,

From *Caroling Dusk* edited by Countee Cullen (New York: Harper & Brothers, 1927).

Or draw a line daring them to cross;
The gods own the searing lightning,
The drowning waters, tormenting fears
And anger of red sins.

Oh, but worse still if you mince timidly—
Dodge this way or that, or kneel or pray,
Be kind, or sweat agony drops
Or lay your quick body over your feeble young;
If you have beauty or none, if celibate
Or vowed—the gods are Juggernaut,
Passing over . . . over . . .

This you may do:
Lock your heart, then, quietly,
And lest they peer within,
Light no lamp when dark comes down
Raise no shade for sun;
Breathless must your breath come through
If you'd die and dare deny
The gods their god-like fun.

SUBSTITUTION

Is Life itself but many ways of thought,
Does *thinking* furl the poets' pleiades,
Is in His slightest convolution wrought
These mantled worlds and their men-freighted seas?
He thinks—and being comes to ardent things:
The splendor of the day-spent sun, love's birth,—
Or dreams a little, while creation swings
The circle of His mind and Time's full girth . . .
As here within this noisy peopled room
My thought leans forward . . . quick! you're lifted clear
Of brick and frame to moonlit garden bloom,—
Absurdly easy, now, our walking, dear,
Talking, my leaning close to touch your face . . .
His All-Mind bids us keep this sacred place!

From *Caroling Dusk* edited by Countee Cullen (New York: Harper & Brothers, 1927).

LADY, LADY

Lady, Lady, I saw your face,
Dark as night withholding a star . . .
The chisel fell, or it might have been
You had borne so long the yoke of men.

Lady, Lady, I saw your hands,
Twisted, awry, like crumpled roots,
Bleached poor white in a sudsy tub,
Wrinkled and drawn from your rub-a-dub.

Lady, Lady, I saw your heart,
And altared there in its darksome place
Were the tongues of flame the ancients knew, ·
Where the good God sits to spangle through.

GWENDOLYN B. BENNETT
(1902)

FANTASY

I sailed in my dreams to the Land of Night
Where you were the dusk-eyed queen,
And there in the pallor of moon-veiled light
The loveliest things were seen . . .

A slim-necked peacock sauntered there
In a garden of lavender hues,
And you were strange with your purple hair
As you sat in your amethyst chair
With your feet in your hyacinth shoes.

Oh, the moon gave a bluish light
Through the trees in the lands of dreams and night.
I stood behind a bush of yellow-green
And whistled a song to the dark-haired queen . . .

From *The New Negro* edited by Alain Locke (New York: Albert and Charles Boni, Inc., 1925).

From *Caroling Dusk* edited by Countee Cullen (New York: Harper & Brothers, 1927).

HATRED

I shall hate you
Like a dart of singing steel
Shot through still air
At even-tide.
Or solemnly
As pines are sober
When they stand etched
Against the sky.
Hating you shall be a game
Played with cool hands
And slim fingers.
Your heart will yearn
For the lonely splendor
Of the pine tree;
While rekindled fires
In my eyes
Shall wound you like swift arrows.
Memory will lay its hands
Upon your breast
And you will understand
My hatred.

SONG

I am weaving a song of waters,
Shaken from firm, brown limbs,
Or heads thrown back in irreverent mirth.
My song has the lush sweetness
Of moist, dark lips
Where hymns keep company
With old forgotten banjo songs.
Abandon tells you
That I sing the heart of a race

Published in *Opportunity* 4 (June 1926).

Published in *Opportunity* 4 (October 1926). Appeared earlier in *The New Negro* edited by Alain Locke (New York: Albert and Charles Boni, 1925).

While sadness whispers
That I am the cry of a soul. . . .

A-shoutin' in de ole camp-meetin' place,
A-strummin' o' de ole banjo.
Singin' in de moonlight,
Sobbin' in de dark.
Singin', sobbin', strummin' slow . . .
Singin' slow; sobbin' low.
Strummin', strummin', strummin' slow. . . .

Words are bright bugles
That make the shining for my song,
And mothers hold brown babes
To dark, warm breasts
To make my singing sad.

A dancing girl with swaying hips
Sets mad the queen in a harlot's eye.
> Praying slave
> Jazz band after
> Breaking heart
> To the time of laughter. . . .
Clinking chains and minstrelsy
Are welded fast with melody.
> A praying slave
> With a jazz band after . . .
> Singin' slow, sobbin' low.
Sun-baked lips will kiss the earth.
Throats of bronze will burst with mirth.
> Sing a little faster,
> Sing a little faster!
> Sing!

SECRET

I shall make a song like your hair . . .
Gold-woven with shadows green-tinged,
And I shall play with my song
As my fingers might play with your hair.

From *Caroling Dusk* edited by Countee Cullen (New York: Harper & Brothers, 1927).

Deep in my heart
I shall play with my song of you,
Gently. . . .
I shall laugh
At its sensitive lustre . . .
I shall wrap my song in a blanket,
Blue like your eyes are blue
With tiny shots of silver.
I shall wrap it caressingly,
Tenderly. . . .
I shall sing a lullaby
To the song I have made
Of your hair and eyes . . .
And you will never know
that deep in my heart
I shelter a song for you
Secretly. . . .

ADVICE

You were a sophist,
Pale and quite remote,
As you bade me
Write poems—
Brown poems
Of dark words
And prehistoric rhythms . . .
Your pallor stifled my poesy
But I remembered a tapestry
That I would some day weave
Of dim purples and fine reds
And blues
Like night and death—
The keen precision of your words
Wove a silver thread
Through the dusk softness
Of my dream-stuff. . . .

From *Caroling Dusk* edited by Countee Cullen (New York: Harper & Brothers, 1927).

TO A DARK GIRL

I love you for your brownness,
And the rounded darkness of your breast,
I love you for the breaking sadness in your voice
And shadows where your wayward eyelids rest.

Something of old forgotten queens
Lurks in the lithe abandon of your walk
And something of the shackled slave
Sobs in the rhythm of your talk.

Oh, little brown girl, born for sorrow's mate,
Keep all you have of queenliness,
Forgetting that you once were slave,
And let your full lips laugh at Fate!

TO USWARD

Let us be still
As ginger jars are still
Upon a Chinese shelf,
And let us be contained
By entities of Self . . .

Not still with lethargy and sloth,
But quiet with the pushing of our growth;
Not self-contained with smug identity,
But conscious of the strength in entity.

If any have a song to sing that's different from the rest,
Oh, let him sing before the Urgency of Youth's behest!

And some of us have songs to sing
Of jungle heat and fires;
And some of us are solemn grown
With pitiful desires;
And there are those who feel the pull
Of seas beneath the skies;

Published in *Opportunity* 5 (1927). Later reprinted in *The Book of American Negro Poetry* edited by James Weldon Johnson, 2d ed., rev. (New York: Harcourt, Brace & Company, 1931).

Published in *Opportunity* 2 (May 1924) and *The Crisis* 28 (May 1924).

And some there be who want to croon
Of Negro lullabies.
We claim no part with racial dearth,
We want to sing the songs of birth!

And so we stand like ginger jars,
Like ginger jars bound round
With dust and age;
Like jars of ginger we are sealed
By nature's heritage.
But let us break the seal of years
With pungent thrusts of song,
For there is joy in long dried tears,
For whetted passions of a throng!

HERITAGE

I want to see the slim palm-trees,
Pulling at the clouds
With little pointed fingers.

I want to see lithe Negro girls,
Etched dark against the sky
While sunset lingers.

I want to hear the silent sands,
Singing to the moon
Before the Sphinx-still face.

I want to hear the chanting
Around a heathen fire
Of a strange black race.

I want to breathe the Lotus flow'r,
Sighing to the stars
With tendrils drinking at the Nile.

I want to feel the surging
Of my sad people's soul
Hidden by a minstrel-smile.

Published in *Opportunity* 1 (December 1923). Later reprinted in *The Book of American Negro Poetry* edited by James Weldon Johnson, 2d ed., rev. (New York: Harcourt, Brace & Company, 1931).

HELENE JOHNSON
(1907)

BOTTLED

Upstairs on the third floor
Of the 135th Street library
In Harlem, I saw a little
Bottle of sand, brown sand
Just like the kids make pies
Out of down at the beach.
But the label said: "This
Sand was taken from the Sahara desert."
Imagine that! The Sahara desert!
Some bozo's been all the way to Africa to get some sand.

And yesterday on Seventh Avenue
I saw a darky dressed fit to kill
In yellow gloves and swallow tail coat
And swirling a cane. And everyone
Was laughing at him. Me too,
At first, till I saw his face
When he stopped to hear a
Organ grinder grind out some jazz.
Boy! You should a seen that darky's face!
It just shone. Gee, he was happy!
And he began to dance. No
Charleston or Black Bottom for him.
No sir. He danced just as dignified
And slow. No, not slow either.
Dignified and proud! You couldn't
Call it slow, not with all the
Cuttin' up he did. You would a died to see him.

The crowd kept yellin' but he didn't hear,
Just kept on dancin' and twirlin' that cane
And yellin' out loud every once in a while.

From *Caroling Dusk* edited by Countee Cullen (New York: Harper and Brothers, 1927).

I know the crowd thought he was coo-coo.
But say, I was where I could see his face,
And somehow, I could see him dancin' in a jungle,
A real honest-to-cripe-jungle, and he wouldn't have on them
Trick clothes—those yaller shoes and yaller gloves
And swallow tail coat. He wouldn't have on nothing.
And he wouldn't be carrying no cane.
He'd be carrying a spear with a sharp fine point
Like the bayonets we had "over there."
And the end of it would be dipped in some kind of
Hoo-doo poison. And he'd be dancin' black and naked
        and gleaming.
And he'd have rings in his ears and on his nose
And bracelets and necklaces of elephants' teeth.
Gee, I bet he'd be beautiful then all right.
No one could laugh at him then, I bet.
Say! that man that took that sand from the Sahara desert
And put it in a little bottle on a shelf in the library,
That's what they done to this shine, ain't it? Bottled him.
Trick shoes, trick coat, trick cane, trick everything—
        all glass—
But inside—
Gee, that poor shine!

MAGALU

Summer comes.
The ziczac* hovers
'Round the greedy-mouthed crocodile.
A vulture beats away a foolish jackal.
The flamingo is a dash of pink
Against dark green mangroves,
Her slender legs rivalling her slim neck.
The laughing lake gurgles delicious music in its throat
And lulls to sleep the lazy lizard,

From *Caroling Dusk* edited by Countee Cullen (New York: Harper & Brothers, 1927).
*The ziczac is an Egyptian species of plover who warns the crocodile of approaching danger by its cry.

A nebulous being on a sun-scorched rock.
In such a place,
In this pulsing, riotous gasp of color,
I met Magalu, dark as a tree at night,
Eager-lipped, listening to a man with a white collar
And a small black book with a cross on it.
Oh, Magalu, come! Take my hand and I will read you
     poetry,
Chromatic words,
Seraphic symphonies,
Fill up your throat with laughter and your heart
    with song.
Do not let him lure you from your laughing waters,
Lulling lakes, lissome winds.
Would you sell the colors of your sunset and the
     fragrance
Of your flowers, and the passionate wonder of your
    forest
For a creed that will not let you dance?

THE ROAD

Ah, little road all whirry in the breeze,
A leaping clay hill lost among the trees,
The bleeding note of rapture streaming thrush
Caught in a drowsy hush
And stretched out in a single singing line of dusky
    song.
Ah little road, brown as my race is brown,
Your trodden beauty like our trodden pride,
Dust of the dust, they must not bruise you down.
Rise to one brimming golden, spilling cry!

Published in *Opportunity* 4 (July 1926). Appeared earlier in *The Book of American Negro Poetry* edited by James Weldon Johnson (New York: Harcourt, Brace and Company, 1922).

TREES AT NIGHT

Slim sentinels
Stretching lacy arms
About a slumbrous moon;
Black quivering
Silhouettes,
Tremulous,
Stencilled on the petal
Of a bluebell;
Ink spluttered
On a robin's breast;
The jagged rent
Of mountains
Reflected in a
Still sleeping lake;
Fragile pinnacles
Of fairy castles;
Torn webs of shadows;
And
Printed 'gainst the sky—
The trembling beauty
Of an urgent pine.

SUMMER MATURES

Summer matures. Brilliant Scorpion
Appears. The Pelican's thick pouch
Hangs heavily with perch and slugs.
The brilliant-bellied newt flashes
Its crimson crest in the white water.
In the lush meadow, by the river,
The yellow-freckled toad laughs
With a toothless gurgle at the white-necked stork
Standing asleep on one red reedy leg.

Published in *Opportunity* 3 (May 1925).

Published in *Opportunity* 5 (July 1927). Later reprinted in *Caroling Dusk* edited by Countee Cullen (New York: Harper & Brothers, 1927).

And here Pan dreams of slim stalks clean for piping,
And of a nightingale gone made with freedom.
Come. I shall weave a bed of reeds
And willow limbs and pale nightflowers.
I shall strip the roses of their petals,
And the white down from the swan's neck.
Come. Night is here. The air is drunk
With wild grape and sweet clover.
And by the sacred fount of Aganippe
Euterpe sings of love. Ah, the woodland creatures,
The doves in pairs, the wild sow and her shoats,
The stag searching the forest for a mate,
Know more of love than you, my callous Phaon.
The young moon is a curved white scimitar
Pierced thru the swooning night.
Sweet Phaon. With Sappho sleep like the stars at dawn.
This night was born for love, my Phaon.
Come.

CARRIE WILLIAMS CLIFFORD
(1882–1958)

THE BLACK DRAFTEE FROM DIXIE

(Twelve Negro soldiers who had served overseas were
lynched upon their return to their homes in the South.)

Upon his dull ear fell the stern command;
And though scarce knowing why or whither, he
Went forth prepared to battle loyally,
And questioned not your faith, O Dixie-land!

And though the task assigned were small or grand,
If toiling at mean tasks ingloriously,

From *The Widening Light* by Carrie Williams Clifford (Boston: Walter Reid Co.,
1922).

Or in fierce combat fighting valiantly,
With poise magnificent he took his stand!

What though the hero-warrior was black?
His heart was white and loyal to the core;
And when to his loved Dixie he came back,
Maimed, in the duty done on foreign shore,
Where from the hell of war he never flinched,
Because he cried, "Democracy" was lynched.

BESSIE CALHOUN BIRD
(1906)

PROOF

Other loves I have known.
One there was which struck suddenly,
Like a great stone
Plunging the waters of a quiet pool
It troubled my being with violent ecstasy . . .
Then easing gradually
It eddied away . . . was gone,
Lost in ever-widening ripples
Of calm, cool
Apathy.

Another came almost imperceptibly,
Like the subtle fragrance of a flower
Wind-scattered in Spring
It claimed my senses delicately;
Suffused me with yearning tenderness
For one enraptured hour . . .
Then being a thing
Infinitely too fragile to last,
At the very dawn of its budding
It passed.

Published in *The Challenge* 2 (Spring 1937).

I am glad, Dear One, that I have known
So much of vagrant love;
Each ephemeral travesty
Has but served to prove
That this which has grown
Oakwise with time,
Storm tested by you and me
Is, and ever shall be
The gift sublime,
The intransmutable verity.

PAULI MURRAY
(1910)

DARK TESTAMENT

1

Freedom is a dream
Haunting as amber wine
Or worlds remembered out of time.
Not Eden's gate, but freedom
Lures us down a trail of skulls
Where men forever crush the dreamers—
Never the dream.

I was an Israelite walking a sea bottom,
I was a Negro slave following the North Star,
I was an immigrant huddled in ship's belly,
I was a Mormon searching for a temple,
I was a refugee clogging roads to nowhere—
Always the dream was the same—
Always the dream was freedom.

From *Dark Testament and Other Poems* by Pauli Murray (Norwalk, Conn.: Silvermine Publishers, 1970.) Copyright 1970 by Pauli Murray. Reprinted by permission of the author.

2

America was a new dream and a new world for dreaming.
America was the vast sleeping Gulliver of the globe.
America was the dream of freedom.
But the dream was lost when campfires grew,
The Bible twisted as white men threw
The Redskins back to mountain pass,
The senses dulled with whiskey flask,
The arrow broken by searing lead.
"Better to die," the Red Man said.

The white slave ran away too soon,
Followed the path of dying moon—
A face forgotten in frontier shack
Where none asked questions, few turned back,
Here was a place where a man could stand
Holding free earth in scrawny hand.
Here was a world where freedom was won
By the hand on an axe, the hand on a gun.

3

Free earth hungered for free men but
Free men soon hungered for gold.
Planters bargained with traders,
    traders bargained with slavers,
Slavers turned toward Africa.
The dream was lost in the quest for gold.

The men of Africa were stalwart men,
Tough as hickory deep in their primal forest,
Their skins the color of tree-bark—
Ebony, bamboo, cocoanut, mango—
Their hair was thick with jungle,
Their eyes were dark as star-fed night.
They were sly and cunning, fearless and cool,
They knew the cry of every forest bird and beast.

Smelters of iron, carvers of wood and ivory,
Weavers and potters of intricate design,
Followers of the honeybird to the honeytree,
Hunters of antelope, lion and elephant,
Some were gentle tribes and some were fiercely brave,

Warriors of the poisoned spear
Testing their strength in battle man for man.
And when they killed the foe, they ate his heart
To make themselves invincible.

Story-tellers all, refusing to be hurried,
Who nightly by the villages fires
Recalled their tribal history,
Evoked ancestral heroes,
Imbued their young with pride.
And every task no matter what its import
Signalled a joyous song and tribal dance.

4

O black warrior,
Hurl a dark spear of song
Borne on a night-wind
Piercing the sorrow-haunted darkness—
Perpetual cycle of grief,
Cruel legacy of endless betrayal,
Frenzied anger beating against
Impenetrable walls of silence!

Ours is no bedtime story children beg to hear,
No heroes rode down the night to warn our
      sleeping villages.
Ours is a tale of blood streaking the Atlantic—
      From Africa to Barbados
      From Haiti to Massachusetts,
      From Rhode Island to Virginia,
      From the red clay of Georgia
      To requiem in Memphis,
      From swampy graves in Mississippi
      To the morgues of Detroit.

Ours is a tale of charred and blackened fruit,
Aborted harvest dropped from blazing bough,
A tale of eagles exiled from the nest,
Brooding and hovering on the edge of sky—
A somber shadow on this native earth,
Yet no faint tremor of her breast
Eludes the circle of our hungered eye.

5

Black men were safe when tom-toms slumbered
'Til traders came with beads and rum,
Bartered and bribed on their slaver's quest,
Killed the watcher, silenced the drum.

Villages screamed in headless horror,
Villages blazed with fiery eye,
Trapped lions roared no greater terror
Than man pinned back on burning sky.
With one great throat the forests thundered,
With one vast body their creatures fled
But man the hunter was now the hunted
Bleeding fresh trails of dying and dead.

Tethered beneath a slave-ship's girth,
The hours throbbed with dying and birth,
Foaming and champing in slime and dung,
Rumbling curses in a jungle tongue,
Torturous writhing of limbs that burst,
Whimpering children choked with thirst,
Vomiting milk from curdled breast,
Rat's teeth sinking in suckling's chest,
Slave ships plunging through westing waves,
Grinding proud men to cringing slaves.

> "Oh running slaves is a risky trade
> When you cross the path of Gov'ment sail,
> They'll smell you five miles down the wind
> For a slaver stinks like a rotting whale.
> And when they spy you, dump your cargo,
> Shove the first black over the rail . . ."

He twists, he spins, he claws at the sun,
He plummets down, dark dagger in the flood,
He sucks in the others one by one
And the foam track crimsons with their blood
As glistening shark fins flash among
The black heads bobbing on the wave,
The slave ship flees and freedom is won
In churning torrent, in fathomless grave.

6

We have not forgotten the market square—
Malignant commerce in our flesh—
Huddled like desolate sheep—
Tumult of boisterous haggling—
We waited the dreadful moment of dispersal.
One by one we climbed the auction block—
Naked in an alien land—

>   Driven by whip's relentless tongue
>   To dance and caper in the sun,
>   Ripple the muscles from shoulders to hips,
>   To show the teeth and bulge the biceps,
>   To feel the shame of a girl whose breasts
>   Are bared to squeeze of a breeder's fists.

Sold! Resold with the same coin
Our unrewarded sweat had borne.
Endless tearing—man wrested from woman
Warm and brown as sunflower heart,
Plucked up, thrust down in untamed earth,
Uprooted, dispersed again—she was too brief a wife.
She sits in frozen grief
And stares with mindless eyes
At fatherless children crying in the night.

7

Trade a king's freedom for a barrel of molasses,
Trade a queen's freedom for a red bandanna,
Or Cherokee-mulattoes in North Carolina,
Or a Creole mistress in Louisiana.
Sell a man's brain for a handful of greenbacks,
Mark him up in Congress—he's three-fifths human,
Mark him down in the record with mules and mortgage,
Sell him long! Sell him short! Cotton's a-boomin'.
Take a black's manhood, give a white God,
Send him 'way down in the dismal woods
Where a black man's tears will not embarrass
A white man's juleps and lofty moods.

A black man down on his knees in the swamp-grass
Sent his prayer straight to the white God's throne,
Built him a faith, built a bridge to this God
And God gave him hope and the power of song.

8

Hope is a crushed stalk
Between clenched fingers.
Hope is a bird's wing
Broken by a stone.
Hope is a word in a tuneless ditty—
A word whispered with the wind,
A dream of forty acres and a mule,
A cabin of one's own and a moment to rest,
A name and place for one's children
And children's children at last . . .
Hope is a song in a weary throat.

> *Give me a song of hope*
> *And a world where I can sing it.*
> *Give me a song of faith*
> *And a people to believe in it.*
> *Give me a song of kindliness*
> *And a country where I can live it.*
> *Give me a song of hope and love*
> *And a brown girl's heart to hear it.*

9

Pity the poor who hate—
Wild brood of earth's lean seasons—
Pity the poor, the land-robbed whites,
Driven by planters to marshy back-lands,
Driven by fevers, pellagra and hookworm,
Driven to hate niggers warm in their cabins,
The nigger fed on scraps from the Big House,
The nigger's hands on a fine tall coach-whip.
The half-white nigger in a rich man's kitchen.

Give 'em a chance they'd burn that nigger,
Burn 'im on a tree in the swamp-lands,
Teach 'im not to eat while white men hungered,
Teach 'im that even God is white
And had no time for niggers' praying.
Teach 'im that the devil is black
And niggers were the sons of evil.

> *Pity slave and serf in their misery,*
> *Bound by common fate to common destiny.*

10

The drivers are dead now
But the drivers have sons.
The slaves are dead too
But the slaves have sons,
And when sons of drivers meet sons of slaves
The hate, the old hate, keeps grinding on.
Traders still trade in double-talk
Though they've swapped the selling-block
For ghetto and gun!

> *This is our portion, this is our testament,*
> *This is America, dual-brained creature,*
> *One hand thrusting us out to the stars,*
> *One hand shoving us down in the gutter.*

Pile up the records, sing of pioneers,
Point to images chipped from mountain-heart,
Swagger through history with glib-tongued traditions,
Say of your grass roots, "We are a hard-ribbed people,
One nation indivisible with liberty and justice for all."

> *Put it all down in a time capsule,*
> *Bury it deep in the soil of Virginia,*
> *Bury slave-song with the Constitution,*
> *Bury it in that vineyard of planters*
> *And poll-taxers, sharecroppers and Presidents.*
> *In coffin and outhouse all men are equal,*
> *And the same red earth is fed*
> *By the white bones of Tom Jefferson*
> *And the white bones of Nat Turner.*

11

Tear it out of the history books!
Bury it in conspiracies of silence!
Fight many wars to suppress it!
But it is written in our faces
Twenty million times over!

> *It sings in our blood,*
> *It cries from the housetops,*
> *It mourns with the wind in the forests,*
> *When dogs howl and will not be comforted,*
> *When newborn lambs bleat in the snowdrifts,*
> *And dead leaves rattle in the graveyards.*
> *And we'll shout it from the mountains.*
> *We'll tell it in the valleys,*
> *We'll talk it in miner's shack,*
> *We'll sing it at the work bench,*
> *We'll whisper it over back fences,*
> *We'll speak it in the kitchen,*
> *We'll state it at the White House,*
> *We'll tell it everywhere to all who will listen—*

We will lay siege, let thunder serve our claim,
For it must be told, endlessly told, and you
     must hear it.
Listen, white brothers, hear the dirge of history,
And hold out your hand—hold out your hand.

12

Of us who darkly stand
Bared to the spittle of every curse,
Nor left the dignity of beasts,
Let none say, "Those were not men
But cowards all, with eyes dull-lidded as a frog's.
They labored long but not from love,
They strove from blind perpetual fear."

Better our seed rot on the ground
And our hearts burn to ash
Than the years be empty of our imprint.
We have no other dream, no land but this;
With slow deliberate hands these years
Have set her image on our brows.
We are her seed, have borne a fruit
Native and pure as unblemished cotton.

Then let the dream linger on.
Let it be the test of nations,
Let it be the quest of all our days,
The fevered pounding of our blood,
The measure of our souls—
That none shall rest in any land
And none return to dreamless sleep.
No heart be quieted, no tongue be stilled
Until the final man may stand in any place
And thrust his shoulders to the sky,
Friend and brother to every other man.

INQUIETUDE

Blue is this night of stars
But over the distant hill
I see lightning dart
        from a dusky cloud.
Discontent tears through me
        like the jagged flame
Which splits the air,
And like the answering thunder
I too would go
Crashing the mountainside
Til, all fury spent,
I sink and let the silver tide
Engulf me.

Published in *The Challenge* 1 (May 1935).

SONG

Because I know deep in my own heart
That every Poet must have his Song,
That Joy and Sorrow are never far apart
And Love, at best, seldom lasts for long;

Because I know that ecstasy and pain
Are twin strings thrummed on the soul's lyre
I will not cry "I Love You!"—but fain
Would say, "I want you always near."

MAE V. COWDERY
(1910)

I SIT AND WAIT FOR BEAUTY

To John Lovell

Long have I yearned and sought for beauty
And now it seems to be a futile race
To strive to look upon the marvel
Of so fair a face.

She is not here with the trees
That bend to wind in endless grace
Nor has she come from a blue sea
In the frothing lace
That breaks upon the shore in white ecstasy.

She did not come on the piercing call
Of wild birds in flight
Nor in young love did I find her
Nor in the wordless wonder of the night
Or with yon' star that holds my breath
Upon a silver spear. Thus I know her to be more than all
These things—than life or death—

Published in *The Challenge* 1 (March 1934).

Published in *The Challenge* 1 (May 1935).

And even though I become a God
With all magic secrets at my command
She will ever hide her face
And elude my grasping hand!

MARGARET WALKER
(1915)

LINEAGE

My grandmothers were strong.
They followed plows and bent to toil.
They moved through fields sowing seed.
They touched earth and grain grew.
They were full of sturdiness and singing.
My grandmothers were strong.

My grandmothers are full of memories
Smelling of soap and onions and wet clay
With veins rolling roughly over quick hands
They have many clean words to say.
My grandmothers were strong.
Why am I not as they?

From *For My People* by Margaret Walker (New Haven, Conn.: Yale University Press, 1942). Reprinted by permission of the author.

KISSIE LEE

Toughest gal I ever did see
Was a gal by the name of Kissie Lee;
The toughest gal God ever made
And she drew a dirty, wicked blade.

Now this here gal warn't always tough
Nobody dreamed she'd turn out rough
But her Grammaw Mamie had the name
Of being the town's sin and shame.

When Kissie Lee was young and good
Didn't nobody treat her like they should
Allus gettin' beat by a no-good shine
An' allus quick to cry and whine.

Till her Grammaw said, "Now listen to me,
I'm tiahed of yoah whinin', Kissie Lee.
People don't never treat you right,
An' you allus scrappin' or in a fight.

"Whin I was a gal wasn't no soul
Could do me wrong an' still stay whole.
Ah got me a razor to talk for me
An' aftah that they let me be."

Well Kissie Lee took her advice
And after that she didn't speak twice
'Cause when she learned to stab and run
She got herself a little gun.

And from that time that gal was mean,
Meanest mamma you ever seen.
She could hold her likker and hold her man
And she went thoo life jus' raisin' san'.

One night she walked in Jim's saloon
And seen a guy what spoke too soon;
He done her dirt long time ago
When she was good and feeling low.

From *For My People* by Margaret Walker (New Haven, Conn.: Yale University Press, 1942). Reprinted by permission of the author.

Kissie bought her drink and paid her dime
Watchin' this guy what beat her time
And he was making for the outside door
When Kissie shot him to the floor.

Not a word she spoke but she switched her blade
And flashing that lil ole baby paid:
Evvy livin' guy got out of her way
Because Kissie Lee was drawin' her pay.

She could shoot glass doors offa the hinges,
She could take herself on the wildest binges.
And she died with her boots on switching blades
On Talladega Mountain in the likker raids.

MOLLY MEANS

Old Molly Means was a hag and a witch;
Chile of the devil, the dark, and sitch.
Her heavy hair hung thick in ropes
And her blazing eyes was black as pitch.
Imp at three and wench at 'leben
She counted her husbands to the number seben.
    O Molly, Molly, Molly Means
    There goes the ghost of Molly Means.

Some say she was born with a veil on her face
So she could look through unnatchal space
Through the future and through the past
And charm a body or an evil place
And every man could well despise
The evil look in her coal black eyes.
    Old Molly, Molly, Molly Means
    Dark is the ghost of Molly Means.

And when the tale begun to spread
Of evil and of holy dread:

From *For My People* by Margaret Walker (New Haven, Conn.: Yale University Press, 1942). Reprinted by permission of the author.

Her black-hand arts and her evil powers
How she cast her spells and called the dead,
The younguns was afraid at night
And the farmers feared their crops would blight.
    Old Molly, Molly, Molly Means
    Cold is the ghost of Molly Means.

Then one dark day she put a spell
On a young gal-bride just come to dwell
In the lane just down from Molly's shack
And when her husband come riding back
His wife was barking like a dog
And on all fours like a common hog.
    O Molly, Molly, Molly Means
    Where is the ghost of Molly Means?

The neighbors come and they went away
And said she'd die before break of day
But her husband held her in his arms
And swore he'd break the wicked charms;
He'd search all up and down the land
And turn the spell on Molly's hand.
    O Molly, Molly, Molly Means
    Sharp is the ghost of Molly Means.

So he rode all day and he rode all night
And at the dawn he come in sight
Of a man who said he could move the spell
And cause the awful thing to dwell
On Molly Means, to bark and bleed
Till she died at the hands of her evil deed.
    Old Molly, Molly, Molly Means
    This is the ghost of Molly Means.

Sometimes at night through the shadowy trees
She rides along on a winter breeze.
You can hear her holler and whine and cry.
Her voice is thin and her moan is high,
And her crackling laugh or her barking cold
Bring terror to the young and old.
    O Molly, Molly, Molly Means
    Lean is the ghost of Molly Means.

BALLAD OF THE HOPPY-TOAD

Ain't been on Market Street for nothing
With my regular washing load
When the Saturday crowd went stomping
Down the Johnny-jumping road,

Seen Sally Jones come running
With a razor at her throat,
Seen Deacon's daughter lurching
Like a drunken alley goat.

But the biggest for my money,
And the saddest for my throw
Was the night I seen the goopher man
Throw dust around my door.

Come sneaking round my doorway
In a stovepipe hat and coat;
Come sneaking round my doorway
To drop the evil note.

I run down to Sis Avery's
And told her what I seen
"Root-worker's out to git me
What you reckon that there mean?"

Sis Avery she done told me,
"Now honey go on back
I knows just what will hex him
And that old goopher sack."

Now I done burned the candles
Till I seen the face of Jim
And I done been to Church and prayed
But can't git rid of him.

Don't want to burn his picture
Don't want to dig his grave
Just want to have my peace of mind
And make that dog behave.

From *Prophets for a New Day* by Margaret Walker (Detroit: Broadside Press, 1970).
Copyright 1970. Reprinted by permission of the author.

Was running through the fields one day
Sis Avery's chopping corn
Big horse come stomping after me
I knowed then I was gone.

Sis Avery grabbed that horse's mane
And not one minute late
Cause trembling down behind her
I seen my ugly fate.

She hollered to that horse to "Whoa!
I gotcha hoppy-toad."
And yonder come the goopher man
A-running down the road.

She hollered to that horse to "Whoa"
And what you wanta think?
Great-God-a-mighty, that there horse
Begun to sweat and shrink.

He shrunk up to a teeny horse
He shrunk up to a toad
And yonder come the goopher man
Still running down the road.

She hollered to that horse to "Whoa"
She said, "I'm killing him.
Now you just watch this hoppy-toad
And you'll be rid of Jim."

The goopher man was hollering
"Don't kill that hoppy-toad."
Sis Avery she said "Honey,
You bout to lose your load."

That hoppy-toad was dying
Right there in the road
And goopher man was screaming
"Don't kill that hoppy-toad."

The hoppy-toad shook one more time
And then he up and died
Old goopher man fell dying, too.
"O hoppy-toad," he cried.

GWENDOLYN BROOKS
(1917)

THE MOTHER

Abortions will not let you forget.
You remember the children you got that you did not get,
The damp small pulps with a little or with no hair,
The singers and workers that never handled the air.
You will never neglect or beat
Them, or silence or buy with a sweet.
You will never wind up the sucking-thumb
Or scuttle off ghosts that come.
You will never leave them, controlling your luscious sigh,
Return for a snack of them, with gobbling mother-eye.

I have heard in the voices of the wind the voices of my
    dim killed children.
I have contracted. I have eased
My dim dears at the breasts they could never suck.
I have said, Sweets, if I sinned, if I seized
Your luck
And your lives from your unfinished reach,
If I stole your births and your names,
Your straight baby tears and your games,
Your stilted or lovely loves, your tumults, your
    marriages, aches, and your deaths,
If I poisoned the beginnings of your breaths,
Believe that even in my deliberateness I was not
    deliberate.
Though why should I whine,
Whine that the crime was other than mine?—
Since anyhow you are dead.
Or rather, or instead,
You were never made.

From *A Street in Bronzeville* by Gwendolyn Brooks. Copyright 1945 by Gwendolyn
Brooks Blakely. Reprinted by permission of Harper & Row, Publishers, Inc.

But that too, I am afraid,
Is faulty: oh, what shall I say, how is the truth to be
    said?
You were born, you had body, you died.
It is just that you never giggled or planned or cried.

Believe me, I loved you all.
Believe me, I knew you, though faintly, and I loved, I
    loved you
All.

THE BEAN EATERS

They eat beans mostly, this old yellow pair.
Dinner is a casual affair.
Plain chipware on a plain and creaking wood,
Tin flatware.

Two who are Mostly Good.
Two who have lived their day,
But keep on putting on their clothes
And putting things away.

And remembering . . .
Remembering, with twinklings and twinges,
As they lean over the beans in their rented back room that
    is full of beads and receipts and dolls and clothes,
    tobacco crumbs, vases and fringes.

From *The Bean Eaters* by Gwendolyn Brooks. Copyright 1959 by Gwendolyn Brooks.
Reprinted by permission of Harper & Row, Publishers, Inc.

THE BIRTH IN A NARROW ROOM

Weeps out of Western country something new.
Blurred and stupendous. Wanted and unplanned.
    Winks. Twines, and weakly winks
Upon the milk-glass fruit bowl, iron pot,
The bashful china child tipping forever
Yellow apron and spilling pretty cherries.

Now, weeks and years will go before she thinks
"How pinchy is my room! how can I breathe!
I am not anything and I have got
Not anything, or anything to do!"—
But prances nevertheless with gods and fairies
Blithely about the pump and then beneath
The elms and grapevines, then in darling endeavor
By privy foyer, where the screenings stand
And where the bugs buzz by in private cars
Across old peach cans and old jelly jars.

THE ANNIAD

Think of sweet and chocolate,
Left to folly or to fate,
Whom the higher gods forgot,
Whom the lower gods berate;
Physical and underfed
Fancying on a featherbed
What was never and is not.

What is ever and is not.
Pretty tatters blue and red,
Buxom berries beyond rot,
Western clouds and quarter-stars,

From *Annie Allen* by Gwendolyn Brooks. Copyright 1949 by Gwendolyn Brooks Blakely. Reprinted by permission of Harper & Row, Publishers, Inc.

From *Annie Allen* by Gwendolyn Brooks. Copyright 1949 by Gwendolyn Brooks Blakely. Reprinted by permission of Harper & Row, Publishers, Inc.

Fairy-sweet of old guitars
Littering the little head
Light upon the featherbed.

Think of ripe and rompabout,
All her harvest buttoned in,
All her ornaments untried;
Waiting for the paladin
Prosperous and ocean-eyed
Who shall rub her secrets out
And behold the hinted bride.

Watching for the paladin
Which no woman ever had,
Paradisiacal and sad
With a dimple in his chin
And the mountains in the mind;
Ruralist and rather bad,
Cosmopolitan and kind.

Think of thaumaturgic lass
Looking in her looking-glass
At the unembroidered brown;
Printing bastard roses there;
Then emotionally aware
Of the black and boisterous hair,
Taming all that anger down.

And a man of tan engages
For the springtime of her pride,
Eats the green by easy stages,
Nibbles at the root beneath
With intimidating teeth.
But no ravishment enrages.
No dominion is defied.

Narrow master master-calls;
And the godhead glitters now
Cavalierly on his brow.
What a hot theopathy
Roisters through her, gnaws the walls,
And consumes her where she falls
In her gilt humility.

How he postures at his height;
Unfamiliar, to be sure,
With celestial furniture.
Contemplating by cloud-light
His bejewelled diadem;
As for jewels, counting them,
Trying if the pomp be pure.

In the beam his track diffuses
Down her dusted demi-gloom
Like a nun of crimson ruses
She advances. Sovereign
Leaves the heaven she put him in
For the path his pocket chooses;
Leads her to a lowly room.

Which she makes a chapel of.
Where she genuflects to love.
All the prayerbooks in her eyes
Open soft as sacrifice
Or the dolour of a dove.
Tender candles ray by ray
Warm and gratify the gray.

Silver flowers fill the eves
Of the metamorphosis.
And her set excess believes
Incorruptibly that no
Silver has to gape or go,
Deviate to underglow,
Sicken off to hit-or-miss.

Doomer, though, crescendo-comes
Prophesying hecatombs.
Surrealist and cynical.
Garrulous and guttural.
Spits upon the silver leaves.
Denigrates the dainty eves
Dear dexterity achieves.

Names him. Tames him. Takes him off,
Throws to columns row on row.
Where he makes the rifles cough,
Stutter. Where the reveille
Is staccato majesty.
Then to marches. Then to know
The hunched hells across the sea.

Vaunting hands are now devoid.
Hieroglyphics of her eyes
Blink upon a paradise
Paralyzed and paranoid.
But idea and body too
Clamor "Skirmishes can do.
Then he will come back to you."

Less than ruggedly he kindles
Pallors into broken fire.
Hies him home, the bumps and brindles
Of his rummage of desire
Tosses to her lap entire.
Hearing still such eerie stutter.
Caring not if candles gutter.

Tan man twitches: for long
Life was little as a sand,
Little as an inch of song,
Little as the aching hand
That would fashion mountains, such
Little as a drop from grand
When a heart decides "Too much!"—

Yet there was a drama, drought
Scarleted about the brim
Not with blood alone for him,
Flood, with blossom in between
Retch and wheeling and cold shout,
Suffocation, with a green
Moist sweet breath for mezzanine.

Hometown hums with stoppages.
Now the doughty meanings die
As costumery from streets.
And this white and greater chess
Baffles tan man. Gone the heats
That observe the funny fly
Till the stickum stops the cry.

With his helmet's final doff
Soldier lifts his power off.
Soldier bare and chilly then
Wants his power back again.
No confection languider
Before quick-feast quick-famish Men
Than the candy crowns-that-were.

Hunts a further fervor now.
Shudders for his impotence.
Chases root and vehemence,
Chases stilts and straps to vie
With recession of the sky.
Stiffens: yellows: wonders how
Woman fits for recompense.

Not that woman! (Not that room!
Not that dusted demi-gloom!)
Nothing limpid, nothing meek.
But a gorgeous and gold shriek
With her tongue tucked in her cheek,
Hissing gauzes in her gaze,
Coiling oil upon her ways.

Gets a maple banshee. Gets
A sleek slit-eyed gypsy moan.
Oh those violent vinaigrettes!
Oh bad honey that can hone
Oilily the bluntest stone!
Oh mad bacchanalian lass
That his random passion has!

Think of sweet and chocolate
Minus passing-magistrate,
Minus passing-lofty light,
Minus passing-stars for night,
Sirocco wafts and tra la la,
Minus symbol, cinema
Mirages, all things suave and bright.

Seeks for solaces in snow
In the crusted wintertime.
Icy jewels glint and glow.
Half-blue shadows slanting grow
Over blue and silver rime.
And the crunching in the crust
Chills her nicely, as it must.

Seeks for solaces in green
In the green and fluting spring.
Bubbles apple-green, shrill wine,
Hyacinthine devils sing
In the upper air, unseen
Pucks and cupids make a fine
Fume of fondness and sunshine.

Runs to summer gourmet fare.
Heavy and inert the heat,
Braided round by ropes of scent
With a hypnotist intent.
Think of chocolate and sweet
Wanting richly not to care
That summer hoots at solitaire.

Runs to parks. November leaves
All gone papery and brown
Poise upon the queasy stalks
And perturb the respectable walks.
Glances grayly and perceives
This November her true town:
All's a falling falling down.

Spins, and stretches out to friends.
Cries "I am bedecked with love!"
Cries "I am philanthropist!
Take such rubies as ye list.
Suit to any bonny ends.
Sheathe, expose: but never shove.
Prune, curb, mute: but put above."

Sends down flirting bijouterie.
"Come, oh populace, to me!"
It winks only, and in that light
Are the copies of all her bright
Copies. Glass begets glass. No
Populace goes as they go
Who can need it but at night.

Twists to Plato, Aeschylus,
Seneca and Mimnermus,
Pliny, Dionysius. . . .
Who remove from remarkable hosts
Of agonized and friendly ghosts,
Lean and laugh at one who looks
To find kisses pressed in books.

Tests forbidden taffeta.
Meteors encircle her.
Little lady who lost her twill,
Little lady who lost her fur
Shivers in her thin hurrah,
Pirouettes to pleasant shrill
Appoggiatura with a skill.

But the culprit magics fade.
Stoical the retrograde.
And no music plays at all
In the inner, hasty hall
Which compulsion cut from shade.—
Frees her lover. Drops her hands.
Shorn and taciturn she stands.

Petals at her breast and knee. . . .
"Then incline to children-dear!
Pull the halt magnificence near,
Sniff the perfumes, ribbonize
Gay bouquet most satinly;
Hoard it, for a planned surprise
When the desert terrifies."

Perfumes fly before the gust,
Colors shrivel in the dust,
And the petal velvet shies,
When the desert terrifies:
Howls, revolves, and countercharms:
Shakes its great and gritty arms:
And perplexes with odd eyes.

Hence from scenic bacchanal,
Preshrunk and droll prodigal!
Smallness that you had to spend,
Spent. Wench, whiskey and tail-end
Of your overseas disease
Rot and rout you by degrees.
—Close your fables and fatigues;

Kill that fanged flamingo foam
And the fictive gold that mocks;
Shut your rhetorics in a box;
Pack compunction and go home.
Skeleton, settle, down in bed.
Slide a bone beneath Her head,
Kiss Her eyes so rash and red.

Pursing lips for new good-byeing
Now she folds his rust and cough
In the pity old and staunch.
She remarks his feathers off;
Feathers for such tipsy flying
As this scarcely may re-launch
That is dolesome and is dying.

He leaves bouncy sprouts to store
Caramel dolls a little while,
Then forget him, larger doll
Who would hardly ever loll,
Who would hardly ever smile,
Or bring dill pickles, or core
Fruit, or put salve on a sore.

Leaves his mistress to dismiss
Memories of his kick and kiss,
Grant her lips another smear,
Adjust the posies at her ear,
Quaff an extra pint of beer,
Cross her legs upon the stool,
Slit her eyes and find her fool.

Leaves his devotee to bear
Weight of passing by his chair
And his tavern. Telephone
Hoists her stomach to the air.
Who is starch or who is stone
Washes coffee-cups and hair,
Sweeps, determines what to wear.

In the indignant dark there ride
Roughnesses and spiny things
On infallible hundred heels.
And a bodiless bee stings.
Cyclone concentration reels.
Harried sods dilate, divide,
Suck her sorrowfully inside.

Think of tweaked and twenty-four.
Fuchsias gone or gripped or gray,
All hay-colored that was green.
Soft aesthetic looted, lean.
Crouching low, behind a screen,
Pock-marked eye-light, and the sore
Eaglets of old pride and prey.

Think of almost thoroughly
Derelict and dim and done.
Stroking swallows from the sweat.
Fingering faint violet.

Hugging old and Sunday sun.
Kissing in her kitchenette
The minuets of memory.

APPENDIX TO THE ANNIAD

leaves from a loose-leaf war diary

1

("thousands—killed in action")

You need the untranslatable ice to watch.
You need to loiter a little among the vague
Hushes, the clever evasions of the vagueness
Above the healthy energy of decay.
You need the untranslatable ice to watch,
The purple and black to smell.

Before your horror can be sweet.
Or proper.
Before your grief is other than discreet.

The intellectual damn
Will nurse your half-hurt. Quickly you are well.

But weary. How you yawn, have yet to see
Why nothing exhausts you like this sympathy.

2

The Certainty we two shall meet by God
In a wide Parlor, underneath a Light
Of lights, come Sometime, is no ointment now.
Because we two are worshipers of life,
Being young, being masters of the long-legged stride,
Gypsy arm-swing. We never did learn how
To find white in the Bible. We want nights
Of vague adventure, lips lax wet and warm,
Bees in the stomach, sweat across the brow. Now.

From *Annie Allen* by Gwendolyn Brooks. Copyright 1949 by Gwendolyn Brooks Blakely. Reprinted by permission of Harper & Row, Publishers, Inc.

MAY MILLER
(1918)

GIFT FROM KENYA

I've come back many times today
To touch the pale wood antelope,
Spindle legs tucked under him,
Tipping his head to danger.
Imagine seeing the pronghorn herd
Run the ridge of a blunted hill
With the skyline copper red.
It is too late to hear the axe
That, in the ruined cedar grove,
Shivered like a death drum note
To fell the trees that would become
Hundreds of antelope.

Some centuries ago
My ancient father knew those trees.
Young and bending in a wind,
He played near the saplings
While the early morning hour whipped
Singing round his loins.
When darkness came and the vultures slept,
In the fragrance of dew-heavy bark
He watched the determined coursing stars.
Come to manhood, in a night of power,
He tracked the curving paths
Leading away from sheltering boughs.

The cedar figurines
Lean upon the years to come.
That man and his way are old in me,
Old in the unborn who wait
To hold the ice-aged heritage
That has no end in single flesh
However wound in death.

From *The Clearing and Beyond* by May Miller (Washington, D.C.: The Charioteer Press, 1974). Copyright 1974. Reprinted by permission of The Charioteer Press.

NOT THAT FAR

Canary Islands

We touched land
White gulls flew on

*

Fishing boats
Everywhere
Everything blooming

*

For all its age
The Dragon Tree remembers
Nothing

*

The boy was too beautiful
To be begging

*

A man of Tenerife
Gave me
His island

Portugal

Once above the sea
And glittering sands
A warrior ruled
Called King

*

Storks red and yellow
On the chimney tops
Below, the women
In black

*

From *Not That Far* by May Miller (Washington, D.C.: The Charioteer Press, 1973). Copyright 1973. Reprinted by permission of The Charioteer Press.

They danced
In silks and velvet
The ceilings fell
Down on their heads

Gibraltar

Great rocks frighten
Little people

Spain

Granada
Seville and Cordoba
But we saw Malaga

*

Warships in
Locked steps on cobblestones
(What was I going to say)

*

A matador buried his sword
In a bank of roses

Tunisia

Dragon seas breathed white death
Scarlet flamingoes flew
Through the madness

*

Now Carthage grows daisies

Egypt

Stone for stone
No questions
Were left for answers

*

It's a skinny bird
You're holding
How old is it

*

I turned down the donkey ride
I wasn't going that far

Rhodes

Something once bloomed
That lit the walls
White Knights slept here

The Holy Land

Along the way
We met a man
Who spoke of
The young boy Jesus

*

Balconies gossiped
A cross is passing

*

A beggar boy
On the Mount of Olives
Held out his lamb to me

Turkey

Remember
The fiery blue of planets
In cool tile
Between two continents

*

Many times I had dreamed
Byzantium Byzantium

*

Minarets
Do stab
The darkness

Yugoslavia

From the tender
The water went too fast
For reflection

*

The spread-wing hills
Rise
Tall and beautiful

*

Time is turning in black hills

Greece

Marble cools
The story

*

Left of one god
A sandaled foot
White broken wings
On the sandal

*

The maidens found the porch
Too heavy for their heads

*

Temples that topped the hill
Turned to dry stone
Dusk

Italy

In Naples
It was beads
The sailors were buying

*

Who walks the shore
That I can't see

*

Ten eagle men went
Up the steps
One came down
Imperator

    *

The saint sat there in bronze
With his blessed toes
Kissed off

Madeira

Go slowly
Like oxen dragging carts
Over ungiving cobblestones

    *

Go slowly
Like time turning wine
In the great vats
To sweeten the air of Madeira

The Trip Back

The ship will never tame
Tiger tails and serpent fangs
But we sailed

    *

Is this home
There's fog over the harbor
And I can't see

MARGARET GOSS BURROUGHS
(1917)

TO SOULFOLK

Soulfolk, think a minute
It is not what is on your head
But rather what is in it.
It is not what you wear
Around your neck
But rather the head
That is on your neck.
Nor is it the cloth
That covers you
But rather the heart
That beats for you
And all of humankind.
Humanity and head and heart
Are the most important part.
Soulfolk, think on that
A minute.

BLACK PRIDE

Black pride, black pride, we remember well
How beautiful you used to be
With your hair thrust high and wide
You walked with awareness in your stride
But black pride why have you gone away?
Some of the things we've seen you do
Certainly have been no credit to you
They've saddened us so much Black Pride
That our souls and our hearts have cried

* * * * *

Black pride, black pride, please tell us
Where have you gone to hide
Happily we thought you'd come to stay
But your actions indicate otherwise
Oh Black pride, young black pride
It saddens us so much today
To find that we lost you along the way

*   *   *   *   *

Black pride, black pride, we were all
So happy to see you in your prime
To know that you had come into your time
Then we saw the black on black crime
This saddened us so much black pride
We were certain that you had died.

*   *   *   *   *

Black pride, black pride, when we saw
Brothers and sisters against sisters and brothers
Children disrespecting fathers and mothers
And hate replacing concern for each other
It really saddened us Black pride
That we had to witness your tragic demise

*   *   *   *   *

Black pride, black pride, we were certain
That you had gone far, far away
When we looked around where you used to stay
And saw the debris, garbage and trash galore
In the streets, on sidewalks and around your door
This sight saddened us Black pride
It looked as if you had really died

*   *   *   *   *

Black pride, black pride, we hear what you say
You admit that you were side-tracked along the way
And now that is all now in the past
You're starting anew on the glory path at last
You say we never should have given you up for dead
And resurrected, you raise your proud black head

*   *   *   *   *

Black pride, black pride, the heart of
Your elders are filled with great joy, Black pride
To know that our children are at our side
Our faith in the future is renewed in you
Black pride, young black pride
Like Moses, you will lead our people over
And through.

ONLY IN THIS WAY

Not by wayout hairdos, bulbous Afro blowouts and certainly
Not by obstreperous naturals, kinky, curly or straight, not by hair . . .
Not by beards or whiskers, scraggy or verdant . . .
Not by dark glasses or frozen facial postures, not by the superficial
Not by dirty jeans with patches sewed on where there are no holes . . .
Not by wearing Che khaki, Mao suits or Nehru jackets . . .
Neither by assuming Huey's or Bobbie's stance
Not by memorizing and repeating Malcolm's or Martin's words . . .
Not by parading as original concepts from Fanon, Marx, Garvey or
    Nkru-ah
Not by claiming the status of worker and disdaining honest labor . . .
Not by blaming the honkie as the cause of it all . . .
Not by placing the blame on the victim for his abject condition . . .
Not by the adulation of material things . . .
Not by making such acquisitions thereof your sole life's ambition . . .
Not by maiming your body and minds through forays into eupho-
    ria . . .
Not by any of those things . . .

Only by starting with self, by knowing and accepting who you are
And what you are and where you've come from and where you are
    going
And charting a course of how you're going to get there . . .
Only by education and learning for yourself and the whole people . . .
Only by each one teaching one, by passing understanding one to the
    other
From person to person and from peoples to peoples . . .
Only by recognition of your singular position . . .
By being aware of the existence of the two great antagonisms
And the reality of the historic and eternal struggle between them . . .

Only by doing your share . . . in exposing the failures and contradic-
tions
Only by serious and concentrated study of the dynamics of social
change
And of the experiences and philosophies of the architects thereof . . .
By becoming convinced that there is one way to liberation
Only by working hard, quietly and persistently can this order
Be altered, changed and turned about completely in interest of work-
ing folk

Only in this way to lay the groundwork for the change to come . . .
For the future . . . for your century.

EVERYBODY BUT ME

"You say that you believe in Democracy for everybody,
Yes, I know, for dogs and cats and others and everybody,
Everybody, but me.

In high sounding words and musty oratory, on Washing-
ton's and Lincoln's birthday.

You government officials, major and minor, effuse bright
praise to our country and all of her glory.

How it was founded and will always be a haven of the free
and I sitting up there listening to you applauded and cheered
with all the rest.

But I was one mighty surprised soul to see when it came to
the test that you did mean everybody, Everybody, but me.

Sure, I read all about it in the history books about how the
founding fathers got together and wrote the Declaration of
Independence cause they didn't want King George stepping
on them and even though I play a part in bringing it about—
they left me out.

They declared that Independence for everybody, Every-
body, but me.

They also got together and wrote a Constitution and a Bill
of Rights saying that everybody had certain rights and priv-
ileges being citizens and that everybody ought to have a job
and a place to live and equal opportunity.

From The Forerunners edited by Woodie King, Jr. (Washington, D.C.: Howard
University Press, 1975).

But when I tried to get my rights and privileges and a job and a house, I was mighty sorry to find that they really did mean everybody, Everybody, but me.

I went to church every Sunday being a pious person and I heard the preacher talking about heaven and eating milk and honey and wearing long white robes and I felt the spirit and shouted out, shouted out that I wanted to be in the number too.

Suddenly I looked up at the wall, saw that all the folks gathered around Jesus had straw blond hair and sky blue eyes and there wasn't a brother among them. I knew again that they did mean everybody, Everybody, but me.

Of course as far back as I hear tell about there have been times when they needed helping out, this is when they had a war and then they sent out a call for everybody, they knew what to use me for and I found that they really did mean everybody, including me.

My father told me that in World War I they sent out a call for everyone including me and we had to go over to fight the Kaiser to keep the world free and safe for Democracy for everybody.

When I got home I was hurt to find that they really did mean everybody, Everybody, but me.

Well putting two and two together you and I can plainly see that those folks down in Washington have never been thinking of you and me, from here on I'm going to be thinking about me. I'm going to get together with you and my sisters and brothers black and white all over the country and over the world and we're going to put up a terrific fight until we win and we will and when we say peace and freedom for everybody it will mean Everybody, everywhere.

It will mean me."

GLORIA C. ODEN
(1923)

THIS CHILD IS THE MOTHER

Black is; slavery was; I am.
Sometimes
when my mind idles
memory taps the subtle gears
of recollection and
I am locked into
my kindergarten years and
seated in that Methodist-simple,
stained glass bosom of
the Lord on a
shining Sunday morning.

Communion Day!
The altar railing drips white.
Behind it, housing the
plum-red blood of Christ,
stacked silver trays
burn in the sun,
flashing their furnace-tried
love and redemption.
Raised above them
the pulpit whereon in
the wit and wisdom of
pastoral years, my father
marches for Jesus striding,
first left, then right;
falling on one knee then
the other as his voice
rises from shout to shout,
beseeching God's lost lambs
home. "Come!" he calls

Published in *The Massachusetts Review* 15 (Summer 1974). Reprinted by permission of the author.

from behind his lectern
standing. "Let whosever will,
come!" he entreats, the
visible sign of The Cross,
his arms outstretching
Heaven's saving offer
of grace.

So is the scene
settling in.
Its mood revives
as a thin uncertain voice
unbosoms a sad
familiar fragment of
song that picks its way
forward from the rear,
urged from throat to throat
by its denomination of
common life experience.
The choir gives response.
At ease in its box
behind my father,
I observe their stiff-
robed bodies ignite and,
slowly, begin to stroke
their flooding fever as
rocking forward and back
they punctuate harmony.

I am no longer at ease.
It will happen soon,
I know: that birth
more terrible than all my
small fears recognize;
that blood-bathed irruption
which is but the beast
in reform of its labyrinth.

It begins in the corners.
On either side
the ministering pulpit
the Elders of the congregation

(sitting self-segregated
by sex and
splendid in their Sunday
formalism of Pilgrim black
and unblemished white)
unlock the piston valves of
their emotion in a
turbulence of heel upon
the hard wood floor.

Antiphonally,
they begin to shout,
to clap shaking hands
and weep.
"Glory be to God!"
comes forth the cry.
"Praise his Holy Name!"
the joyous response.
"My Strength and My Redeemer!"
is the rejoinder.

The church is awash
with sun and singing.
Antique dervishes
invade the aisles in
compulsive pavane:
history is metamorphized
within the furlongs of
my vision.

Now it happens:
she moves.
That tall woman
immediately in front of me
who hatted and wreathed in
a tonnage of black veiling
has been sitting like
some megalith of
slowed time
mute and motionless,
unresponsive to the
joy in flux

about her. But,
now she moves.
Her center can no
longer hold against
the store of grace
wedded to her days.

With the lightning's thrust
it has cleaved her.
She jerks and twists
whiplashed by memories
that rip her headgear
from her and force her
arms up, overhead, in
tight-fisted supplication.
Pushing against some
unseen weight, slowly,
she raises her bowed head
until, bursting free
at last it falls
back upon her shoulders.
She opens her mouth.
Out of it,
rocketing upwards,
as if from her toes,
jets an explosive cry that
crashes and beats
against the ceiling
like some crazed bird
in a frenzy of wing
for distance.

This is that moment
to which I am frozen.
This, that awesome time
when, more profoundly
than by pigment, I am
informed of my
blood heritage; and
when, as I burrow
into the protective folds
of my mother,
the outermost margins

of my mind began
to struggle with
the unexplained metaphor
in color,
the mysterious verdures
in history,
the fierce physics of
that soothing fountain
outpouring
from her side.

NAOMI LONG MADGETT
(1923)

DEACON MORGAN

His artificial feet calumped in holy rhythm
down the center aisle of Calvary Baptist Church
to Deacons' Row in front.
He knelt to pray before he took his chair.

Little and popeyed in our pew,
we never ceased to marvel
that he could strut when he got happy,
walk the narrow straitly,
and even drive a car.
Surely an understanding Jesus
has laid His hands on him.

Oh, lowlier than angels,
More visible than Holy Ghost,
he was our credible atonement,
our certainty of Paradise
who, having sinned we thought
and had his limbs cut off for punishment,
was welcome still in the abundant household
of a loving Father.

From *Exits and Entrances* by Naomi Long Madgett (Detroit: Lotus Press, 1978).
Reprinted by permission of the author.

EXITS AND ENTRANCES

Through random doors we wandered
into passages disguised as paradise
and out again, discarding,
embracing hope anew, discarding again:
exits and entrances to many houses.

Without new joy we sang,
without grace we danced,
our hump-backed rhythms colliding,
with our sanity,
our beauty blanching in a hostile sun.

How should we, could we
sing our song in a strange land?

Through random doors we have come
home to our kingdom, our own battleground,
not with harps, not with trumpets even,
but armed with the invincible sword and shield
of our own names and faces.

MIDWAY

I've come this far to freedom and I won't turn back.
I'm climbing to the highway from my old dirt track.
I'm coming and I'm going
And I'm stretching and I'm growing
And I'll reap what I've been sowing or my skin's not black.

I've prayed and slaved and waited and I've sung my song.
You've bled me and you've starved me but I've still grown strong.

From *Exits and Entrances* by Naomi Long Madgett (Detroit: Lotus Press, 1978). Reprinted by permission of the author.

From *Star by Star* by Naomi Long Madgett (Detroit: Harlo Press, 1965). Reprinted by permission of the author.

You've lashed me and you've treed me
And you've everything but freed me
But in time you'll know you need me and it won't be long.

I've seen the daylight breaking high above the bough.
I've found my destination and I've made my vow;
    So whether you abhor me
    Or deride me or ignore me,
Mighty mountains loom before me and I won't stop now.

NOMEN

(To Femi Sodipo and my African-American ancestors)

"What's in a name?"
(Shakespeare)

My sunlight came pre-packaged
from the corner store
a few days old
and always overpriced

but somehow I brought it safely
past thieves in dingy doorways
beyond fly-spattered mailboxes
with broken locks
            to my father's many-mansioned home.

Too many tombstones have been toppled,
too many pigeons have already fouled
the names and dates no longer legible.

So I will keep the name my father gave me
being neither anonymous nor poor
and having no need to let myself be robbed
a second time.

From *Exits and Entrances* by Naomi Long Madgett (Detroit: Lotus Press, 1978).
Reprinted by permission of the author.

NEW DAY

"Keep a-inchin' along, keep a-inchin' along,
Jesus'll come bye an' bye.
Keep a-inchin' along like a po' inchworm,
Jesus'll come bye an' bye."
                                    (Negro spiritual)

She coaxes her fat in front of her
like a loaded market basket with defective wheels.
Then she pursues it, slowly catches up, and
the cycle begins again.
Every step is a hardship and a triumph.

As she inches her way along in my direction
I sense the stretchings and drawings of
her heavy years. I feel the thunderous
effort of her movement reverberating
through a wilderness of multiple betrayals.

As gently as I can, I say, "Good Morning, Sister,"
as we come face to face, and wonder
if she understands at all what I am saying.

BLACK WOMAN

My hair is springy like the forest grasses
That cushion the feet of squirrels—
Crinkled and blown in a south breeze
Like the small leaves of native bushes.

My black eyes are coals burning
Like a low, full, jungle moon
Through the darkness of being.
In a clear pool I see my face,
Know my knowing.

From *Exits and Entrances* by Naomi Long Madgett (Detroit: Lotus Press, 1978).
Reprinted by permission of the author.

From *Pink Ladies in the Afternoon* by Naomi Long Madgett (Detroit: Lotus Press,
1972). Reprinted by permission of the author.

My hands move pianissimo
Over the music of the night:
Gentle birds fluttering through leaves and grasses
They have not always loved,
Nesting, finding home.

Where are my lovers?
Where are my tall, my lovely princes
Dancing in slow grace
Toward knowledge of my beauty?
Where
Are my beautiful
Black men?

MARGARET DANNER
(1915)

A GRANDSON IS A HOTICEBERG

A grandson is
not
the wing-sprouting cherub
that I, as a doting grandmother
have persisted in seeing and showing.

A grandson is a
                    hot
                        ice
                            berg,
that one cannot retain or disdain,
with all the half submerged knowing grinnings,
lusty leerings and/or jeerings
that the name implies.

Published in *Black World* 20 (September 1971). Reprinted by permission of the
author.

And as an added distraction or attraction
(according to ones politics)
this grandson is a

        BLACK

            hot

                ice

                    berg,

with bushy head hung down
and lengthy legs sprawled up
over the easiest-to-dirty chair.

And stubby fingernails thrown out in
"V for victory"
and grubby fists thrust to the polluted air
in cries of
"POWER TO THE PEOPLE . . . FIGHT"

and King Kong combs rearing up out of his
"this is an *AFRO . . . MAN*" hair.
And orangegreengoldblue
SHIKIS
and ebony with ivory eyed
TIKIS
and rather than the
"Yes mam, grandmother"
that he had been taught;
a jolting of "aints . . . wonts"
and other igniting Black language revolts,
and defyings of

        "RIGHT ON

              MOTHERS

                      MOTHER,

      DYNAMITE . . ."

THE RHETORIC OF LANGSTON HUGHES

While some "rap" over this turmoil
of who was Blackest first
and the ins and outs of the Spirituals
and the Blues
and how many of us have or have not
paid our dues;

Langston Hughes (in his traveling)
has sung to so many for so long
and from so very Black a Power
that we have clearly seen the "angles"
and dedicated ourselves
to be unraveling.

AT HOME IN DAKAR

When the African Arts,
home again,
became hosts of the hour,
their essence breezed into holidays,
holidays for those
dressed in their tans, browns, and charcoal grays, of the West;

and for those robed in their brighter power apparel;
and even for those who had much less than the
seven bright yards of M'bou bous
with the (seemingly) seven bright yards of turban to match.
For a flash, their battered sandals and tattered sacs had not mattered.

The Art objects (rejoicing in being "at home")
kept lending themselves
until their valid guests were jeweled.

Published in *Black World* 20 (September 1971). Reprinted by permission of the author.

Published in *Negro Digest* 15 (July 1966). Reprinted by permission of the author.

Not one felt too poor
and what with the incessant drumming
we all went on Tribute-to-African-Art inclinations,
Fabio, Fuller, Drake, and Langston Hughes
dancing through the streets.
Yes, I danced, too;
emotions thrumming that the dazzling grace of Blacks
could finally be felt in all its impact.

Yes, I danced; flinging out
my sheer lace (peach shifting to tangerine) M'bou bou
feeling neither too ill nor too old.

KATTIE M. CUMBO
(1938)

NOCTURNAL SOUNDS

Trembling November winds,
steam whistling in tenement pipes
breathing of slumbering neighbors
cracking walls, dripping faucets,
soft music from the flat below,
transistorized repetition of
yesterday's history.

Nocturnal sounds.

Loneliness caressing the night
and its sound is loud and penetrating.
Bursting in the eardrums like love
bursts in the heart of a new bride.

Nocturnal sounds.

From *Nine Black Poets* edited by R. Baird Shuman (Durham, North Carolina: Moore Publishing Company, 1968). Reprinted by permission of the author.

Fire engines rushing to right here,
no where. Speeding cars, noisy buses,
a laughter.

Nocturnal sounds.

Sleep comes to close the ears of
the mind to night sounds of this world.

DOMESTICS

Damit blackman
what are you going to
do to get your woman
from the kitchen of
the Jew?

BLACK SISTER

Black skin against bright green,
beautiful sister, hair a mess.
Don't you know you don't need that
wig? You are so beautiful, ancient
African queen—black sister.

Your bold features, your strong limbs,
your feet that stomp sand into deserts,
Sahara! Your sturdiness. Oh, but oh
why not, why not more sureness. More
sureness to enhance, enrich your blackness?

Black skin against green, touches of red,
black. Oh beautiful sister, Queen of the
Nile, beautiful ancient African queen,
black sister.

From *Nine Black Poets* edited by R. Baird Shuman (Durham, North Carolina: Moore Publishing Company, 1968). Reprinted by permission of the author.

From *Nine Black Poets* edited by R. Baird Shuman (Durham, North Carolina: Moore Publishing Company, 1968). Reprinted by permission of the author.

Rich rivers run through you, your veins, your teeth of ivory, your eyes, your smile. Oh beautiful sister, think, let's think about the empires, the richness. You must have more sureness and think more about your blackness.

And boy, you have now become a man. So brother, proclaim the beauty that you see, in your black sister.

THE MORNING AFTER . . . LOVE

clouds fill the sky
the breeze is cool
work a demanding task

i walk

my mind is relaxed
my body, remembering
the morning after love

a feeling fills my heart
like a cup of calm black
mist, refreshing

i walk

a new day, remembering
for a short spell
your embrace.

life trying to take on new
meaning, a dirty world reaching
for lustre.

I smell chrysanthemums from
tomorrow months.

and blinding rain drops smell
of perfume
on the morning after . . . love.

i walk.

I'M A DREAMER

I dream of Serenity,
Peace,
Calmness.

Of loving,
being,
sharing,
having.

I'm a dreamer.

I dream of living,
helping,
receiving,
giving.

I'm a dreamer.

One who sleeps
away reality.

CEREMONY

At the ceremony of *Emobo**
I feel your embrace,
your breath upon my face;

I hear the royal command,
see the dances, the chiefs,
the ritual.

Uzoma in Shivon‡ members oppose
one another in mock battle, but
it is I who die
       who die from loneliness,
from wanting.

---

*According to a Benin legend, *Arbebor*, "most loved wife," sacrificed herself for her king-husband; the ceremony referred to here celebrates that act.
   ‡These are seven warriors who comprise the "Council of War Chiefs" and who are king makers.

Spirits of dead kings invoke their
blessings.

It is the 13th moon.
Traditional leaves are placed
on your lap
      Son of the *Oba*†

for me, it is just the end of
another *Bini*** year.

A lonely year it was
I relive the *Izwoba*‡‡
the beautiful celebration
of dying year,
then rebirth.

As Muslims in the north
fast for Ramadan,
I wait for the new year.

---

†*Oba* is the king of the Benin empire in modern Nigeria.
**Bini is a native of Benin which is both a city in Nigeria and a tribe.
‡‡This refers to a feast in honor of the king and the coming new year.

SARAH WEBSTER FABIO
(1928–1979)

BACK INTO THE GARDEN

It's a hell

creeping back into
the garden, shedding
your badly worn skin,
starting anew;

worming into the
apple unrelent-
ingly until you
touch the hard core:

and always in mind
the thought and risk of
your being bitten
in two before

you've gotten far,
boring feverishly,
and all you've left
are split ends.

It's a hell!

But making it
the shiny seed's
your prize and
genesis.

From *A Mirror: A Soul* by Sarah Webster Fabio (San Francisco: Julian Richardson, Success Publishers, 1969).

TO TURN FROM LOVE

No,
I cannot
turn from love,
in affirmation,
with measured
finesse, like some
dull fuzzed cocoon
metamorphosing into a
bright-winged butterfly,
a tight-brown bud
transforming, with
sunburst halo, into
a chrysanthemum,
a five-o'clock
blossoming, with
daily gusto, into
full bloom.

No.
If I must
turn from love,
it will be with
the cadence of an
addict flinging poppy
from tremorous grasp
while retched with
the effort of breaking
the habit, or a
gravedigger turning
daisy-filled clods
on a fresh made
bed.

From *Dices or Black Bones* edited by Adam David Miller (New York: Houghton Mifflin Company, 1970).

ALL DAY WE'VE LONGED FOR NIGHT

In this room, holding hands,
joining in the small talk, our faces
with other languid faces mingling
in the smoke-soft light dulling
edges of day's end;

The string quartet plucking
sad notes from our sighs echoing
beneath the low ceiling and tingling
on the crystal rims of our olive-drowned
martinis as we take smooth sips, aah!

And outside, on the veranda,
under the milky-way canopy
of night, where our high
dreams—sandman bound—bump
their sleepy heads, we know

Only through these dreams
are we ourselves: all that we
may hope to be, locked in
our day-long longing for night.

From *Dices or Black Bones* edited by Adam David Miller (New York: Houghton Mifflin Company, 1970).

MARI EVANS

DAUFUSKIE

(Four Movements)

ebb
with the flow
of this soft movement

people
Being

gullah counterpoint
jabbing the swamp
underbreath
gullah laughter
taming the fetid forests
mosshung lairs for
bony blackkneed ghosts
silent tracking their grands

ebb
with the flow
of this soft movement

saltdamped
feet

moving to water rhythms
white sanded thru dimness
keening mysteries
saying the road
devouring the distances from
here to there

the ebb
and flow
of this soft movement

now the circle
be
unbroken

Jake

Jake the best damn cap'n in the world
   O gaaahd
the best damn cap'n in the world
    just been runnin the boat
    for the last twenny years
    for the last twenny years
    O gaaahd

He boat turn over with he wife
    You tell'm
He ride the breakers sideways
   in the storm
Smooth as m'hand I say that Jake
   and he caint swim

But he the best damn cap'n in the world
   O gaaahd
   the best damn cap'n in the world

The People Gather

They had it together
   and they laid it out

          Easy.

     Womans in the kitchen
     with the cookin

     Mens in the yard
     with the whiskey

     Chuhrens in the front
     with Jamesbrown

Didnt have to look at me
        with they eyes

But once.

Janis

Sand evy'where over
Janis sweepin
Sweepin d'dirt right out d'door
Janis ain playin
Janis grabbin d'dishes
Janis wipin d'sink wipe d'sink real dry
Janis workin
Janis ain playin
Janis get out d'polish
Gon spray on d'shine
Sweepin d'floor, places she miss any
Turnin aroun
Thats James Brown she singin
Janis in d'new house
Janis glad
Janis in d'new house
she' glad
she' glad

HOW WILL YOU CALL ME, BROTHER

How will you call me, brother
in the badtime . . .

I have been away so long I
do not know
the big drum's voice and you
have bought their murmuring
for so many years my voice is foreign
in your ear

Published in *Black World* 23 (September 1974). Reprinted by permission of the author.

Published in *Black World* 21 (September 1972). Reprinted by permission of the author.

"We own the night" but they
    own WHI TRadio
      WHI TV
        WHI TUnion

In the moment when their poison blurs the sun
and the air is heavy in my nostrils
I will need the comfort of your Blackness

How will you call me, brother
      in the badtime . . .

Have you armed your children and
sent the old ones to the woods
Have you fled the concrete compounds
for the safety of the night and
felt the softblack of your cousin
like a tree in turbulence
beside you

How will you call me, brother
      in the badtime . . .

Like carcasses that have begun to stink you
have outlived their need
you fill the air with curses and your foot
is heavy in the land
they pull their face and hide
behind the opaque of their souls gathering
blessings to come forth, armored
in the name of the FatherSonandHolyGhost
with an act of purification

How will you call me, brother
      in the badtime . . .

Have you armed your children?

. . . AND THE OLD WOMEN
GATHERED
(The Gospel Singers)

and the old women gathered
and sang His praises
standing
resolutely together
like supply sergeants who
have seen
everything
and are still
Regular Army: It
was fierce and
not melodic and
although we ran
the sound of it
stayed in our ears . . .

ALICE S. COBB
(1942)

THE SEARCHING

The chains that bind my thinking
That dare me to speak
Once scarred my great-grandmother
On that journey inhumanly bleak.
The words I mutter
The piece covering my hair
Bespeak of all I've suffered
And the decades of despair.

From *I Am a Black Woman* by Mari Evans (New York: William Morrow & Company, 1970). Reprinted by permission of the author.

From an unpublished volume *To Break These Chains* by Alice S. Cobb. Copyright 1976 by the author. Used by permission of the author.

So I look to a mountain undiscovered
Where destiny's urgent quest
Offers a private balcony
Where a *black* woman can protest.
Where she dare speak truth defiantly
Revivify soul ridiculed and undressed
Where she dare preen and reaffirm
Her womanness.

ANGELA DAVIS

Angela Davis
Tall, fair and wiry-haired,
Black people prayed and hoped for you.

"The only fair trial would have been no trial,"
        she said,
And I believe you!

Tell me pretty Angela of the oppressor's hand.
How he chained a people to labor in a foreign land.
Tell me pretty Angela of the slave-master's plan.
How he twisted the black mind to not believe he was human.

Angela Davis
tall, fair and wiry-haired
Blow my mind!
Oh, wake my deadened senses to the work to be done.
In the cause of freedom
The battle is yet to be won.

From *Blood of Africa* by Alice S. Cobb (Madison, Wisc.: FAS Publishing Co., 1975).
Reprinted by permission of the author.

JUNE JORDAN
(1936)

POEM FOR NANA

what will we do
when there is nobody left
to kill?

40,000 gallons of oil gushing into
the ocean
But I
sit on top this mountainside above
the Pacific
checking out the flowers
the California poppies orange
as I meet myself in heat

               I'm wondering

where's the Indians?

               all this filmstrip territory
               all this cowboy sagaland:
               not
               a single Indian
               in sight

40,000 gallons gushing up poison
from the deepest seabeds
every hour
40,000 gallons
while
experts international
while
new pollutants
swallow the unfathomable
still:

   no Indians

I'm staring hard around me
past the pinks the poppies and the precipice
that let me see the wide Pacific

unsuspecting
even trivial
by virtue of its vast surrender

I am a woman searching for her savagery
even if it's doomed

Where are the Indians?

Crow Nose
Little Bear
Slim Girl
Black Elk
Fox Belly

the people of the sacred trees
and rivers precious to the stars that told
old stories to the night

how do we follow after them?

falling
snow before the firelight
and buffalo as brothers
to the man

how do we follow into that?

*

They found her face down
where she would be dancing
to the shadow drums that humble
birds to silent
flight

They found her body held
its life dispelled
by ice
my life burns to destroy

Anna Mae Pictou Aquash†
slain on The Trail of Broken Treaties

---

†The Trail of Broken Treaties was an American Indian protest movement of the early 1970s. All the treaties negotiated between Native Americans and the United States government have been broken by the U.S. and this fact gave the movement its name. Aquash was a member of the American Indian Movement, participated in the occupation of Wounded Knee in 1973, and was murdered—under mysterious circumstances—in 1976.

bullet lodged in her brain/hands
and fingertips
dismembered

who won the only peace
that cannot pass
from mouth to mouth
                    *

And memory should agitate
the pierced bone crack
of one in pushed back horror
pushed back pain
as when I call out looking for my face
among the wounded coins
to toss about
or out
entirely
the legends of Geronimo
of Pocahontas
now become a squat
pedestrian cement inside the tomb
of all my trust

as when I feel you isolate
among the hungers of the trees
a trembling
hidden tinder so long unsolicited
by flame

as when I accept my sister dead
when there should be instead
a fluid holiness
of spirits wrapped around the world
redeemed by women
whispering communion
                    *

I find my way by following your spine

Your heart indivisible from my real wish
we
compelled the moon into the evening when
you said, "No,

I will not let go
of your hand."

*

Now I am diving for a tide to take me everywhere

Below
the soft Pacific spoils
a purple girdling of the globe
impregnable

*

Last year the South African Minister of Justice
described Anti-Government Disturbances as
quote Part of A Worldwide Tend Toward the
Breakdown of Established Political and Cultural
Orders unquote.

*

God knows I hope he's right.

*

JAYNE CORTEZ
(1936)

ORISHA*

Across the flesh and feeling of soledad
tornados of blackness
patoised in its beauty
in its luminous fuchsia lagos nights
ruby darkness

From *Scarifications* by Jayne Cortez (New York: Bola Press, 1973). Copyright 1973 by Jayne Cortez. Reprinted by permission of the author.
*The Orisha are the goddesses and gods of the Yoruba people of Western Nigeria.

criss-crossing in front of the music
in front of my pigeontoed solitude
another bush of praise
another battle ground for accents
insurrecting against brainwash and breakdowns
white bucks and famished lyrics
spellbound and peglegged
on cartridges of gunpowder teeth
Windpipes of burgundy lands
burning veins of respect forward into the blues
into pulsating ear of my cobra skin heart
immense in its infancy of these few words
Orisha Orisha Satchmo Orisha

PHRASEOLOGY

I say things to myself
in a bitch of a syllable
an off tone wisp remarkable
in weight and size
completely savage to the passing of silence
through mass combinations of moisture
uncaked in pockets of endless phraseology
moving toward sacred razors
like air like untangled bush
over a piece of dead scar
instant in another smashed ear lobe
shivering between word echoes of
word shadows
jugular veins of popular contradictions
well dressed and groomed in the mirror of language
transparent and useless against
the impulsive foam
of a spastic

From *Scarifications* by Jayne Cortez (New York: Bola Press, 1973). Copyright 1973 by Jayne Cortez. Reprinted by permission of the author.

ORANGE CHIFFON

If orange chiffon sadness
flowed from my chin of three bumps
and sat in the armpit of a worn-out douche bag
looking back at the system
opening like unfamiliar smells of dead cimarrons
in my two hands of empty tribal reserves
the cap and blanket of my thirst
    would i hold back
my jelly-bean shrine of menstrual blood
to wipe skag from curve
of a lone pubic hair
and sink into anesthesia of my launch pad
    would i push back the desert
and begin my shake dance with a flask
of empty buzzard grunts
if orange chiffon sadness
flowed from my uka of purple hearts
and my shadow half the size of two dates
broke

UNDER THE EDGE OF FEBRUARY

Under the edge of february
in hawk of a throat
hidden by ravines of sweet oil
by temples of switch blades
beautiful in its sound of fertility
beautiful in its turban of funeral crepe
beautiful in its camouflage of grief
in its solitude of bruises
in its arson of alert

From *Scarifications* by Jayne Cortez (New York: Bola Press, 1973). Copyright 1973, 1978 by Jayne Cortez. Reprinted by permission of the author.

From *Scarifications* by Jayne Cortez (New York: Bola Press, 1973). Copyright 1973, 1978 by Jayne Cortez. Reprinted by permission of the author.

Who will enter its beautiful calligraphy of blood

Its beautiful mask of fish net
mask of hubcaps mask of ice picks mask
of watermelon rinds mask of umbilical cords
changing into a mask of rubber bands
Who will enter this beautiful beautiful mask of
punctured bladders moving with a mask of chapsticks

Compound of Hearts   Compound of Hearts

Where is the lucky number for this shy love
this top-heavy beauty bathed with charcoal water
self-conscious against a mosaic of broken bottles
broken locks   broken pipes   broken
bloods of broken spirits broken through like
broken promises

Landlords   Junkies   Thieves
enthroning themselves in you
they burn up couches they burn down houses
and infuse themselves against memory
every thought
a pavement of old belts
every performance
a ceremonial pickup
how many more orphans   how many neglected shrines
how many stolen feet   stolen guns
stolen watchbands of death
in you how many times

Harlem

hidden by ravines of sweet oil
by temples of switch blades
beautiful in your sound of fertility
beautiful in your turban of funeral crepe
beautiful in your camouflage of grief
in your solitude of bruises in
your arson of alert
beautiful

SO MANY FEATHERS

You danced a magnetic dance
in your rhinestones and satin banana G-strings
it was you who cut the river
with your pink diamond tongue
did the limbo on your back
straight from the history of southern flames
onto the stage where your body
covered in metallic flint
under black and green feathers strutted
with wings of a vulture paradise on your head
strutted among the birds
until you became terror woman of all feathers
of such terrible beauty
of such fire
such flames
all feathers Josephine
This Josephine
exploding red marble eyes in new york
this Josephine
breaking color bars in miami
this Josephine
mother of orphans
legion of honor
rosette of resistance
this Josephine before
splitting the solidarity of her beautiful feathers

Feather-woman of terror
such feathers so beautiful
Josephine
with your frosted mouth half-open
why split your flamingos
with the death white boers in durban south africa
Woman with magnificent face of Ife mask
why all the teeth for the death white boers in durban

From *Mouth on Paper* by Jayne Cortez (New York: Bola Press, 1977). Copyright 1977 by Jayne Cortez. Reprinted by permission of the author.

Josephine you had every eyelash in the forest
every feather flying
why give your beaded snake-hips
to the death white boers in durban
Josephine didn't you know about the torture chambers
made of black flesh and feathers
made by the death white boers in durban
Josephine terror-woman of terrible beauty of such feathers
I want to understand why dance
the dance of the honorary white
for the death white boers in durban

After all Josephine
I saw you in your turquoise headdress
with royal blue sequins pasted on your lips
your fantastic legs studded with emeralds
as you kicked as you bumped as you leaped in the air
then froze
your body breaking lightning in fish net
and Josephine Josephine
what a night in harlem
what electricity
such trembling
such goose pimples
so many feathers
Josephine
dancer of the magnetic dancers
of the orange flint pelvis of the ruby navel
of the purple throat
of the feet pointing both ways
of feathers now gone
Josephine Josephine
I remember you rosette of resistance
southern flames
Josephine of the birdheads, ostrich plumes
bananas and sparkling G-strings
Josephine of the double-jointed knees
double-jointed shoulders double-jointed thighs
double-jointed breasts double-jointed fingers
double-jointed toes double-jointed eyeballs
double-jointed hips doubling

into a double squat like a double star into a giant double snake
with the double heartbeats of a young girl
doubling into woman-hood
and grinding into an emulsified double spirit
Josephine terror-woman of feathers i remember
Josephine of such conflicts i remember
Josephine of such floating i remember
Josephine of such heights i remember
Josephine
of so many transformations i remember
Josephine
of such beauty i remember
Josephine of such fire i remember
Josephine of such sheen i remember
Josephine
so many feathers i remember
Josephine Josephine

IN THE MORNING

Disguised in my mouth as a swampland
nailed to my teeth like a rising sun
you come out in the middle of fish-scales
you bleed into gourds wrapped with red ants
you syncopate the air with lungs like screams from yazoo
like X rated tongues
and nickel plated fingers of a raw ghost man
you touch brown nipples to knives
and somewhere stripped like a whirlwind
stripped for the shrine room
you sing to me through the side face of a black rooster

In the morning in the morning in the morning
all over my door like a rooster
in the morning in the morning in the morning

From *Mouth on Paper* by Jayne Cortez (New York: Bola Press, 1977). Copyright 1977 by Jayne Cortez. Reprinted by permission of the author.

And studded in my kidneys like perforated hiccups
inflamed in my ribs like three hoops of thunder through a screw
a star-bent-bolt of quivering colons
you breathe into veiled rays and scented ice holes
you fire the space like the flair of embalmed pigeons
and palpitate with the worms and venom and wailing flanks
and somewhere inside this fever
inside my patinaed pubic and camouflaged slit
stooped forward on fangs
in rear of your face
you shake to me in the full crown of a black rooster

In the morning in the morning in the morning

Masquerading in my horn like a river
eclipsed to these infantries of dentures of diving spears
you enter broken mirrors through fragmented pipe spit
you pull into a shadow ring of magic jelly
you wear the sacrificial blood of nightfall
you lift the ceiling with my tropical slush dance
you slide and tremble with the reputation of an earthquake
and when i kick through walls
to shine like silver
when i shine like brass through crust in a compound
when i shine shine shine
you wail to me in the drum call of a black rooster

In the morning in the morning in the morning
gonna kill me a rooster
in the morning
early in the morning
way down in the morning
before the sun passes by
in the morning in the morning in the morning

In the morning
when the deep sea goes through a dogs bite
and you spit on tip of your long knife

In the morning in the morning
when peroxide falls on a bed of broken glass
and the sun rises like a polyester ball of menses
in the morning

gonna firedance in the petro
in the morning
turn loose the blues in the funky jungle
in the morning
I said when you see the morning coming like
a two-headed twister
let it blow let it blow
in the morning in the morning
all swollen up like an ocean in the morning
early in the morning
before the cream dries in the bushes
in the morning
when you hear the rooster cry
cry rooster cry
in the morning in the morning in my evilness of this morning

I said
disguised in my mouth as a swampland
nailed to my teeth like a rising sun
you come out in the middle of fish-scales
you bleed into gourds wrapped with red ants
you syncopate the air with lungs like screams from yazoo
like X rated tongues
and nickel plated fingers of a raw ghost man
you touch brown nipples into knives
and somewhere stripped like a whirlwind
stripped for the shrine room
you sing to me through the side face of a black rooster

In the morning in the morning in the morning

GRINDING VIBRATO

Blues Lady
with the beaded face
painted lips
and hair smeared
in the oil of texas

You were looking good and sounding beautiful
until the horseman wanted your thunder
until the boa constrictor wanted your body
until syringes upright hyenas
barbwired your meat to their teeth
pushing behind your ears
inside your mouth
between your vagina
scabs the size of quarters
scabs the size of pennies
the size of the shape of you
all pigeon holes and spider legs colonized woman
funky piece of blood flint
with blue graffitied arms
a throat of dead bees

and swollen fingers that dig into a swamp of broken purrtongue

Spotted stripped blues lady
who was looking good and sounding beautiful
with those nasal love songs
those strident battle-cry songs
that copper maroon rattle resonator
shaking from your feet to your eyes
the sound of water drum songs
grinding vibrato songs to work by to make love by
to remember you by
Blues song lady who was looking good and sounding beautiful
until you gave away your thunder
until you gave up your spirit
until you barbwired your meat to teeth

From *Mouth on Paper* by Jayne Cortez (New York: Bola Press, 1977). Copyright 1977 by Jayne Cortez. Reprinted by permission of the author.

and became the odor of hyenas
uprooted woman with the embalmed face
pall bearer lips
and hair matted in the mud of texas
how many ounces of revolution do you need
to fill the holes in your body
or
is it too late to get back your lightning
is it too late to reconstruct your song blues song sister tell me
is it too late for the mother tongue in your womanself to insurrect

DELLA BURT
(1944)

SPIRIT FLOWERS

Spirit flowers are our lives,
We move in the
promise of the future.
We watch the ones
born unto us
walk, talk, dance, sing
grow
into the futures we've dreamed.
Sometimes losing faith
we bemoan
the wind which blows too strongly
losing our perfection.
We berate the sun
which shines too brightly
baking us black.
We deny love
tormenting our waking hours.
We kill the dream
leaving goals unattended.
But then the gentle breeze blows;
The sun breaks open our smiles;

The dream is reborn
Our love blossoms and
we are fulfilled.
The blue sky and warm sunshine
caress our shoulders
and wrap us in security
making us believers again.
We create
and what we create
is our future.
Spirit flowers we are.

A LITTLE GIRL'S DREAM WORLD

I remember the time
he dared me to understand
being Second to One
But I wasn't supposed to
use the label.
Labels don't mean a thing;
They don't accurately describe.
I understood.

I remember the time
he dared me to believe
We're honest and earnest,
We're different, special
What we have builds confidence
can't be swayed
Dared me to believe in a love that said
"WAIT."

I believed.
I understood.
I waited.
Now I die a slow death of
non-labels and honesty
Bereft of words to support the vacuum
Wanting labels and words for

now they bear a special kind of
reality
On my believing and my honesty
I choke on words
I can't see
        feel
                a love gone by.
Could it be that
it never
was?

ON THE DEATH OF LISA LYMAN

I had become callous like most
Numbed by statistics:
Viet Nam wounded, captured, dead
Foreign train wreck—100 killed
Landslide—ten houses swallowed up
Earthquake—100 foundations shaken.
Chicago wreck—44 dead, 300 injured—
This time it's not the same.

Through those nameless entities
I see Lisa
and those numbers
become people
dying, dead.
And I can't even say
"I know how it is"
Because I don't.
I can only try to feel for
once-living, now-dead people
and the living
they leave behind.

I want to talk about it
but I can't—
must seem hard, cold, callous
Nobody seems to understand
that I keep seeing Lisa's face.
Talk is too unreal.

FAREEDAH ALLAH
[Ruby C. Saunders]

HUSH, HONEY

HUSH! YO'MOUTH
IT IS TIME TO BE QUIET
AND SOFT SPOKEN
WELL MANNERED
REFINED
SPEAKING SELDOM
AND ONLY WHEN NECESSARY
SPEAKING FINE GOOD WORDS
WHEN NECESSARY

HUSH! HONEY!
IT IS TIME TO BURY
BELULAH
AND BIG MAYBELLE
AND TINY MAE
AND CALDONIA
IT IS TIME TO BURY
LOUD MOUTH, CUSSING MAMAS
WHO WILL SLAP YOU DOWN
IF YOU GET IT WRONG
HANDS ON HIPS
SALLY WALKER
MOUTH FLYING
LIPS FLIPPING

"DON'T YOU TELL ME TO SHUT UP
WHO YOU, NEGRO? WHO YOU THINK YOU IS?"

HUSH, HONEY
BE QUIET
SISTER
"BE CALM BE COOL AND BE COLLECTIVE"

CLOSE YOUR BIG UGLY MOUTH
CAN'T YOU SEE HOW UGLY YOU BE
YOU'RE BAD   ALRIGHT

YOU LOOK BAD!
YOU SOUND BAD!

YOU MAKE THE MAN FEEL SO SMALL
HE HAS TO KICK YOU   KICK YOU
BEAT YOU   BEAT YOU
LEAVE YOU   LEAVE YOU
LEAVE YOU TO KEEP FROM KILLING
YOU
THE MOTHER OF HIS BABIES

CLOSE YOUR UGLY MOUTH,
BLACK WOMAN
JUST HUSH!
UP!

YOU SOUND LIKE A SAVAGE
YOU LOOK LIKE A SAVAGE
YOU BE MAKING MOVEMENTS LIKE
A BABOON

QUEEN MOTHER
QUEEN MOTHER
THE WIFE OF THE MAKER OF THE PLANET
AND THE MOON
QUEEN MOTHER
QUEEN MOTHER

MADE INTO A SAVAGE BEAST
FOLLOWING THE WAYS OF THE
MONKEY WOMAN,
MISS ANN!
QUEEN MOTHER
LOST TO ALL KNOWLEDGE OF YOUR
BEAUTIFUL BLACK SELF
HUSH, HONEY!

TAKE YOUR HANDS OFF YOUR HIPS!
UNCROSS YOUR LEGS AND ANKLES!
PULL-UP STRAIGHT IN THAT CHAIR!
YOU ARE THE QUEEN OF THIS PLANET!
YOU GAVE BIRTH TO THE GOD OF THIS UNIVERSE!
YOU ARE THE QUEEN OF THIS PLANET!
STOP TALKING LIKE A FILTHY SLUT!

STOP SHAKING YOUR BACKSIDE IN
STRANGE MEN'S FACES!

MR. MUHAMMAD HAS TOLD THE WORLD
YOU'RE THE GREATEST!
TOLD THE WORLD—
YOU'RE THE GREATEST!
YOU'RE THE BEST!
YOU'RE THE BEST!
BLACK WOMAN IN AMERICA!
YOU'RE THE BEST!

CLOSE YOUR FILTHY MOUTH!
HUSH — HONEY!
EVERYTHING YOU THINK
HAS ALREADY BEEN THOUGHT AND SAID
EVERYTHING YOU KNOW IS KNOWN

THE NIGHT DEPARTS
THE MORNING BRIGHTENS
THE SUN RISES IN THE EAST
THE STARS SHINE
THE MOON REFLECTS LIGHT FROM THE SUN
THE FRUIT TREES GROW
AND THE UNIVERSE
IT CONTINUES
IN THE TRINITY OF TIME, SPACE, AND MOTION
WHEN YOU ARE QUIET, BLACK WOMAN
ALLAH IS GOD
MASTER WALLACE FARD MUHAMMAD
TO WHOM PRAISES ARE FOREVER DUE
WHEN YOU, BLACK WOMAN, SPEAK NOT!
THE MOST HONORABLE ELIJAH MUHAMMAD
IS THE LAST MESSENGER OF ALMIGHTY ALLAH

WHEN YOU SPEAK, BLACK WOMAN, SPEAK
FINE WORDS
GOOD WORDS
ALL PRAISES ARE DUE
ALL PRAISES ARE DUE

EVERYTHING WILL BE
AND ALL THAT IS UGLY ABOUT YOU WILL
BE GONE

WHEN YOU ARE QUIET
SOFT SPOKEN
REFINED
BEAUTIFUL
SITTING ON THE THRONE
NEXT TO YOUR LORD
THE KING

LISTEN—LISTEN—
LISTEN—BLACK WOMAN
LISTEN—TO—THE PRAISES
LISTEN—TO—THE PRAISES

ALL PRAISES ARE DUE TO ALLAH FOR THE LAMB

ALL PRAISES ARE DUE TO ALLAH FOR THE LAMB

CINDERELLA

I WILL BE PATIENT WHILE MY LORD
PUNISHES ME FOR I HAVE SINNED
AGAINST HIM.

AND SO I WAIT
AND SUFFER THE PAINS
OF NEW GROWTH
OF NEW HEALTH
OF NEW BEAUTY
OF NEW DESIRES
OF NEW DREAMS

I WAIT AND PRAY AND FAST AND SUFFER
BECAUSE
I HAVE KNOWN LOVE
AND   MAN
AND   UNDERSTAND
THE LAW OF NATURE
AND   WOMAN
AND   WOMAN SHOULD
BE WITH HER MAN
AND A JOY TO HIM
AND WITH HER MAN

AND A COMFORT
AND WITH HER MAN
AND LOVING HIM
BEING MADE WHOLE BY HIM
PROTECTED—SHELTERED—RESPECTED
PROTECTED—SHELTERED—RESPECTED

AND WOMAN IS A GIFT FOR MAN
FROM HIS LORD HIS KING HIS MASTER
WOMAN IS
WOMAN IS
WOMAN IS A GIFT FOR MAN

SO I PRAY
SO I FAST
SO I SUFFER THE PAINS OF NEW GROWTH—NEW HEALTH
NEW BEAUTY—NEW LIFE—NEW DESIRES—NEW DREAMS

I WILL BE PATIENT
WHILE MY LORD PUNISHES ME
FOR I HAVE SINNED AGAINST HIM

AND I WAIT

CLEAN-UP TIME
MADE NEW BY ELIJAH
MADE NEW BY ELIJAH
PURIFIED BY THE FIRE
PURIFIED BY THE FIRE

ALL PRAISES ARE DUE
ALL PRAISES ARE DUE

FOR I HAVE SINNED AGAINST HIM
AND WOMAN
        WOMAN
SHOULD BE PURE BEAUTIFUL
YOUTH NEVER ALTERING IN AGE
A GARDEN OF PARADISE FOR HER MAN

SO I WAIT
AND WORK HARD IN THE VINEYARD OF MY SOUL
CRYING NIGHTLY TO MY LORD
ALL PRAISES ARE DUE
ALL PRAISES ARE DUE

FOR I HAVE SINNED AGAINST HIM
ALMIGHTY ALLAH
ALL AND ALL
ALMIGHTY ALLAH   I HAVE SINNED
AGAINST HIM

I WILL BE PATIENT
I WILL BE PATIENT
WAITING FOR A KING
CROWN PRINCE
IN GLORY

MY KING
MY GLORY

I WILL BE PATIENT
WHILE MY LORD PUNISHES ME
FOR I HAVE SINNED AGAINST HIM.

I WILL BE PATIENT

"MIRROR, MIRROR ON THE WALL
WHOSE THE FAIREST OF THEM ALL?
CINDERELLA", CINDERELLA
CINDERELLA, CINDER—ELLA
BLACK GIRL
BLACK GIRL
MGT
MGT
MGT

ALL PRAISES ARE DUE TO ALLAII FOR
THE LAMB

ALL PRAISES ARE DUE TO ALLAH FOR
THE LAMB

FUNKY FOOTBALL

The 'Kat' can play ball, Man
The 'kat' can play
Remember when
Remember when
And how . . .
And How . . .
The kats could play
No 'prettyboy' stuff
No "Starlight"
No Starbright
Those 'kats' had to jump into the stuff
Play like hell then, Man

The Kats could play
Remember when
Remember when
And how
And how
Could run 50 yards
With two dudes on his back
The quarterback could
Throw, run and block
And no body messed with the line
The line was bad
Heavy, Kats, broke the scales at
Three Hundred pounds
Remember
Remember
When, man

Yeah! . . . I still play
Little, semi pro . . .
In the league, sandlot, you know
Lots of kats we used to play
Turned pro . . . making MONEY
Cash Bills
Saw so-and-so and li'boy and
'Choo-the train' playing on TeeVee
With the Rams

And "Shoot", my man, I know a dude
On the Colts, and two playing for
New York, . . . and Who?
Yeah! I know him . . . I know the Kat!
Little Boy's sister got two kids by him
That's a mean running back, Jack
Saw him bring in two in the first half
Yeah!
I'm still playing a little
Now & then . . . in the league
Little semi-pro . . .
I ain't going to get messed up, you know
Can't dig no broken bones, ribs
and scratches on my face
My women don't like it
Yeah! man . . . (laughing)
Remember
Remember
When . . .

The brothers were mean on the field
Man . . . no 'pretty boystuff'
                "Starlight/starbright"
Your ass had to play some ball
And roll in the mud, Jack . . .
Yeah, yeah . . .
Remember . . .
Remember . . .
When . . .
When . . .
And how . . .
And how . . .

Jean?
Yeah! I married her
We got four boys
And two girls

Joan?
Yeah! . . . I still see her now & then

Bettye?
She married some kat
Who is locked up now

Mary Louise?
I still see her now & then
When I can get away . . . (laughing)

How's your stuff?
Yeah! what? . . .
Jimmy Small's sister
Damn! I didn't know that
You got four girls, too . . .
Damn!

You still playing "END", man?
Yeah, I remember
      I remember when
           When . . .
Look, I got to split
Come on over, Sunday
We can watch the pro's
Double Hitter
See . . . 'so-and-so' . . . kick dust
Yeah! The kat can play, man
The kat can play some ball
Check you later
Check you, man
Gotta make it on in
My women don't like my being out late
(laughing)
Got Ta stay in shape
I'm going on in and lift a few weights
(laughing)
Sunday . . . Football . . .
See you then . . .
Yeah, man
Hell, no, Baby!
They can't win!

YOU MADE IT RAIN

You made it rain, Lady
You made it rain
The rains poured for days down on the lowly earth
Stripping the Queenly trees of their Fall dresses
Dresses of yellow gold red brown green and purple
Leaves covered the ground
After you made it rain, Lady
After you made it rain

Were you so jealous of the Queenly trees
Changing their summer greens for the many colored
Beautiful Fall Robes
You were jealous, I believe, Madame Moon
So, you made it rain

And at night you come out to laugh
In your pale silver colorless beauty
Madame Moon
You laugh
At the bare brown oaks and spruces
Queenly naked branches of the earth
Standing proudly
Watching the earthly creatures walk on their discarded
Robes of golden red yellow brown leaves
You laughed
Throwing your dark curls back
Becoming full faced
Robed in black
Madame Moon, you laughed

And the Sun came up from up behind your clouds to kiss the
Earth, showing the world the Queens in their soft
Brown nakedness.

Madame Moon, shall I tell how you gathered up the
Waters from the standing city seas, lakes
Evaporated their essences
Mist rising because of your jealous envy
The clouds gathered in the water and poured
A river of your bitter tears down on Her Majesties
The black brown Trees

You made it rain, Lady
Because of you it rains, Madame Moon
Because of you and your envy of the mighty trees
The Earthly Queens
Because of you, Madame Moon
It rains.

THE GENERATION GAP

I takes up for my colored men
Let me tell you, chile
I takes up for me colored men
Been doing it for quite a while.

I don't let these whitefolks tell me
Nothing!
Jesus Christ above
Anything that Rap Brown does
He's doing it out of love.

I tuns on my TV set
Cause my FM needs some fixing
I hears the news everyday
Just to see what Charley be thinking.

Don't you show no disrespect
Standing in my face.
Jesus Christ lawd's my saviour
Colored men got lots to take.
And they takes it too
I tell you
They takes it too
I say
Sing their praises bless the lawd
Makes me want to shout!

From *We Speak as Liberators* edited by Orde Coombs (New York: Dodd, Mead & Company, 1970). Reprinted with permission of the author.

I don't wear my hair all nappy
Don't throw my fists up in the air
I can't wear them African garments
On my subway job, no how.
But I knows that
You's in colleges and schools
All over this land
Got good job and houses, senators,
Congressmen, the vote . . . plans!
Now just because this is so
And the white folks calls you news
Remember . . . Tom . . . and . . . Aunt Jemima
Bent low to pay your dues.

LAWD, DESE COLORED CHILLUM

I get my degree
The Spring of '52
Walked all over this town.

Got a Brooks Brothers' suit
Shoes brand new
I was gonna knock the Whiteman down.

I had learned me some languages too
French I.
And French II.
Got a *bad* hat or two.

Finally got a job The Winter of '52

I practiced in the mirror
Knew just what to do
How to act like Charley
And speak like him too.

I left home early
In the morningtime
Proud as I could be

From *We Speak as Liberators* edited by Orde Coombs (New York: Dodd, Mead & Company, 1970).

Whitewashed
Grinning
9-to-5
Bluecollar
Job
Me.
    A nappy-headed boy
    Some son of a mother . . .
    Said
        "HEY, BROTHER!"
Lawd, dese Chillum won't let you be
White for nothing.

CAROLYN M. RODGERS
(1942)

POEM FOR SOME BLACK WOMEN

i am lonely.
all the people i know
i know too well

there was comfort in that
at first but now
we know each others miseries
    too well.
we are
    lonely women, who spend time waiting for
    occasional flings

we live with fear.
we are lonely.
we are talented, dedicated, well read
    BLACK, COMMITTED,

we are lonely.

From *How I Got Ovah* by Carolyn Rodgers. Copyright 1971 by Carolyn Rodgers. Reprinted by permission of Doubleday & Company, Inc.

we understand the world problems
Black women's problems with Black men
    but all
we really understand is
    lonely.

when we laugh,
we are so happy to laugh
we cry when we laugh
    we are lonely.
we are busy people
always doing things
fearing getting trapped in rooms
loud with empty . . .
            yet
knowing the music of silence/hating it/hoarding it
loving it/treasuring it,
    it often birthing our creativity
          we are lonely

being soft and being hard
supporting our selves, earning our own bread
soft/hard/hard/soft/
knowing that need must not show
          will frighten away
knowing that we must
walk back-wards nonchalantly on our tip-toesssss
    into
happiness,
    if only for stingy moments

we know too much
we learn to understand everything,
to make too much sense out
of the world,
of pain
          of lonely . . .

we buy clothes, we take trips,
we wish, we pray, we meditate, we curse, we crave, we coo, we caw,

          we need ourselves sick, we need, we need
we lonely we grow tired of tears we grow tired of fear
we grow tired but must al-ways be soft and not too serious . . .

not too smart not too bitchy not too sapphire
not too dumb not too not too not too
a little less a little more

add here detract there

.lonely.

MASQUERADE

I

you think you
need me. think
that i
will complete some picture for you.
total up and be the sum
of something, your thing . . .
but it's a lie you know
you've almost come up on
the truth about yourself
and you want me to hold
you/hold the truth off
when the pain comes
of lying too much.
when the awkward moments
descend from closing ones eyes too often
you want me to present my self
for the wrapping.
you want me to wrap your self
up in me/i in you and we
will hide behind each other
and that will be the only
truth between us.
we, us ducking and hiding and
running and blinding ourselves.

From *How I Got Ovah* by Carolyn Rodgers. Copyright 1975 by Carolyn Rodgers. Reprinted by permission of Doubleday & Company, Inc.

II

i could help you.
i could become the vital
part of your struggle
whenever the truth comes
too near
i could divert you
with my body at first,
perhaps later with marriage and
a child
something to weigh you
or divert your attention.
you know how women do.
i could find some thing
that would be sufficient
and then you would be able
to smile.

III

and of course
you promise to do
the same for me.
you promise to lie to me
about me to me to others. . . .
we promise to present a
united front to our friends
to the world.
we promise not to expose
but to preserve each other's
weakness.
i will forgive
and we will both
forget
gracefully . . .
except of course at
the times when we must
most painfully remind each other
of the function we are
                              performing
for each other lest one of us

forgets one day
and steps one step too far from
our masquerade.

we could be together only
if i promised to keep my mouth
shut and speak on cue.
you propose to pay me with
the hard and softness of your body.
that is what you bait me with.
your soft mouth and your unconsciously
deceitful face.

it is not enough for me.
it is not enough for you.
together we must plunge
deeper into our pain for more—
for the more pain we attempt to escape
the more joy we automatically negate
for it is through pain that we
ultimately realize the specific beautiful or ugly
innards of
our
selves.

JESUS WAS CRUCIFIED OR:
IT MUST BE DEEP
(an epic pome)

i was sick
and my motha called me
tonight yeah, she did she
sd she was sorri
i was sick, but what
  she wanted tuh tell
me was that i shud pray or
have her (hunky) preacher

From *How I Got Ovah* by Carolyn Rodgers. Copyright 1969 by Carolyn Rodgers. Reprinted by permission of Doubleday & Company, Inc.

pray fuh me, she sd. i
had too much hate in me
she sd u know the way yuh think is
got a lots to do
wid the way u feel, and i
agreed, told her i WAS angry a lot THESE days
and maybe my insides was too and she sd
     why it's somethin wrong wid yo mind girl
that's what it is

      and i sd yes, i was aware a lot
lately and she sd if she had evah known educashun
woulda mad me crazi, she woulda neva sent me to
school (college that is)
she sd the way i worked my fingers to the bone in
this white mans factori to make u a de-cent some-
bodi and here u are acting not like decent folks
     talking bout hating white folks & revolution
& such and runnin round wid Negroes
    WHO CURSE IN PUBLIC!!! (she sd)
THEY COMMUNIST GIRL!!! DON'T YUH KNOW
THAT???
  DON'T YUH READ*THE NEWSPAPERS??????
       (and i sd)
i don't believe—(and she sd) U DON'T BELIEVE IN
       GOD NO MO DO U?????
u wudn't raised that way! U gon die and go tuh HELL
and i sd i hoped it wudn't be NO HUNKIES there
and she sd
what do u mean, there is some good white people and
some bad ones, just like there is negroes
and i says i had neva seen ONE (wite good that is) but
she sd negroes ain't redi, i knows this and
deep in yo heart you do too and i sd yes u right
negroes ain't readi and she sd
why just the utha day i was in the store and there was
uh negro packin clerk put uh colored woman's ice cream
in her grocery bag widout wun of them "don't melt" bags
   and the colored ladi sd to the colored clerk
"how do u know mah ice cream ain't gon tuh melt befo I
git home."

clerk sd. "i don't" and took the ice cream
back out and put it in wun of them "stay hard"
bags
and me and that ladi sd see, ne-groes don't treat
nobody right why that clerk packin groceries was un
grown main, acted mad. white folks wudn't treat yuh that
way. why when i went tuh the BANK the otha day to de-
posit some MONEY
this white man helped me fast and nice. u gon die girl
and go tuh hell if yuh hate white folks. i sd, me and
my friends could dig it . . . hell, that is
she sd du u pray? i sd sorta when i hear Coltrane and
she sd if yuh read yuh bible it'll show u read genesis
revelation and she couldn't remember the otha chapter
i should read but she sd what was in the Bible was
happnin now, fire & all and she sd just cause i didn't
       believe the bible don't make it not true
                                        (and i sd)
       just cause she believed the bible didn't make it true
and she sd it is it is and deep deep down
in yo heart u know it's true
                                        (and i sd)

  it must be deeep
she sd i gon pray fuh u tuh be saved. i sd thank yuh
     but befo she hung up my motha sd
     well girl, if yuh need me call me
i hope we don't have to straighten the truth out no mo.
i sd i hoped we didn't too
                     (it was 10 P.M. when she called)
she sd, i got tuh go so i can git up early tomorrow
and go tuh the social security board to clarify my
record cause i need my money.
work hard for 30 yrs. and they don't want tuh give me
$28.00 once every two weeks.
              i sd yeah . . .
don't let em nail u wid no technicalities
              git yo checks . . . (then i sd)

     catch yuh later on Jesus, i mean motha!
          it must be
                     deeeeep . . . .

U NAME THIS ONE

let uh revolution come. uh
state of peace is not known to me
anyway
since i grew uhround in chi town
where
howlin wolf howled in the tavern on 47th st.
and muddy waters made u cry the salty nigger blues,
    where pee wee cut lonnel fuh fuckin wid
    his sistuh and blood baptized the street
    at least twice ev'ry week and judy got
    kicked outa grammar school fuh bein pregnant
    and died trying to ungrow the seed
        we was all up in there and
        just livin was guerilla warfare, yeah.

let uh revolution come.
couldn't be no action like what
i dun already seen.

LINDA PIPER
(1949)

SWEET ETHEL

Sweet Ethel was a roaming gal
You could see her on many a different street
Every night of the week
Sweet Ethel roamed the street

They got her
They got her
And she'll never
Walk the streets no more

From *How I Got Ovah* by Carolyn Rodgers. Copyright 1969 by Carolyn Rodgers. Reprinted by permission of Doubleday & Company, Inc.

If you needed a friend
To help you make it through the night
There was Sweet Ethel
Standing on Lyons, Scott and Right

They got her
They got her
And she'll never
Walk the streets no more

Sweet Ethel was a pretty gal
The prettiest gal there was
Not many a gal
Can do for you what Sweet Ethel does

They got her
They got her
And she'll never
Walk the streets no more

One night in the heat of July
The man came and got Sweet Ethel
One night in the heat of July
The man came and got Sweet Ethel

They got her
They got her
And she'll never
Walk the streets no more

MISSIONARIES IN THE JUNGLE

In the clearing stands
A three story white brick structure
With manicured lawns
And clean polished floors
Little white nuns
March up and down the corridors
Administering to garrulous black ghetto residents.

CAROLE C. GREGORY
(1945)

LOVE LETTER

Dear Samson,
I put your hair
in a jar
by the pear tree
near the well.
I been thinkin'
over what I done
and I still don't think
God gave you
all that strength
for you to kill
my people.

Love — Delilah

REVELATION

I

An old woman in me walks patiently to the hospital,
I felt ridiculous,
I was mad about my life,
it was never in harmony with Momma's,
and now her 300 pressure pushed life every which a way,
I couldn't stand her god,
I wanted to hurt her spoiled sons,
but I smiled and fed Momma potatoes, peaches,
the softest food I could find,
why didn't I give her the tobacco she asked for?

Published in *Conditions* 5 (August 1979). Copyright 1979 by Carole Clemmons Gregory. Reprinted by permission of the author.

Published in *Conditions* 5 (August 1979). Copyright 1979 by Carole Clemmons Gregory. Reprinted by permission of the author.

II

Momma had cut through,
I flew home Christmas and heard her
talking about Harriet Tubman on a Seagram's calendar
and asking didn't Sojourner Truth look like Grandma?
a little darker though,
not talking no Jesus to me,
she had exchanged the Christian truth for the real truth
and just asked if I'd fix the tree.
The white man that molested your brother's grandchild
who was playing Mary in the Nativity play,
you understood him too late.
Only nine and five, sisters walking home from school
into a slum once a neighborhood of choir members, garden keepers,
coming home they faced his knife and sucked his desire,
their father searches to kill the man.

At the hospital
I watch the room fill with those faithful lovers—
grandmothers with no switches in their hands,
silent about your brother's grandgirls,
always silent about sex,
glad to see me even though I am too grown for my own good,
they had rehearsed the Nativity play
the same as nothing had happened,
expecting the molested child to say Mary's lines.

III

Momma, a unselfish woman,
soft-voiced and brown in an apron
and setting a table with the Lord's Prayer,
once a child sharecropper whose father was driven
from the land to the Ohio steel mills,
Momma grew up not liking artificial flowers,
married, bore children, watched her husband leave,
she loved the end of winter,
birds pulling Spring out as worms,
the earth in her fingers planting-red morning glories,
petunias, sunflowers decorating our yard,
braiding our hair, proud of my brothers,
she held her head up as we moved into the projects.

IV

My brother, a Central State graduate in elementary education,
shot heroin while teaching his sixth grade class,
he started his habit in Black Power meetings
denouncing mothers like Momma as apolitical women.
For years Momma hid his secret,
one Christmas I slept on the sofa,
at 3:00 am in the morning
my youngest brother came in and overcharged
the other for heroin,
their fight waking me.

At coffee the sunrise,
I questioned Momma til she dug out
her son's needle.
"No," my brother said, "I am not on,"
later that day he was fighting with
our younger brother.
I saw Momma run between them
at the top of the stairs,
Momma screaming, "You should say brother, that's enough,"
all three of them falling down the stairs,
Momma's head landing at my feet.

In the new year the mothers
walked to the Mayor's office
with the name and address of the drug dealers,
next week the dealers moved to another address.

V

I felt rough from the needs that took me away,
weakened from comfortable white minds,
afraid to come home so broken,
afraid to lose you, Momma
confused and painful like my brother's arms,
but contemptuous of his needle.
I walk to the store for a pop,
Arabs own the corner store now,
we still stand outside.

I grow older,
agreeing with my Uncle, no new kidney,
"I want your mother to pass sweetly,"
and the fear spreads more,
til everybody saw me and said I was fine
and looked so good
and when am I coming back to stay.

A FREEDOM SONG FOR THE BLACK WOMAN

For the woman
African in ancestry,
woman of intelligence
to raise generations
victoriously through Jim and Jane Crow,
the poets sing few songs.
We gathered to search for you,
a Nigerian brother with a white mother,
four Caribbean sisters who say
women from their country
watch their men be bought
by white women during tourist season,
Black American women with African features
and mulatto women alike
turn to our brothers to ask
the meaning of their new/old custom.
Why do you reject us?
The brothers say this is a class for
African Religion and Philosophy,
not personal questions,
Jim Crow racism is our struggle,
not Jane Crow sexism.
Our texts say African men marry
to have sons to assure their immortality,
the sisters say the men
in socialist dreams or capitalist chains
on the African continent, Caribbean or the Americas
try to seduce every woman in the race.

The Nigerian brother says this is polygamy,
no one hears him,
they ask,
"*How can he be African if his mother is white?*"

           * * * * * * * * * * * *

      Voices from the past echo,
      "*I belong to this race . . .*
      After all, friend, do we not belong
      to one of the best branches of
      the human race? And yet, how have our
      people been murdered in the South,
      and their bones scattered at the grave's mouth! . ."
      Frances Watkins Harper writes to William
      Still her link on the Underground Railroad.

* * * * * * * * * *

Slowly Black women organize
as our men lose their consciousness of race
to pursue Adolf Hitler's theory of Aryan superiority,
any white body can be a rite of passage,
male or female transport.
Aryan superiority blooms
again and threatens Africa
as in the day Napoleon's soldiers
shot their cannon at the head
and broad nose of the Sphinx,
we buy bleaching cream, straightening combs,
plastic surgery to straighten our noses.
Or a white wife
tames the Black man's struggle for freedom,
the chairman of Afro-American Studies
is African from the continent and an Establishment school,
married to an understanding, "unique human being,"
whom we never see
except in her husband's decisions
against the discipline, Black futures,
in his treachery and class snobbery,
in his contempt for anything
not European or fascist.

Black women
see how these mercenary women
conceal their loathing as they mark Black men
for death and looting by men of white races.
                    * * * * * *

     Voices from the past declare,
     "*I found that white men who had created a race of
     mulattoes by raping and consorting with Negro
     women were still doing so wherever they could,
     these same white men lynched, burned and tortured
     Negro men for doing the same thing with white
     women; even when the white women were willing
     victims.*"
     Ida Wells-Barnett writes anti-lynching words
     falling off America's deaf ears,
     We revive Black Reconstruction
     our enemies burned to the ground
     like our churches, schools, homes—
     unavenged rape
     removes our fears
     of being called "unfeminine,"
     we are the strong women.

          THE GREATER FRIENDSHIP BAPTIST CHURCH

               mothers
               cranking the machine,
               adding milk to make ice cream,
               summer in church,
               the women
               sell golden fried chicken,
               potato salad and fresh greens
               to buy new choir robes,
               our grandmothers
               carry switches from trees,
               we feel love
               in the Greater Friendship Baptist Church,
               love no other place
               has for us.

Black children
believing in miracles,
oblivious to our mothers aging,
doing domestic work
and our fathers getting fired
so white men can work for their families,
we go back for seconds,
another scoop of ice cream
our smiles receive.

JO ANN HALL-EVANS
(1934)

CAPE COAST CASTLE REVISITED

Though you are a continent and two seasons away,
I again wander your once Castle ruins
Remembering now quiet cannons
Facing the same seas,
Which brought my shackled forefathers from those shores
To suffer the forbidden ways of this strange, distant land.

I am drawn deeper
Until the burning, blinding African sun is no more.
Lured
By chilling, centuries-old memories etched into your crumbling
   innards.
Intrigued
By craggy, winding courses into our haunting histories.

Though I am a continent and two seasons away,
I am chilled and fearful, yet strengthened
Remembering your dank, dark dungeons,
Recognizing your indomitable spirits,
Which have obviously sustained your children's child
To face the still shackling ways of this strange, distant land.

SEDUCTION

SENSUOUS
SLOE EYED
SOFT LIPPED
SWIVEL HIPPED
SISTER OF SOUL.

SALACIOUS
SMOOTH SHOULDERED
SWIFT TONGUED
SLY SHUCKIN'
SON OF SATIN.

AW . . .
SH . . . IT
SE . . . DUC . . . ED!!

JOHARI M. KUNJUFU
(1936)

CEREMONY

libation.

hey sisters, we the color of our men
who are sun like the sun feeding African soil
supposed to be the Mothers of the earth
the Mothers of Generations of life
like when we was real

but what we doin
now in this place?
what about the babies? our Children?
where are they?
why they lookin to know who we are
and can't find us
cause we have nothin good to tell them
while we fakin
while we think we aint female?

libation.

when we was real
we never had orphans
and children in joints
or sons who thought they was daughters in the streets
we wont build a nation with hit men
and useless males wishin they wore dresses and
teachin our sons to
switch their generations away before they
are even old enough to pour them out

libation.

when we was real
we never had women lovers
we *always* knew what Man meant
and *that* was natural
we wont build a nation with
trippers out on smoke and
lesbians wishin they wore pants and
teachin our daughters to
close up their centers before they
are even old enough to give out life

libation.

come spirits
cleanse us up in this place
drive out the non sense from our minds
and the crap from our dreams

libation.

make us remember that what we need is *with* men
that Children are the next life
and eternal as they come
before we chase ourselves to the final death

libation.

make us remember who we are
so our babies will come when we start them
and come through us clean
so our sons will know their manhood
so our daughters will know their womanhood

so we will not keep screamin and dyin in confusion
lost to ourselves and what we need to do

libation.

bring us back to the real

we the color of our Men like the sun in the soil
we the Mothers of the earth
the Mothers of the Generations of Life

we the
libation.

RETURN

things begin again
on homeland
this time

and you are

all Africa warm earth mojo
through me
deep.

the earth is soft and full
with cricket sound
underneath our sound

grass covering is still
while we move

and the sound we make makes
life
for these minutes

and the earth is warm deep soft and full
when the quietness bursts

THE PROMISE

i am warm
great
i am undulating life

my sons are coming home

and they will not
remember the cold tribes
the years
far away within the snow
and dying trees

they will not remember
the stripes and the lashes
whip stroking across
the sunless days

they will only know me

IRMA McCLAURIN
(1945)

THE MASK

Hanging on the wall, an iron face watches me.
Snakes crawl up his cheeks
his eyes sink back to a land
where tales of warriors and empires
weave into ancient tapestries, knotted to my blood.
He speaks to me beneath the tunes of billie and bessie.
I hear him *hum** the intervals in Coltrane,
reverberating the tales of men sold;
of women sold leaving earthen huts;

Published in *Obsidian* 3 (Summer 1977). Copyright 1976 by Irma McClaurin. Revised version used by permission of the author.
*All italicized words should be sung.

of children seized from villages
and brought to ships *waiting* on the water Niger.
Blue waters witnessing:
more *blues* than the brownblack veins on billie's arms.
More *blues* than the broken body of bessie waiting
on a dusty southern backroad.
More *blues* than the last visions of 'Trane.
More *blues* than me walking through neon cities
walking through red southern fields,
not knowing where I belong.
The mask contains a deeper blues than those I know,
carving out my heart with yesterday's pain.

TO A GONE ERA

(My College days — Class of '73)

The eye of this storm is not quiet.
It sees brown frames inside the city cutting themselves on jagged
     loves
and knows. This is a mean place.
Once we sought to change this world with matches.
Striking our visions against straw promises
we summoned fire gods and burnt jewish stores
built upon our parent's tragedies; Dodged bullets
and walked carefully among the ashes
sifting for our childhood
friends and looking for a place called future.
This is a mean place
there are no children here,
only troubled spirits wandering in and out of childlike bodies.

We read books and communed with the "others"
in their land; we spoke their blunted language,

From *Black World* 4 (September 1975). Copyright 1975, 1978 by Irma McClaurin.
Reprinted by permission of the author.

hung our anger on coathooks in dusty ivy hallways
becoming a new minstrel tradition: blacks in whiteface
shadows tapdancing in cornfields.
CHANGE?
We collected barbed words, shot them
through poems with poison edges, used wisdom
of kings & malcolms to ignite bonfires, rising
to taunt the overcast sky divining our destruction.

Now the voices that once strung themselves like pearls
across the city's neck haunt the bruised nights.
Their sorrow sings through the cracked tenement walls.

I, WOMAN

And I, woman, cloaked in blues
sit knitting prison days
reflecting on the ice pick stabbing
the beating heart beneath aging skin.
Holding my thighs apart
he tried to reach this black mouth
that has spit seeds: buried in the mississippi,
hung on magnolias.
I, woman, watch these patches of my life fraying.
I have run too often.

Yet inside this body black women,
Tubman and Truth,
cast spells. Freedom
I swear I heard them on that lonely night
singing "steal away" and—stumbling,
fearful—I ran, hid.

Sitting before this jury, sweating
in this hotbox of hate
I swear I hear those sisters still humming.

(For JoAnn Little and other oppressed women)

Published in *Obsidian* 3 (Summer 1977). Copyright 1976, 1978 by Irma McClaurin.
Revised version used by permission of the author.

AUDRE LORDE
(1934)

COAL

I
is the total black, being spoken
from the earth's inside.
There are many kinds of open
how a diamond comes into a knot of flame
how sound comes into a words, coloured
by who pays what for speaking.

Some words are open like a diamond
on glass windows
singing out within the crash of sun
Then there are words like stapled wagers
in a perforated book—buy and sign and tear apart—
and come whatever wills all chances
the stub remains
an ill-pulled tooth with a ragged edge.
Some words live in my throat
breeding like adders. Others know sun
seeking like gypsies over my tongue
to explode through my lips
like young sparrows bursting from shell.
Some words
bedevil me.

Love is a word, another kind of open.
As the diamond comes into a knot of flame
I am Black because I come from the earth's inside
Now take my word for jewel in the open light.

"Coal" is reprinted from *Coal*, poems by Audre Lorde, with the permission of W. W. Norton & Company, Inc. Copyright 1968, 1970, 1976 by Audre Lorde.

CHAIN

News item: Two girls, fifteen and sixteen, were sent to foster homes, because they had borne children by their natural father. Later, they petitioned the New York courts to be returned to their parents, who, the girls said, loved them. And the courts did so.

I

Faces surround me that have no smell or color no time
only strange laughing testaments
vomiting promise like love
but look at the skeleton children
advancing against us
beneath their faces there is no sunlight
no darkness
no heart remains
no legends
to bring them back as women
into their bodies at dawn.

Look at the skeleton children
advancing against us
we will find womanhood
in their eyes
as they cry
which of you bore me
will love me
will claim my blindness as yours
and which of you marches to battle
from between our legs?

II

On the porch outside my door
girls are lying
like felled maples in the path of my feet
I cannot step past them nor over them
their slim bodies roll like smooth tree trunks

"Chain" is reprinted from *The Black Unicorn*, poems by Audre Lorde, with the permission of W. W. Norton & Company, Inc.

repeating themselves over and over
until my porch is covered with the bodies
of young girls.
Some have a child in their arms.
To what death shall I look for comfort?
Which mirror to break or mourn.

Two girls repeat themselves in my doorway
their eyes are not stone.
Their flesh is not wood nor steel
but I cannot touch them
Shall I warn them of night
or offer them bread
or a song?
They are sisters. Their father has known
them over and over. The twins they carry
are his. Whose death shall we mourn
in the forest
unburied?
Winter has come and the children are dying.
One begs me to hold her between my breasts
Oh write me a poem mother
here, over my flesh
get your words upon me
as he got this child upon me
our father lover
thief in the night
do not be so angry with us. We told him
your bed was wider
but he said if we did it then
we would be his
good children if we did it
then he would love us
oh make us a poem mother
that will tell us his name
in your language
is he father or lover
we will leave your words
for our children
engraved on a whip or a golden scissors
to tell them the lies
of their birth.

Another says mother
I am holding your place.
Do you know me better than I knew him
or myself?
Am I his daughter or girlfriend
am I your child or your rival
you wish to be gone from his bed?
Here is your granddaughter mother
give me your blessing before I sleep
what other secrets
do you have to tell me
how do I learn to love her
as you have loved me?

SUMMER ORACLE

Without expectation
there is no end
to the shocks of morning
or even a small summer.

Now the image is fire
blackening the vague lines
into defiance across the city.
The image is fire
sun warming us in a cold country
barren of symbols for love.

Now I have forsaken order
and imagine you into fire
untouchable in a magician's coat
covered with signs of destruction and birth
sewn with griffins and arrows and hammers
And gold sixes stitched into your hem
your fingers draw fire
but still the old warlocks shun you
for no gourds ring in your sack

"Summer Oracle" is reprinted from *The Black Unicorn*, poems by Audre Lorde, with the permission of W. W. Norton & Company, Inc.

no spells bring forth peace
and I am still fruitless and hungry
this summer
the peaches are flinty and juiceless
and cry sour worms.

The image is fire
flaming over you burning off excess
like the blaze planters start
To burn off bagasse from the canefields
After a harvest.

The image is fire
the high sign that rules our summer
I smell it in the charred breezes blowing over
your body
close
hard
essential
under its cloak of lies.

HARRIET

Harriet there was always somebody calling us crazy
or mean or stuck-up or evil or black
or black
and we were
nappy girls quick as cuttlefish
scurrying for cover
trying to speak trying to speak
trying to speak
the pain in each other's mouths
until we learned
on the edge of a lash
or a tongue
on the edge of the other's betrayal

"Harriet" is reprinted from The Black Unicorn, poems by Audre Lorde, with the permission of W. W. Norton & Company, Inc.

that respect
meant keeping our distance
in silence
averting our eyes
from each other's face in the street
from the beautiful dark mouth
and cautious familiar eyes
passing alone.

I remember you Harriet
before we were broken apart
we dreamed the crossed swords
of warrior queens
while we avoided each other's eyes
and we learned to know lonely
as the earth learns to know dead
Harriet Harriet
what name shall we call our selves now
our mother is gone?

NATURALLY

Since Naturally Black is Naturally Beautiful
I must be proud
And, naturally,
Black and
Beautiful
Who always was a trifle
Yellow
And plain though proud
Before.

I've given up pomades
Having spent the summer sunning
And feeling naturally free

Published in *Negro Digest* 17 (September/October 1968). Reprinted by permission of the author.

(if I die of skin cancer
oh well—one less
black and beautiful me)
Yet no Agency spends millions
To prevent my summer tanning
And who trembles nightly
With the fear of their lily cities being swallowed
By a summer ocean of naturally woolly hair?

But I've bought my can of
Natural Hair Spray
Made and marketed in Watts
Still thinking more
Proud beautiful black women
Could better make and use
Black bread.

THE WOMAN THING

The hunters are back from beating the winter's face
in search of a challenge or task
in search of food
making fresh tracks for their children's hunger
they do not watch the sun
they cannot wear its heat for a sign
of triumph or freedom.
The hunters are treading heavily homeward
through snow that is marked
with their own bloody footprints.
Emptyhanded the hunters return
snow-maddened, sustained by their rages.

In the night after food they may seek
young girls for their amusement. But now
the hunters are coming
and the unbaked girls flee from their angers.

From *Coal* by Audre Lorde (New York: W.W. Norton & Company, 1978). Copyright 1968, 1970, 1976. Reprinted by permission of the author.

All this day I have craved
food for my child's hunger.
Emptyhanded the hunters come shouting
injustices drip from their mouths
like stale snow melted in sunlight.

Meanwhile the womanthing my mother taught me
bakes off its covering of snow
like a rising blackening sun.

GAYL JONES
(1949)

3—31—70

Part IV of Journal

   She said the Jehovah Witness man
gave her the cane to walk with.
   "I showed him my stick. And then
Sunday when he came to get me
for church, he drove up and had this cane.
I hope they don't think I'm going every
Sunday . .
   "They don't do like we do.
They have Sunday school but
they don't divide them up into
classes. The preacher teaches
everybody. When you go away
from there you know everything
that was said. Hell's not fire
like I used to think it was. It's
something else. They told me what
it was and then
they pointed it out in the bible.

Published in *Obsidian* 2 (Winter 1979). Copyright 1977 by Gayl Jones. Reprinted by permission of Harold Matson Co., Inc.

They always tell you something and
you don't believe them and they
point it out in the bible. It's
in the bible. I don't remember.
They teach Sunday school out of
The Watch Tower. You know
The Watch Tower they go around
selling? Well, I never looked at
it before, but it's got lessons in
it. One of the questions
in it said, what is hell? and
then it told what hell was, and
then it told where you could find it in
the bible. Hell
ain't fire like I always thought
it was."

"I thought it was too," my
mother said. "Fire and brimstone."

"Well, it's not," my aunt said.
"I read what it was. I read
it right in there and then right
in the bible. I was reading it
and looking at television like a
fool. That's why I don't remember.
But it ain't fire. If it's just
that then people can do what-
ever they want to do if that's
all it is."

"I thought it was fire," my
mother said.

"I'll show you the next time
I come," my aunt said.

"When we drove by
here," my aunt said, "I
pointed out the house. He
brings *Watch Towers* all
around the neighborhood. That is his
job. He said you must be at work
all the time then. I told him
you were sick, and were probably
in the bed asleep."

"Colored and white sell *The
Watch Tower*," my mother said.
   "The white out there
treat you like you're the same
as they are. They started
doing that everwhere now though.
They come over and start talking
to you just like you're the same as
they are."
   (I am combing my aunts hair.
It is in a bush now.)
   "She's making you an afro,"
my mother says.
   "You would look pretty with an
afro," I say.
   (I start greasing it and platting
it up.)
   "I look topsy," my aunt says.
   "Do you remember—?"
my mother asks. "She used to wear
a head full of platts even when she was
in the tenth grade."
   "I never would have thought
of her," my aunt says.
   "I wouldn't have either
until she started making platts."
   "When you comb it out
it'll be an afro," I say.
   "She was dark wasn't she?"
my aunt says.
   "Yes. I was a little girl. I used
to think she was pretty," my mother said.
   "I did too," my aunt said.
   "There was a girl who came
into the doctor's office once," my
mother said. "She was real dark,
but she had the prettiest face.
I thought she had one of the prettiest
faces I've ever seen."
   My aunt said yes they can.
   I think, Black is beautiful.

I think how in the black fashion
magazines they are using the
darker girls now. They used to not.
I am thinking how beautiful black
is. I am thinking they are from a
different generation than me, but
I understand them. I am not
saying anything. I am combing
beautiful hair.

My aunt looked in the mirror
when she had the bush and laughed.

"You're laughing, but it
looks nice to her," my mother
said meaning me.

"You'd look pretty in an afro,"
I say.

Somebody rings the doorbell
and my father goes to the door.
We three women are in the bedroom
off from the front room, two older
generation women, and one younger
generation woman. Whoever rings
the doorbell does not come in.

"Who was it?" my mama asks,
but my daddy doesn't hear her.

"Probably somebody selling
The Watch Tower or potatoe
chips," I say.

"Potatoe Chips?" my aunt
asks.

"There were kids selling potatoe
chips," I say.

"Oh," she says.

"Do they have a record of
it down at the courthouse?" my
father asked.

"Yes if somebody didn't
pay them to take it out," my
aunt said.

"They would in Versailles,"
my father said, "but they wouldn't
here . . . I'll get you a lawyer.
They're all crooked."

TRIPART

1.

a very friendly
prison
this is—
white kids discussing politics
and suddenly your nerves have a finished
form (half-digested rage)—
white power goes in and out of Kennedy airport
flight unknown

2.

the telephone keeps ringing
the cop keeps swinging his nightstick
and conversing with negroes
(and never knows they are blackmen)
Who is Uncle Thomas?
a nigger with pocket money.

3.

connecticut has trees
and white has two faces:
may you go to Chicago when you die.
i'll be in Harlem with Allah's
blessings
in a restaurant
dealing with humanity

From *Soulscript* edited by June Meyer Jordan. Copyright 1970 by June Meyer Jordan. Used by permission of Doubleday & Company, Inc.

SATORI

disturbed by consciousness
god created creation
he traced our lives in ink
ink is made of soot and glue
and the old man sits with
an empty mind:
this is Buddhahood
this is the second christ
(Is He still alive?
Yes.
How old is He?
Eighty.
He's still a child.)

we pray over our beer
and i spring from the
Buddha's forehead,
black as jesus.

MANY DIE HERE

Many die here.
I follow the footprints of strangers
to the tombs of strangers.
I squat with cupped hands.
To the living people
my back is turned.
I look to Zen for validation
I look to the three christs:
but there are trucks in the forest
loaded down with carcasses.

From *Soulscript* edited by June Meyer Jordan. Copyright 1970 by June Meyer Jordan. Used by permission of Doubleday & Company, Inc.

From *Soulscript* edited by June Meyer Jordan. Copyright 1970 by June Meyer Jordan. Used by permission of Doubleday & Company, Inc.

there are naked children
running, dancing toward the water,
splashing being baptized by their unknown
fathers
i, who have revoked all ritual,
picking prayers from my teeth,
i see the shining lake and the
cool children:
my god is a black giant.
i slid down the rocks
with mud in my mouth,
herding the cattle and goats of others.
i met a bearded man
who said, "You are young,
but you have the spirit of the dead;
learn from me; learn from the
living people."
i answered, "You are one who
will soon have to do the dying."

(nests, hanging empty
skulls of birds
the man, in old sandals)

i laugh and laugh:

when you are old and without place or people
i will come riding my donkey along the road
to annoy you with its braying.
You, who have let my people die without a name.

ALICE WALKER
(1944)

REVOLUTIONARY PETUNIAS

Sammy Lou of Rue
sent to his reward
the exact creature who
murdered her husband,
using a cultivator's hoe
with verve and skill;
and laughed fit to kill
in disbelief
at the angry, militant
pictures of herself
the Sonneteers quickly drew:
not any of them people that
she knew.
A backwoods woman
her house was papered with
funeral home calendars and
faces appropriate for a Mississippi
Sunday School. She raised a George,
a Martha, a Jackie and a Kennedy. Also
a John Wesley Junior.
"Always respect the word of God,"
she said on her way to she didn't
know where, except it would be by
electric chair, and she continued
"Don't yall forgit to *water*
my purple petunias."

From *Revolutionary Petunias and Other Poems* by Alice Walker. Copyright 1972 by Alice Walker. Reprinted by permission of Harcourt Brace Jovanovich, Inc.

ONCE

i

Green lawn
a picket fence
flowers—
My friend smiles
she had heart
that Southern
jails
were drab.

Looking up I see
a strong arm
raised
the Law
Someone in America
is being
protected (from me).

In the morning
there was
a man in grey
but the sky
was blue.

ii

"Look at that
nigger with those
white folks!"
    My dark
Arrogant friend
turns calmly, curiously
helpfully,
        "Where?" he
            asks.

From *Once* by Alice Walker. Copyright 1968 by Alice Walker. Reprinted by permission of Harcourt Brace Jovanovich, Inc.

It was the fifth
arrest
In as many
  days
How glad I am
that I can
look
surprised
        still.

iii

Running down
Atlanta
      streets
With my sign
I see heads
    turn
Eyes
    goggle
"a nice girl
  like her!"

A Negro cook
assures
      her mistress—

But I had seen
the fingers
near her eyes
  wet with
    tears.

iv

One day in
Georgia
Working around
the Negro section
My friend got a
letter
in
the mail

—the letter
said
   "I hope you're
having a good
time
fucking all
     the niggers."

"Sweet," I winced.
    "Who
       wrote it?"

"mother."
        she
        said.

That day she sat
   a long time
a little black girl
in pigtails
on her lap

Her eyes were very
Quiet.

She used to tell the big colored ladies
her light eyes just
the same
"I am alone
my mother died."
Though no other
letter
came.

V

It is true—
I've always loved
the daring
     ones
Like the black young
man
Who tried
to crash

All barriers
at once,
    wanted to
swim
At a white
beach (in Alabama)
Nude.

vi

Peter always
thought
the only way to
"enlighten"
southern towns
was to
introduce
    himself
to
the county
sheriff
    first thing.

Another thing
Peter wanted—
was to be
cremated
    but we
couldn't
    find him
when he needed it.

But he was just a kid
    seventeen.

vii

I
never liked
white folks
really
it
happened quite
suddenly
one
day
A pair of
amber
eyes
I
think
he
had.

viii

I don't think
integration
entered
into it
officer

You see
there was
this little
Negro
girl
Standing here
alone
and her
mother
went into
that store
there

then—
    there came by
this little boy
  here
without his
  mother
& eating
  an
ice cream cone
—see there it is—
  strawberry

Anyhow

           and the little
           girl was
           hungry
           and
           stronger
           than
           the little
           boy—
           Who is too
           fat
           really,
              anyway.

ix

Someone said
      to
        me
that
    if
     the South
rises
     again
it will do so
     "from
the grave."

Someone
    else
       said
if the South
  rises
    again
he would
     "step on
      it."

Dick Gregory
said that
  if the
    South
     rises
  again
  there is
    a
  secret
   plan.

But I say—
  if the
     South
rises
  again
It will not
  do
   so
in my presence.

X

"but I don'
really
  give a fuck
Who
  my daughter
   marries—"
the lady
was
adorable—

it was in a
tavern
i remember
her daughter
sat there
beside her
tugging
at
her arm
sixteen—
very shy
        and
very pim
        pled.

xi

then there
was
the charming
        half-wit
who told
the judge
re: indecent exposure
"but when I
step out
   of the
   tub
I look
 Good—
just because
my skin
is black
don't mean
it ain't
pretty
        you old bastard!
what will we
finally do
with
prejudice

some people like
to take a walk
after a bath.

xii
"look, honey
said
the
blond
amply
boobed
babe
in the
green
  g
string

"i like you
sure
i ain't
prejudiced

but the
lord didn't
give me
legs
like
these
because
he
wanted
to see'm
dangling
from a
poplar!"

"But they're so
   much
       prettier
          than mine.

Would you really mind?"
he asked
wanting her to dance.

xiii

I remember
seeing
a little girl,
dreaming—perhaps,
  hit by
    a
  van truck

"That nigger was
in the way!" the
man
    said
     to
understanding cops.

      But was she?
      She was
        just eight
          her mother
            said
      and little
            for
        her age.

xiv

then there was
the
picture of
the
bleak-eyed
little black
girl
waving the
american
flag

holding it
gingerly
with
the very
tips
of her
fingers.

EARLY LOSSES: A REQUIEM

Part I

Nyanu was appointed
as my Lord. The husband chosen
by the elders
before my birth.
He sipped wine with
my father
and when I was born
brought a parrot as
his gift
to play with me.
Paid baskets of grain
and sweet berries
to make me fat
for his pleasure.

Omunu was my playmate
who helped consume
Nyanu's gifts.
Our fat selves grew
together
knee and knee.
It was Omunu I wished
to share my tiny
playing house.

From *Good Night, Willie Lee, I'll See You in the Morning* by Alice Walker. Copyright 1975, 1979 by Alice Walker. First published in *The Iowa Review*. Used by permission of The Dial Press.

Him I loved as the sun
must seek and chase
its own reflection
across the sky.
My brothers, before you
turn away—

The day the savages came
to ambush our village
it was Nyanu who struggled
bravely
Omunu ran and hid
behind his parents' house.
He was a coward but
only nine
as was I; who trembled
beside him as we two
were stolen away
Nyanu's dead body
begging remembrance
of his tiny morsel
taken from his mouth.
Nor was I joyful that he was dead
only glad that now I would not have
to marry him.

Omunu clasped my hands
within the barkcloth pouch
and I his head
a battered flower
bent low
upon its stalk
Our cries pounded back
into our throats
by thudding blows
we could not see
our mothers' cries
at such a distance
we could not hear
and over the miles
we feasted on homesickness
our mothers' tears and

the dew
all we consumed of homeland
before we left.

At the great water Omunu fought
to stay with me
at such a tender age
our hearts we set
upon each other
as the retreating wave
brings its closest friend
upon its back.
We cried out in words
that met an echo
and Omunu vanished
down a hole that
smelled of blood and
excrement and death
and I was "saved"
for sport among
the sailors of the crew.
Only nine, upon a ship. My mouth
my body a mystery
that opened with each tearing
lunge. Crying for Omunu
who was not seen
again
by these eyes.

Listen to your sister, singing
in the field.
My body forced to receive
grain and wild berries
and milk so I could seem
a likely wench
—my mother's child
sold for a price. My father's
child again for sale.
I prayed to all our Gods
"Come down to me."
Hoist the burden no child
was meant to bear

and decipher the prayer
from within each song
—the song despised—
my belly become a stronghold
for a stranger
who will not recall
when he is two
the contours of
his mother's face.
See the savages turn back
my lips
and with hot irons
brand me neck and thigh.

I could not see the horizon
for the sky
a burning eye
the sun, beloved in the shade,
became an enemy
a pestle pounding long
upon my head.
You walked with me.
And when day sagged into night
some one of you of my own
choice
shared my rest. Omunu
risen from the ocean
out of the stomachs of whales
the teeth of sharks
lying beside me sleeping
knee and knee.
We could not speak always
of hearts
for in the morning if they
sold you
how could I flatten
a wrinkled face?
The stupor of dread
made smooth the look
that to my tormentors
was born erased.

I mourned for you. And if you died
took out my heart upon my lap
and rested it.

See me old at thirty
my sack of cotton weighted
to the ground. My hair
enough to cover a marble
my teeth like rattles
made of chalk
my breath a whisper
of decay.
The slack of my belly
falling to my knees.
I shrink to become a tiny size
a delicate morsel
upon my mother's knee
prepared like bread. The shimmering
of the sun a noise
upon my head.

To the child that's left
I offer a sound
without a promise
a clue
of what it means.

The sound itself is all.

Part II

The Child

A sound like a small wind
finding the door of a
hollow reed
my mother's farewell
glocked up from the back
of her throat

the sound itself is all

all I have
to remember a mother
I scarcely knew.

"Omunu" to me; who never knew
what "Omunu" meant. Whether home
or man or trusted God. "Omunu."
Her only treasure,
and never spent.

PINKIE GORDON LANE
(1939)

ON BEING HEAD OF THE
ENGLISH DEPARTMENT

I will look with detachment
on the signing of contracts,
the ordering of books,
and making of schedules—
will sing hymns of praise
to the negative, when
it is necessary, to survive.

And if the morning
light freezes in the East,
a dawn-covered eye
will tell me I am cold
to your pleas, but never whore
to the spirit. I will
write poems in the blue—
frosted lake.

If I disdain poetasters
announcers, and the gods
of mediocrity, knowing
that they too insist on living,
it is because I hand you
the bread and the knife
but never the music and the art
of my existence.

From *The Mystic Female* by Pinkie Gordon Lane (Fort Smith, Arkansas: South and West, 1978). Reprinted by permission of the author.

You will not swallow me or absorb me:
I have grown too lean for that.
I am selfish, I am cruel,

   I am love.

WHEN YOU READ THIS POEM

(For Citizens Opposed to [Book] Censorship, Baton Rouge)

The earth turns
like a rainbow
And the smell of autumn
drifts down   Yellow
leaf on my arched back

The light touches
I see it with my skin
feel it lean
That furrow of trees
casts its shadow—long
as the night, the wind,
the river

Truth has many faces
My friends, don't honor me
Without passion
I will not be
wheat in the summer's fire
I will not lie fallen
like autumn fruit
or die in the evening sun

Listen,
Let us band together
and fight evil   We
cannot let it burn
the earth   We
cannot let it guide
the sun

Copyright *The Black Scholar*. Reprinted by permission of the author.

The world is a bird
in flight

When you read this poem,
love me

SEXUAL PRIVACY OF
WOMEN ON WELFARE

The ACLU Mountain States Regional Office came across a
welfare application used in . . . (a certain state) for women
with illegitimate children. Among the questions:

—When and where did you first meet the defendant (the
child's father).
—When and where did intercourse first occur.
—Frequency and period of time during which intercourse
occurred.
—Was anyone ever present. If yes, give dates, names, and
addresses.
—Were preventive measures always used.
—Have you ever had intercourse with anyone other than the
defendant. If yes, give dates, names, and addresses.

THE PRIVACY REPORT, American Civil Liberties Union
Foundation, Vol. IV, No. 3, Oct., 1976.

When and where did you first
confront loneliness?
When and where did you resist
the urge to die?
Did you pull a blind around
your sorrow?
Was anyone present? If yes, give
names and dates and addresses.
Did you survive?
Were preventive measures always
used?

Copyright MS. Magazine. Reprinted by permission of the author.

Who listened to the rage of your
silent screams? Give the frequency
and period of time,
dates and names and addresses . . .

Will you promise never to breathe ice?
To follow the outline
of a city street whose perspective
darkens with the morning light?

Document.

MIGRATION

The winter birds
are flying from the North
to embrace our swamps
our rain-trapped fields/
My backyard trees hang
heavy and Louisiana
is a depot for this alien flock/
Their noisy forms slice the air
in restless flight
translated out of need/

The autumn mist mud-packs
the earth/   Caladiums,
their once firm stalks
reaching high, now bend
to snake the grass and wait
for death/   Hibiscus
forks the air to reach
the sky—a last count
before frost/   I know

Published in *Callaloo* 2 (Spring 1976). Reprinted by permission of the author.

the time to seek
new ground, when what
I wanted, felt, erupts
from leaning's desert ice/
flocks to a new Spring
and Southern warmth/

Winter's frost a forgotten
land, and time a revolving
flame/

WHO IS MY BROTHER?

My friend, your face
is showing
Where are your roots?
We will expose them
like valleys that lie hidden
in darkness

I have eyes in the back
of my head   They see
things I don't want to know
Secrets burn
like the August sun

Your hands speak
in known tongues
articulating the distance
in your weathered eyes

Go wipe your feet in ashes
The sun has always been red

Published in *Obsidian* 1 (Winter 1975). Reprinted by permission of the author.

NOCTURNE

Listening for the sound
of my own
voice
I hear only the brainwaves
at 1:00 a.m.
on a quiet Baton Rouge
night   The silence
is unbelievable
only the rumble of a distant
truck on a highway
not that close to home
A dead man walks
the avenue
his coattail caught
in the wind's draft
and the color of blue
everywhere

NIKKI GIOVANNI
(1943)

NIKKI-ROSA

childhood remembrances are always a drag
if you're Black
you always remember things like living in Woodlawn
with no inside toilet
and if you become famous or something
they never talk about how happy you were to have your mother
all to yourself and
how good the water felt when you got your bath from one of those

Published in *Obsidian* 1 (Winter 1975). Reprinted by permission of the author.

From *Black Judgement* by Nikki Giovanni (Detroit: Broadside Press, 1968). Reprinted by permission of the author.

big tubs that folk in chicago barbecue in
and somehow when you talk about home
it never gets across how much you
understood their feelings
as the whole family attended meetings about Hollydale
and even though you remember
your biographers never understand
your father's pain as he sells his stock
and another dream goes
and though you're poor it isn't poverty that
concerns you
and though they fought a lot
it isn't your father's drinking that makes any difference
but only that everybody is together and you
and your sister have happy birthdays and very good christmasses
and I really hope no white person ever has cause to write about me
because they never understand Black love is Black wealth and they'll
probably talk about my hard childhood and never understand that
all the while I was quite happy

WOMAN POEM

you see, my whole life
is tied up
to happiness
its father cooking breakfast
and me getting fat as a hog
or having no food
at all and father proving
his incompetence
again
i wish i knew how it would feel
to be free

its having a job
they won't let you work

From *Black Feeling, Black Talk/Black Judgement* by Nikki Giovanni (Detroit: Broadside Press, 1968; New York: William Morrow & Company, 1970). Reprinted by permission of the author.

or no work at all
castrating me
(yes it happens to women too)

its a sex object if you're pretty
and no love
or love and no sex if you're fat
get back fat black woman be a mother
grandmother strong thing but not woman
gameswoman romantic woman love needer
man seeker dick eater sweat getter
fuck needing love seeking woman

its a hole in your shoe
and buying lil sis a dress
and her saying you shouldn't
when you know
all too well—that you shouldn't

but smiles are only something we give
to properly dressed social workers
not each other
only smiles of i know
your game sister
which isn't really
a smile

joy is finding a pregnant roach
and squashing it
not finding someone to hold
let go get off get back don't turn
me on you black dog
how dare you care
about me
you ain't got no good sense
cause i ain't shit you must be lower
than that to care

its a filthy house
with yesterday's watermelon
and monday's tears
cause true ladies don't
know how to clean

its intellectual devastation
of everybody
to avoid emotional commitment
"yeah honey i would've married
him but he didn't have no degree"

its knock-kneed mini skirted
wig wearing died blond mamma's scar
born dead my scorn your whore
rough heeled broken nailed powdered
face me
whose whole life is tied
up to unhappiness
cause its the only
for real thing
i
know

MOTHER'S HABITS

i have all
my mother's habits
i awake in the middle of night
to smoke a cigarette
i have a terrible fear of flying
and i don't like being alone
in the dark
sleep is a sport we all
participate in
it's the scourge of youth
and a necessity of old age
though it only hastens the day
when dissolution is inevitable
i grow tired
like my mother doing without

From The Women and the Men by Nikki Giovanni (New York: William Morrow and Company, 1975). Reprinted by permission of the author.

even one small word
that says i care
and like my mother i shall fade
into my dreams
no longer caring
either

KNOXVILLE, TENNESSEE

I always like summer
best
you can eat fresh corn
from daddy's garden
and okra
and greens
and cabbage
and lots of
barbecue
and buttermilk
and homemade ice-cream
at the church picnic
and listen to
gospel music
outside
at the church
homecoming
and go to the mountains with
your grandmother
and go barefooted
and be warm
all the time
not only when you go to bed
and sleep

From *Black Judgement* by Nikki Giovanni (Detroit: Broadside Press, 1968). Reprinted by permission of the author.

PATRICIA PARKER

FROM THE CAVITIES
OF BONES

*This at last is bone of my bones and flesh of my flesh; she shall be
called Woman, because she was taken out of Man.*
—Genesis 1:23

from cavities of bones
   spun
     from caverns of air
i, woman—bred of man
taken from womb of sleep;
i, woman that comes
before the first.

to think second
to believe first
   a mistaken conundrum
     erased by the motion of years.
i, woman, i
   can no longer claim
   a mother of flesh
   a father of marrow
I, Woman, must be
   the child of myself.

From *Dices or Black Bones* edited by Adam David Miller (New York: Houghton
Mifflin, 1970). Reprinted by permission of the author.

I FOLLOWED A PATH

Do not go gentle into that good night.
                    —DYLAN THOMAS

I followed a path.
    the path—it led
to somewhere. Curved
around space leading
me from my youth.
I met an old man.
"Old man, give back
my youth."
He gave me a
gold pitcher
with a hole in it.

I followed a path.
    the path—it led
to marbles & jacks
& dolls, mother,
house, school, love.
I met a little girl.
"Little girl, give back
my youth."
She ran away.
Her mother had told her not to speak
to strangers.

I followed a path.
    the path—it led
to a mirror.
I saw a face - not mine.
A face with lines
leading to pain & joy,
song and dances.
I wanted to dance again.
I skipped over guilt;
I laughed at failure.
For one moment,
I chased the lines away.

From *Dices or Black Bones* edited by Adam David Miller (New York: Houghton Mifflin, 1970). Reprinted by permission of the author.

THERE IS A WOMAN IN THIS TOWN

there is a woman in this town

she goes to different bars
sits in the remotest place
watches the other people
drinks til 2 & goes home—alone

some say she is lonely
some say she is an agent
none of us speak to her

Is she our sister?

there is a woman in this town

she lives with her husband
she raises her children
she says she is happy
& is not a women's libber

some say she is misguided
some say she is an enemy
none of us know her

Is she our sister?

there is a woman in this town

she carries a lot of weight
her flesh triples on her frame
she comes to all the dances
dances a lot; goes home—alone

some say she's a lot of fun
some say she is too fat
none of us have loved her

Is she our sister?

there is a woman in this town

From *Movement in Black: The Collected Poetry of Pat Parker* (Oakland, Calif.: Diana Press, 1978). Reprinted by permission of the author.

she owns her own business
she goes to work in the day
she goes home at night
she does not come to the dances

some say she is a capitalist
some say she has no consciousness
none of us trust her

Is she our sister?

there is a woman in this town

she comes to all the parties
wears all the latest men's fashions
calls the women mama
& invites them to her home

some say she's into roles
some say she hates herself
none of us go out with her

Is she our sister?

there is a woman in this town

she was locked up
she comes to many meetings
she volunteers for everything
she cries when she gets upset

some say she makes them nervous
some say she's too pushy
none of us invite her home

Is she our sister?

there is a woman in this town

she fills her veins with dope
goes from house to house to sleep
borrows money whenever she can
she pays it back if she must

some say she is a thief
some say she drains their energy
none of us have trusted her

Is she our sister?

once upon a time, there was a dream
a dream of women. a dream of women
coming together and turning the world
around. turning the world around and making it over.
a dream of women, all women being sisters.
a dream of caring; a dream of protection, a dream
of peace.
once upon a time there was a dream
a dream of women. for the women who rejected the
dream, there had only been a reassurance. for the
women who believed the dream—there is dying, women,
sisters dying
once upon a time there was a dream, a dream of women
turning the world all over and it still lives—
it lives for those who would be sisters

it lives for those who need a sister
it lives for those who once upon a time had a dream.

SONIA SANCHEZ
(1934)

MEMORIAL

1. The supremes-cuz they dead

the supremes done gone
and sold their soul
to tar
        zan and other
honky/rapers
                They sing rodgers

From *Homecoming* by Sonia Sanchez (Detroit: Broadside Press, 1970). Reprinted by permission of the author.

and hart songs
as if we didn't
have enough andrew
sisters spitting their
whiter than mr.
clean songs in our faces.
YEAH.
       the supremes
                    done gone

and bleached out
                    their blk/ness
and all that is heard
is
         me. tarzan
         u.   jane
and
        bwana.
              bwana.
                    bwana.

2. bobby hutton

i didn't know bobby
hutton in fact it is
too hard to re
cord all the dying
young/blks.
           in this country.
but   this i do know.
                he was
part of a long/term/plan
for blk/people.
          he was denmark
          vesey.
malcolm.
       garvey. all the
dead/blk/men
          of our now/time
and ago/time.

           check it out. for
bobby wd be living today.
Panther/jacket/beret
and all.
          check it out & don't let
it happen again.
               we got enough
blk/martyrs for all the
yrs to come
         that is, if they
still coming
         after all the shit/
yrs of these
         white/yrs   goes down

3. rev pimps

    Sisters
git yr/blk/asses
out of that re/
        volution/
              ary's
bed.
  that ain't no revolutionary
thing com/munal
          fuck/ing
  ain't nothing political
bout fucking.
        that's a white/
thing u doing Sisters.
            and that so/
called/ brother there
screwing u in tune to
          fanon
        and fanon
     and fanon
        ain't no re
           vo/lution/
           ary

the game he's running
ain't called no

                        post/office

cuz. u show me
a revolutionary/fuck &
i'll send my ass   C.O.D.
to any Revolutionary.

                        u dig?

POEM AT THIRTY

it is midnight
no magical bewitching
hour for me
i know only that
i am here waiting
remembering that
once as a child
i walked two
miles in my sleep.
did i know
then where i
was going?
traveling. i'm
always traveling.
i want to tell
you about me
about nights on a
brown couch when
i wrapped my
bones in lint and
refused to move.
no one touches
me anymore.
father do not
send me out
among strangers.

From *Homecoming* by Sonia Sanchez (Detroit: Broadside Press, 1970). Reprinted by permission of the author.

you you black man
stretching scraping
the mold from your body
here is my hand.
i am not afraid
of the night.

SUMMER WORDS FOR A SISTER ADDICT

the first day i shot dope
was on a sunday.
           i had just come
home from church
           got mad at my mother
cuz she got mad at me.   u dig?
             went out. shot up
behind a feeling gainst her.
             it felt good.
gooder than dooing it.   yeah
              it was nice.
i did it.   uh. huh.   i did it.   uh. huh.
i want to do it again.   it felt so gooooood.
           and as the sister
           sits in her silent/
           remembered/high
           someone leans for
           ward gently asks her:
              sister.
               did u
              finally
           learn how to hold yr/mother?
and the music of the day
             drifts in the room
to mingle with the sister's young tears.
        and we all sing.

From *Homecoming* by Sonia Sanchez (Detroit; Broadside Press, 1970). Reprinted by permission of the author.

LUCILLE CLIFTON
(1936)

THE LOST BABY POEM

the time i dropped your almost body down
down to meet the waters under the city
and run one with the sewage to the sea
what did i know about waters rushing back
what did i know about drowning
or being drowned

you would have been born into winter
in the year of the disconnected gas
and no car   we would have made the thin
walk over Genesee hill into the Canada wind
to watch you slip like ice into strangers' hands
you would have fallen naked as snow into winter
if you were here i could tell you these
and some other things

if i am ever less than a mountain
for your definite brothers and sisters
let the rivers pour over my head
let the sea take me for a spiller
of seas   let black men call me stranger
always   for your never named sake

From *Good News about the Earth* by Lucille Clifton. Copyright 1972 by Lucille
Clifton. Reprinted by permission of Random House, Inc.

MY MAMA MOVED AMONG THE DAYS

My Mama moved among the days
like a dreamwalker in a field;
seemed like what she touched was hers
seemed like what touched her couldn't hold,
she got us almost through the high grass
then seemed like she turned around and ran
right back in
right back on in

MISS ROSIE

When I watch you
wrapped up like garbage
sitting, surrounded by the smell
of too old potato peels
or
when I watch you
in your old man's shoes
with the little toe cut out
sitting, waiting for your mind
like next weeks grocery
I say
when I watch you
you wet brown bag of a woman
who used to be the best looking gal in Georgia
used to be called the Georgia Rose
I stand up
through your destruction
I stand up

From *Good Times* by Lucille Clifton. Copyright 1969 by Lucille Clifton. Reprinted by permission of Random House, Inc.

From *Good Times* by Lucille Clifton. Copyright 1969 by Lucille Clifton. Reprinted by permission of Random House, Inc.

PATRICIA JONES
(1951)

I DONE GOT SO THIRSTY THAT MY MOUTH WATERS
AT THE THOUGHT OF RAIN

i done got so thirsty that my mouth waters
at the thought of rain
let it come down on into me/ like this pain
let it just intensify my eyes
let the will slip away in an avalanche of tears
all choked up
all choked up
all choked up
been dancing on a dream too long
& found myself lost in this desert/ no
lovers tonight/ not a one
no rain for days
got too much sun/ burning through my heart
every bone/ muscle/ corpuscle
aches
aches
aches
been running through these streets
looking for a coolness/ a coolness
been running through these streets
looking for your face/ your face/ that
soft smile/ long gone/ cross that barrier
past tense
songs rolling on the tongues of angels
i don't hear them/ off at a distance/ six
men beat up on one/ bottle breaks/ blue lights
flashing/ get the cops/ GET THE COPS/ a
screaming/ through the dancing music
a quick mambo baby 'fore i goes

From *Ordinary Women* edited by Patricia Jones (New York: Ordinary Women Books, 1978). Reprinted by permission of the author.

yeah
& the tight lips of the drunken women
they walk past the windows/ broken/ like
the windows/ oh these women/ bellies so swollen
tongues don't move 'cept to curse/ oh these
women broken/ like glass gouged into the
face of the pendejito who was in the wrong
place on the wrong saturday night
come on
come on
come on
come on rain/ come on water/ down this dry
throat/got no time for dying like this/ in
the sun/ give me some greenery/ some fertility
tell me bout female forms & what happens to
them when they are abandoned
all you get is sticks & mud/ drying

i been thirsty so long that my mouth feels
like parchment/ got words written cross it/ dead
stories bout dead feelings/ dried up/ dead
i been this thirsty so long that my hands are
crusts of brown bread flaking out into the
fields eaten by dying men/ no sustenance
no dreams/ dancing

i been thirsty been dry been drinking in the
sun/ no moisture/ not a drop of blood saliva
all of it taken out of me removed/ the removal
of fingers/ the loss of touch/ what is velvet &
how am i to know your lips/ the whore's short skirt
reveals soft flabby knees that bulge with fat wishes
loss of taste/ what makes me come/ nothing/ i just
do it/ for the money/ for the time passing/ no man's
hands can ever move me/ again/ my voice is the dryest
wind/ hard sound/ diamonds on the sidewalk/ what is in her
hair/ that scent/ god only knows/ what ever did he do
this for/ why are you looking at the other way/ what happened
here/ just this desert dry sand falling falling on the
orphan and the whore/ some want light in the darkness
candles have turned my soul to ashes/ what kinds of
movements/ slow/ slow/ slow i've been so thirsty/ so truly

in need of liquids/ water/ wine/ whiskey/ leche con dulces
dulces/ sweet water on my tongue/ need to move these female
forms round over this dry ground/ need to get down eighth
avenue without seeing broken women pass by/ as bottles break
cross the pendejo's throat & the cops come
too late

i've been thirsty so long my mouth dreams
at the thought of water dancing
dancing in the blood of women dripping
on the sidewalk like flooded houses
wasted of time and touch

WHY I LIKE MOVIES

for Charlotte

1.

I like movies because
people get to mug their faces in movies
or walk around with bad posture
and no one yells
"Stop that mugging" or "Stand up straight!"

2.

I like movies because
faces become monuments to promise.

3.

I like movies because
they spark nationalistic conversations
such as
"I never go to French movies, they're
so pretentious and intellectual."
or
"Italians must be terribly affected by sex.
Just think of those voluptuous women, always
waiting. Anna Magnani, what a face!"

or
"There's nothing like an American movie musical.
All that razzle dazzle disguising the petit anguish
beneath the smiles. Blah, blah, blah."

4.

I like movies because
they say a lot about the Other.
Like Black Folks in America. Those natives in Tarzan
movies with processes and straightened hair. That buffoon
rolling his eyes towards the coming thunder or talking
casually to spooks, saints and children. The women who
tended the house of the seemingly rich with gestures meant
for either tenderness or reproach. Secrets studded in
their enormous flesh.

5.

I like movies because
I never saw myself in them.
I saw the dreams of a people
who looked like spooks, saints
and acted like children.

6.

I like movies because
as the last reel winds back upon itself:
image on image
time turns away
a revolution terrified of the dark.

SHERLEY ANNE WILLIAMS
(1944)

THE EMPRESS BRAND TRIM: RUBY REMINISCES

He was still Uncle
Jack to me the first
time they come to New
York and I knew she
was special cause he
didn't run his women
in front of us kids.
She rehearsed that first
record right there in
our parlor and I
stayed out of school to
watch her. I didn't know
it then but my whole
life changed. She didn't look
no older than me—
bigger and darker,
sure, but no older,
and I was a teen-
ager then. I watched
her and my whole life
changed.

I was with her
in Chicago that
first time when she bought
them dark glasses cause
folks recognized her
over and over
in the streets; and that
night in Concord when
she chased the Klan out
from behind our tent.

Just cussed them out while
the mens stood shaking
in their pants; she went
on with her number
like it was routine—
cept she "never
heard of such shit."

She
loved womens and she
loved mens. The womens
was on the Q.T.,*
of course; Jack wouldn't play
that. But wasn't nothing
he could do about
the mens. She'd go to
a party and pick out the
finest brown. "I'mo
give you some Empress
Brand Trim. Tonight you
pay homage to the
pussy Blues made."
And they always did.

SAY HELLO TO JOHN

I swear I ain't done what Richard
told me bout jumpin round and stuff.
And he knew I wouldn't do nothin to make the baby
come, just joke, say I'mo cough

this child up one day.
So in the night when I felt the water tween
my legs, I thought it was pee and I laid
there wondering if maybe I was in a dream.

---

*Q.T. means quiet and is used here in the sense of sly or sneaky.

From *The Peacock Poems* by Sherley Williams (Middletown, Conn.: Wesleyan University Press, 1977). Reprinted by permission of the author.

Then it come to me that my water broke and I went
in to tell Ru-ise. *You been havin pains?*
she ask. I hear her fumblin for the light.
Naw, I say. Don't think so. The veins

stand out along her temples. *What time
is it?* Going on toward four o'clock.
*Nigga, I told you:
You ain't havin no babies, not*

*in the middle of the night.
Get yo ass back to bed.
That ain't nothin but pee.* And what
I know bout havin kids cept what she said?

Second time it happen, even she
got to admit this mo'n pee.
Add the pain when it come, wa'n't bad
least no mo'n I eva expect to see

again. I remember the doctor smilin,
sayin, Shel, you got a son.
His bright black face above me
saying, Say hello to John.

THE HOUSE OF DESIRE

I

This is really the story of a
sista who was very too-ga-tha
in everythang but life. You
see she was so too-ga-tha
she had nothang but
strife. Everyone thought

From *The Peacock Poems* by Sherley Williams (Middletown, Conn.: Wesleyan University Press, 1977). Reprinted by permission of the author.

because she was so
too-ga-tha she didn't
feel pain and the men she went
with felt just the same. They got
to-gatha with her and then, once they
were, left in most un-togatha ways.

Her end was a black one without pain,
tears of strife. She finally
concluded there's no earthly
use in bein too-ga-tha
if it don't put some
joy in yo
life.

II

this city-light

Oh, I see myself as I was
then skinny little
piece a woman dying to
get to Frisco and change. I
couldn't see the worn patches on
my coat, only the suede and
once late at night I climbed through
a window into a room.
It was bare the pot up in
smoke and the nigga was gone.

I see myself as I was then
skinny little woman-girl
sitting in a third floor room
a voice floats up from the street
calling me to prayer and once
in answer I went to the
door. There was an old woman
there crying Belle. Belle. Belle I
wet myself and falling up
the stairs.

(He asked once to tease
what I did *jes fo* fun. You
don't smoke you don't drink you don't

fuck, was the way it was phrased
and the words, no I don't fuck
unless it's with you, never
got said and I passed it all
off as one more hip joke.

                    Oh,
I could say more—there was
the day we crossed the Bridge, we were
perched on the back of the truck.
I never saw the bay quite
like that again: Oakland a
dream city I was leaving
behind; Frisco a city
of dreams I wanted to make
mine—but these three things would still
stay the same. I came to the
city to live on a hill.
I am the bird that was plucked.
I am the woman that was

III

the peacock poem

1.
                We are
ready for the night
have done the final
chores spoken of the
earlier rap emptied
ashtrays cleared the notes
and records from the
floor. Tiredness pulls
at my legs heavies
my hands as I wash
my face then shrug off
the robe. I bump the
bed in darkness and
fumble at the sheets.

Asleep you reach for me your body
curves around mine. You breathe even and

quiet now and briefly touch my breast my hip. I
believe you know it is my hand you
hold know my neck beneath your
lip.
And I am
satisfied:
You love me.

2.
He say
I'm beautiful and
for real chant about
my blackness cause that's
another way of
saying for real for
beautiful for him
and the purple dusk
of every winter
evenin belong just
only to me and
to him. I lay up
beside him and it's
us togetha in our own selves house
in our own selves bed in the dark. the
dark and ahhhhh. it be so good. good to be
beautiful to be real be for him to be
more than one. It's enough. I
know my man lovin
the way
I
struts my stuff.

IV

*What is love if it is only
known through words saying it would
be hard for me to leave you?*

Some words, seldom spoken
and then whispered only, I

sigh in dreaded visions, smoke
engendered dreams of what might
be or is:

Love, in trying
for good, can jam what it seeks
to free, be *too* instead of
so. And when that trick comes down
"I" just isn't big enough to
cover the distance between
"love" and "you."

Postscript

I offer my
body in the silence of
love-get/love-give to fill in
sexual satisfaction
the space between the words I
have put on this page.

V

the house of desire

The house feels unfinished like
a bird whose feathers have molted or one
that's been stuffed. The wind whistles
under the doors and the toilets run.

There's a voice at the window that calls me
by a name only the brotha should know.
I'd have to leave my house to answer
yet one night I was tempted to go.

The brotha says I got a good
house here. He don't know that night's
temptation, the voice, like a devilish wind
slippin in the window that doesn't bolt right.

The house old as me. They don't make
em like this no more and, like the brotha
say, I got a son. Think
about the sun when the light gatha

in the windows and the floors is all clean,
about you and the house waitin
for your son to come in; your child needs
this house. The brotha is right—comin

on strong like he usually do—but
sometimes I think if he really cared,
then . . . would he leave me so much on my own
to cry and get scared?

DRIVING WHEEL

myth story and life

I want you to come on, baby,
here's where you get
yo steak, potatoes and tea.

first story

The darkened bedroom, the double bed,
the whispers of the city night,
against it her voice, husky, speaking
past the one soft light.

> I am   through you   wholly woman. You
> say I am cold   am hard   am vain. And
> I know I am fool and bitch. And black.
> Like my mother before me and my
> sisters around me. We share the same
> legacy   are women to the same
> degree.

And I ain't even touched what's between us.
A sullen, half tearful thought.
Others lay below the surface of her mind,
rushing, gone, finally caught.

From *The Peacock Poems* by Sherley Williams (Middletown, Conn.: Wesleyan University Press, 1977). Reprinted by permission of the author.

Not circumstance; history
keeps us apart. I'm black. You black. And
how have niggas proved they men? Fightin
and fuckin as many women as
they can. And even when you can do
all the things a white man do you may
leave fightin behind but fuckin stay
the same.

For us it's havin babies and how
well we treats a man and how long we
keep him. And how long don't really have
that much to do with how well. I just
can't be a woman to yo kinda man.

second song

my man is a fine fine man
the superman of his time
   the black time   big time
in a mild mannered disguise
revealed only as needed:
   the heart steel   heart stone   heart
and its erratic beating.

      Inner and outer
rine and heart and running.
Running.   Hanging.   Caught by that powerful joint.
But my man can pull his ownself's coat
come at last to see that dick is just the same old rope.

         Yeah.

      A mild mannered
   disguise: laughing country boy astride
      a laughing goat.

first fable

We do not tell ourselves all the things we
know or admit, except perhaps in dreams,
oblique reminiscence, in sly yearnings, all
the people we feel ourselves to be.

<pre>
                                       Except
perhaps in dreams   the people we
feel . . .
</pre>

Three. A prideful panther who
stalks a white wolf, a goatish rooster who was lured on
by a grey fox and a head, a body
and, lying to one side, a heart.
The head, the heart, the body had always
been apart. The rooster called
them Humpty Dumpty things and urged
the panther to attack. The rooster was accustomed
to command, ruling the panther through
words he had taught the panther to
talk; the words only said what he wanted
the panther to know. He would crow
or blow upon his horn
and the panther would forget
all the questions he had ever known.
And once in a while, just for show,
the rooster would allow the panther
to have his way.
Now, the panther thought it too good
a body to waste, too good a brain to be
forever cut from its source.
        Let's put them together, man,
he called. You begin with the heart.
        But the rooster
knew that rebuilt Humpty Dumpty men have a
way of taking worlds apart, have new ways of
putting them together again. He lived in the world
of putting them together again. He lived in the world
of already was and it was all he ever wanted
to know.
    Not so fast, the rooster cried.

But the panther had already touched the heart
and for the first time he realized
that Not So Fast meant Don't Go. He
could feel something new, something
indefinable pumping through him. The rooster's
words failed to sway him. The rooster, angered,

sank his talons into the panther's shoulder.
The panther turned and, instinctively,
went upside the rooster's head.
The rooster absorbed the first blow;
but he was smart enough to know it was coming.
But the second was a surprise, beyond
his comprehension. He died with a question
Why   still unspoken.

                    . . . in glancing asides
we are seen, or in oblique reference. And still
left to answer is how we can pull it all together.

fourth life

They lie up in the darkened bedroom
and listen to the whispers of the city night;
each waits upon the other
to make the final move to the light
or toward the door. They have met
history; it is them. Definitions from the past
—she bitch and fool; he
nigga and therefore jive—seem the last

reality. And, once admitted, mark
the past as them. They are defeated.
She moves to strap on her shoes.

     You said,

                    and he speaks.
voice and hand holding her seated,
his head moving into the circle of light.

     You said we are more than the
     sum jiveness, the total foolishness.
     You are wholly woman, right? Isn't that
     more than bitch?

          What do it matter, huh?

His hand holds her, holds the wary
wearied question. He speaks, slow:

Matter a helluva lot. We can't
get together less we stay together.

His lips brush her cheek; she buries

her fingers in his bush. The question will always
be present, so too the doubt it leaves in its wake.
To question and to answer is to confront. To deal.
History is them; it is also theirs to make.

MAYA ANGELOU
(1928)

WOMAN ME

Your smile, delicate
rumor of peace.
Deafening revolutions nestle in the
cleavage of
your breasts
Beggar-Kings and red-ringed Priests
seek glory at the meeting
of your thighs
A grasp of Lions, A lap of Lambs.

Your tears, jeweled
strewn a diadem
caused Pharaohs to ride
deep in the bosom of the
Nile. Southern spas lash fast
their doors upon the night when
winds of death blow down your name
A bride of hurricanes, A swarm of summer wind

Your laughter, pealing tall
above the bells of ruined cathedrals.
Children reach between your teeth
for charts to live their lives.
A stomp of feet, A bevy of swift hands.

From *Oh Pray My Wings Are Gonna Fit Me Well* by Maya Angelou. Copyright 1975 by Maya Angelou. Reprinted by permission of Random House, Inc.

STILL I RISE

You may write me down in history
With your bitter, twisted lies,
You may trod me in the very dirt
But still, like dust, I'll rise.

Does my sassiness upset you?
Why are you beset with gloom?
'Cause I walk like I've got oil wells
Pumping in my living room.

Just like moons and like suns,
With the certainty of tides,
Just like hopes springing high,
Still I'll rise.

Did you want to see me broken?
Bowed head and lowered eyes?
Shoulders falling down like teardrops,
Weakened by my soulful cries.

Does my haughtiness offend you?
Don't you take it awful hard
'Cause I laugh like I've got gold mines
Diggin' in my own back yard.

You may shoot me with your words,
You may cut me with your eyes,
You may kill me with your hatefulness,
But still, like air, I'll rise.

Does my sexiness upset you?
Does it come as a surprise
That I dance like I've got diamonds
At the meeting of my thighs?

Out of the huts of history's shame
I rise
Up from a past that's rooted in pain
I rise
I'm a black ocean, leaping and wide,
Welling and swelling I bear in the tide.

From *And Still I Rise* by Maya Angelou. Copyright 1978 by Maya Angelou. Reprinted by permission of Random House, Inc.

Leaving behind nights of terror and fear
I rise
Into a daybreak that's wondrously clear
I rise
Bringing the gifts that my ancestors gave,
I am the dream and the hope of the slave.
I rise
I rise
I rise.

MY ARKANSAS

There is a deep brooding
in Arkansas.
Old crimes like moss pend
from poplar trees.
The sullen earth
is much too
red for comfort.

Sunrise seems to hesitate
and in that second
lose its
incandescent aim, and
dusk no more shadows
than the noon.
The past is brighter yet.

Old hates and
ante-bellum lace, are rent
but not discarded.
Today is yet to come
in Arkansas.
It writhes. It writhes in awful
waves of brooding.

From *And Still I Rise* by Maya Angelou. Copyright 1978 by Maya Angelou. Reprinted by permission of Random House, Inc.

SEPIA FASHION SHOW

Their hair, pomaded, faces jaded
bones protuding, hip-wise
The models strutted, backed and butted,
Then stuck their mouths out, lip-wise.

They'd nasty manners, held like banners,
while they looked down their nose-wise,
I'd see 'em in hell, before they'd sell
me one thing they're wearing, clothes-wise.

The Black Bourgeois, who all say "yah"
When yeah is what they're meaning
Should look around, both up and down
before they set out preening.

"Indeed" they swear, "that's what I'll wear
When I go country-clubbing,"
I'd remind them please, look at those knees
you got a Miss Ann's scrubbing.

ON DIVERSE DEVIATIONS

When love is a shimmering curtain
Before a door of chance
That leads to a world in question
Wherein the macabrous dance
Of bones that rattle in silence
Of blinded eyes and rolls
Of thick lips thin, denying
A thousand powdered moles,
Where touch to touch is feel
And life a weary whore
    I would be carried off, not gently
    To a shore,
    Where love is the scream of anguish
    And no curtain drapes the door.

From *Just Give Me A Cool Drink of Water 'Fore I Diiie* by Maya Angelou (New York: Random House, 1971). Reprinted by permission of G. W. Purcell Assoc. Ltd.

From *Just Give Me A Cool Drink of Water 'Fore I Diiie* by Maya Angelou (New York: Random House, 1971). Reprinted by permission of G. W. Purcell Assoc. Ltd.

NTOZAKE SHANGE
(1948)

NAPPY EDGES (A CROSS COUNTRY SOJOURN)

st. louis/ such a colored town/ a whiskey
black space of history & neighborhood/ forever ours/
to lawrenceville/ where the only road open
to me/ waz cleared by colonial slaves/ whose children never
moved/ never seems like/ mended the torments of the Depression
the stains of demented spittle/ dropped from lips of crystal women/
still makin independence flags/
    from st. louis/ on halloween's eve to the veiled prophet/
usurpin the mystery of mardi gras/ made it mine tho the queen
waz always fair/ that parade/ of pagan floats & tambourines/
commemoratin me/ unlike the lonely walks wit liberal trick or
treaters/ back to my front door/ bag half empty/
    my face enuf to scare anyone i passed/ a colored kid/
whatta gas

    1) here
        a tree
        wonderin the horizon
        dipped in blues &
        untended bones
        usedta hugs drawls
        rhythm & decency
        here a tree
        waitin to be hanged

    sumner high school/ squat & pale on the corner/ like
our vision/ waz to be vague/ our memory
of the war/ that made us free to be forgotten
becomin paler/ a linear movement from south carolina
to missouri/ freedmen/ landin in jackie wilson's yelp/ daughters of
the manumitted swimmin in tina turner's grinds/ this is chuck
berry's town/ disavowin misega-nation/ in any situation/ & they let

---

From *Nappy Edges* by Ntozake Shange (New York: St. Martin's Press, 1978). Reprinted by permission of St. Martin's Press, Inc.

us be/ electric blues & bo diddley's cant/ rockin pneumonia &
boogie-woogie flu/ the slop & short-fried heads/ runnin always to
the river

/ from chambersbourg/ lil italy/ i passed everyday
at the sweet shoppe/ & waz afraid/ the cops raided truants/
regularly/ after dark i wd not be seen/ wit any other colored/
sane/ lovin my life/
in the 'bourg/ seriously expectin to be gnarled/
hey niggah/ over here/
& behind the truck lay five hands claspin chains/
round the trees/ 4 more sucklin steel/
hey niggah/ over here
this is the borderline/
a territorial dispute/
hey/ niggah/
over here/
cars loaded wit families/ fellas from the factory/ one or two
practical nurses/ black/ become our trenches/ some dig into cement
wit elbows/ under engines/ do not be seen/ in yr hometown/ after
sunset we suck up our shadows/

2) i will sit here
my shoulders brace an enormous oak
dreams waddle in my lap
round to miz bertha's where lil richard
gets his process
run backwards to the rosebushes/ a drunk man/ lyin
down the block to the nuns in pink habits
praying in a pink chapel
my dreams run to meet aunt marie
my dreams draw blood from ol sores
these stains & scars are mine
this is my space
i am not movin

DARK PHRASES

lady in brown

dark phrases of womanhood
of never havin been a girl
half-notes scattered
without rhythm/ no tune
distraught laughter fallin
over a black girl's shoulder
it's funny/ it's hysterical
the melody-less-ness of her dance
don't tell nobody don't tell a soul
she's dancin on beer cans & shingles

this must be the spook house
another song with no singers
lyrics/no voices
& interrupted solos
unseen performances

are we ghouls?
children of horror?
the joke?

don't tell nobody don't tell a soul
are we animals? have we gone crazy?

i can't hear anythin
but maddening screams
& the soft strains of death
& you promised me
you promised me . . .
somebody/anybody
sing a black girl's song
bring her out
to know herself
to know you
but sing her rhythms
carin/struggle/hard times

From *For Colored Girls Who Have Considered Suicide When the Rainbow Is Enuf* by Ntozake Shange. Copyright 1975, 1976, 1977 by Ntozake Shange. Reprinted by permission of Macmillan Publishing Co., Inc.

sing her song of life
she's been dead so long
closed in silence so long
she doesn't know the sound
of her own voice
her infinite beauty
she's half-notes scattered
without rhythm/no tune
sing her sighs
sing the song of her possibilities
sing a righteous gospel
the makin of a melody
let her be born
let her be born
& handled warmly.

lady in brown
i'm outside chicago

lady in yellow
i'm outside detroit

lady in purple
i'm outside houston

lady in red
i'm outside baltimore

lady in green
i'm outside san francisco

lady in blue
i'm outside manhattan

lady in orange
i'm outside st. louis

lady in brown
& this is for colored girls who have considered suicide
but moved to the ends of their own rainbows.

everyone
mama's little baby likes shortnin, shortnin,
mama's little baby likes shortnin bread
mama's little baby likes shortnin, shortnin,
mama's little baby likes shortnin bread

little sally walker, sittin in a saucer
rise, sally, rise, wipe your weepin eyes
an put your hands on your hips
and let your backbone slip
o, shake it to the east
o, shake it to the west
shake it to the one
that you like the best

                    lady in purple
you're it

NO MORE LOVE POEMS #1

                    lady in orange
ever since i realized there waz someone callt
a colored girl an evil woman a bitch or a nag
i been tryin not to be that & leave bitterness
in somebody else's cup/come to somebody to love me
without deep & nasty smellin scald from lye or bein
left screamin in a street fulla lunatics/whisperin
slut bitch bitch niggah/get outta here wit alla that/
i didnt have any of that for you/i brought you what
joy i found & i found joy/honest fingers round my
face/with dead musicians on 78's from cuba/or live
musicians on five dollar lp's from chicago/where i
have never been/& i love willie colon & arsenio
rodriquez/especially cuz i can make the music loud
enuf/so there is no me but dance/& when i can
dance like that/there's nothin cd hurt me/but i get
tired & i haveta come offa the floor & then there's
that woman who hurt you/who you left/three or
four times/& just went back/after you put my heart
in the bottom of yr shoe/you just walked back to
where you hurt/& i didnt have nothin/so i went to
where somebody had somethin for me/but he waznt

From *For Colored Girls Who Have Considered Suicide When the Rainbow Is Enuf* by
Ntozake Shange. Copyright 1975, 1976, 1977 by Ntozake Shange. Reprinted by permis-
sion of Macmillan Publishing Co., Inc.

you/ & i waz on the way back from her house in
the bottom of yr shoe/so this is not a love poem/
cuz there are only memorial albums available/& even
charlie mingus wanted desperately to be a pimp/
& i wont be able to see eddie palmieri for months/
so this is a requium for myself/cuz i have died in a
real way/not wid aqua coffins & du-wop cadillacs/
i used to joke abt when i waz messin round/but a
real dead lovin is here for you now/cuz i dont know
anymore/how to avoid my own face wet wit my
tears/cuz i had convinced myself colored girls had no
right to sorrow/& i lived & loved that way & kept
sorrow on the curb/allegedly for you/but i know i did
it for myself/
i cdnt stand it
i cdnt stand bein sorry & colored at the same time
it's so redundant in the modern world

FRANK ALBERT & VIOLA BENZENA OWENS

she waited on the 7th floor
corner flat   her children   wanderin
from room to room   ghosts   ghost children
effie   althea   rosalie
          diptheria deserted
blonde colored girls   bright-migrant
children never runnin carolinian hills
never utterin   gullah accents
          slurrin words like bajans
mountain folk

they wandered
rosalie   althea   effie   in white
lace dresses   starched for the wake
celebrated births on 52nd street   swallowed
like placenta   when there is nothin/ else

From *Nappy Edges* by Ntozake Shange (New York: St. Martin's Press, 1978). Reprinted by permission of St. Martin's Press, Inc.

when you rear yr young in dark closets
like a stray cat
  she waited by the door
opened to aunties from his side of the family
uncles from charleston   a loyal bartender   &
children in bodies
      only hintin of ochre soil
she lingered by the corrupted window
by the fire escape   soot-sprinkled plants
laughed at her   meticulous   ventures
washin
sills   diapers   the carpenter's trousers
her hair
  languid in the nape of the neck
a thick wad of soft nap   above the mole
she wanted a 'bob'   a fashionable diversion
to save pushin thick braids off her chest
while she leaned
     over steamin laundry
     the baby
     the father
     & the graves
she waited for him at the kitchen
table heaped with buttered rice n okra
heaped with linen napkins from the allendale wedding
the children in bodies gorged themselves
on halves of biscuits   they prided
themselves for lovin him   the father
they waited   & she drew sketches
of her mother   who had died   her sisters
who had died   her father who had died
in jacksonville & left her to speak
too proper for a workman   too poor
for somethin better   the carpenter
was solid   was handsome   was kind &
delivered her north
delivered her too many to suckle
& still sass him   she waited/ her hair
so heavy   her head hung down
to fondle the baby
warm the baby

move the baby from colored manhattan
take the baby north to freedom
to the bronx   she waited for deliverance
for him to return
from tendin the fire
from passin for irish
from the bar where faster women rolled
from the garveyites sneering at pale
    niggahs all livin together
in special wings of tenements

she waited & mumbled
  'his eye is on the sparrow
  & i know he's watchin me/ he's watchin me'
she poured grease over turnip greens
asked the haitian roomer to move
for workin voodoo on the baby
dyin   from scarlet fever
warm the baby pray   save
the child
    he loved his own
    he loved his own

she sweat & brought breath to his blood
he lied in the world   he looked over his
shoulder   every step   to see
the burnin cross   feathers/ ruins of farms
his father's tools   she waited
by the bed
    fingerin his tuskegee photo
the carpenter's shop   the colored pioneers
the baby was purple/ foamin at the mouth
she waited   for christ
to reveal himself   she sang
          compulsively
to soothe the baby
ease his entry
the door never opened
he lay in the cellar   fractured   crumbled
over   un-even casing   the carpenter
crawled without his body   thru sicilian ashes/
jewish cadavers moanin in the beams/

he crawled to his children
rosalie   althea   effie in lace dresses starched for the wake
roamin from room to room   swallowed like placenta
his   woman   waitin   receivin   the   spirits
carolina screams/ branded up country slaves/ raging

   he made the journey
    to deliver her   to freedom
     the carpenter   tendin   to his   own
      movin   north

THADIOUS M. DAVIS
(1944)

IT'S ALL THE SAME

   My Grandmama
dont believe they walked in space:
"In the desert someplace,
Child, where your sense?"
dont believe they traveled to the moon
"On a mountain somewhere,
Child, watch what I say!"

   My Grandmama
wont admit there're still Albinos:
"Now we fight for it, they done stopped
stealing our color for sunning oil."
wont admit they let blacks go to Africa:
"What, for this here country to c'lapse?"

   On Sunday morning
her old-time preacher preaches the old word:
"And the Sun *do* move!
And the Moon *do* shine!"
And my righteous grandmama,
stronger than a matter-of-fact,
leads the Amen chorus:
"Tell it . . . Tell it . . .
Tell the Gospel Truth, Rev."

REMEMBERING FANNIE LOU HAMER

Precious night-blooming cereus
You flowered once in Mississippi
Red clay blistered your bare feet
Kept you burnt-out sharecropping
But you blossomed out of Ruleville
A new field worker
Losing job, house, family, health
A new field worker committed in strength
Organizing, registering, mobilizing
Teaching us how to flower in battle
How to free our lives ourselves
How to move powerful in love
How to make "joyful noises" for ourselves

In the barren morning after you
Silences inside match the flowerless clay
We won't blossom the same any more
And we won't sing the old hymns
Because your passing into Mississippi dust
Teaches us
It's not for our song
We will be remembered
But for strong new growth
Under midnight moons

DOUBLE TAKE AT RELAIS DE L'ESPADON*

On the Ile de Gorée, M. Diop elegant
in steel-gray cardigan
bowed his greeting, waved me be seated
inside a shaded courtyard opening to the sea
With quiet ceremony he offered me tea
Senegalese style   hot and sweet
served neat like shots of whiskey
His fine manner and regal bearing
subdued the space around us

*Relais de l'Espadon is a tourist hotel on Gorée, an island three miles off the coast of
Senegal. Gorée is known as "the island of the slave trade."

In a generous flourish of slender sepia hands
he adopted me, one of the lost tribe
Graced with relief from a tourist's day
I dreamed of a long time coming
then blossomed reclaimed
A Wolof daughter admiring his formal ease
that bore no trace of my many fathers
shuffling through Louisiana mud
my fathers bent by labor, bowed in servility

After lunch, we sat thigh-to-thigh
riding the ferry to Dakar
Ignoring moisture and heat, we struggled to speak
His flawless French   but no English
drew hesitant response
Our language: gestures
flowing reserves of sudden caring
I followed his eyes scanning the wake
Gorée, golden globe of afternoon, flickered into view
And I began the long journey backward
Relais de l'Espadon   slaver's mansion
stood restored, a sunlit pastel
yellow walls and rose shutters
jailing stone patios swept by sea air
Salt water welled within old wounds
preserved memories   my father's house of many rooms
Blood and bone stiffened before we sighted port
I surrounded myself with a prison of kin
My human fortress still fighting sea and separation

M. Diop disappeared into the city
His straight proud back, graceful and controlled,
left me wondering
    Is he the father I might have had
    Is he the son who shackled my father and me

"HONEYSUCKLE WAS THE SADDEST ODOR OF ALL, I THINK."

Quentin Compson in Faulkner's
The Sound and the Fury

I wanted to be a nature poet
And write hauntingly of
Southern landscapes
Lush with brilliant birds
Animals green framed in hanging moss
Musky magnolia floral curtains
Under spiraling
Hot blue white moon spaces
Faulkner's wisteria
Lemon scented verbena
Sculptured yards luminous on
Twilight canvas blending
Cable's bayou parish
In painted midnight readings

I forgot "Poplar trees bear a
Strange Fruit"
Deep roots
Strong limbs
Flexing
Spreading
North
Searing cultured descendants of
Fiery abolitionists

In frigid light
School buses plow
Push thunder through
Brick-lined rotaries
Spinning salt-snow
Pebble bouquets

Published in *Obsidian* 4 (Spring 1978).

In frozen dark
Spit slices my pores
Hard glass fragments
Jagged tears
Remnants of
My poetic eye

ASANTE SANA,* TE TE

Laughing eyes followed
the gold everywhere in our circle
gold rings reflecting red
afternoon sun

Precious links in a chain
surviving the crossing

Laughing eyes followed
the gold in my ears

I do not know how to say in Fulani
My great-grandmother preserved the ritual
My great-grandmother Te Te
Three weeks after my birth
Great-grandmother Te Te
pierced my ears
and named me Marée Nage

---

*"Many thanks" in Swahili.

MELBA JOYCE BOYD
(1950)

SUNFLOWERS AND SATURDAYS

daddy sits
in his brown
leather chair
back straight,
brow tight
behind the
rims of
his glasses.
he studies
my puzzles
with precise
algebraic
words,
printed perfectly
balanced
with the
center of
the page.

his hair
waves into
even black
curves,
streaked with
silver
as smooth as
my child-
hood
cuddled in
his lap
on a saturday
afternoon
sneaking a sip
of beer

studying the
red scar
above his
right eye
fixed on
the cross-
word puzzle
or speck
of dust
diving into
the tv
screen.

the summers
were longer then,
when i kept
frogs
and turtles
in the shade
of the sunflowers
and the
quaking aspen
daddy planted
my third
spring.

still an
ignorant child
sulking justice,
i build
poems
from chipped
and narrow
fractions.
daddy reads
with the
ambiance
of sunflowers
and saturdays,
yesterday
afternoon.

WHY?

katherine
is warm,
chocolate marsh-
mallow
floating on
the turquoise
carpet,
pretending it
is a pond
her toys
must travel
around
to reach
the party
in the right
angle
of her
room.

she bridges
the journey
because pooh
bear
is afraid
the monster
pacing the kitchen
will crash
the door,
crushing the
moment.

but
katherine cups
her tears
in the brown
mole
from her
father,
twinkling in

her right
eye,
thru the
lashes
her mother
dispenses daily,
like aspirin.

questions
peal off
her tongue
elliptic,
like her
goldfish
vanishing into
the curve
of the bowl:
what lives
beyond?
what hides
behind?
why can't
crooked clowns
cartwheel
away
with the snow?

and why
do teardrops
dry in
the pockets
of my
cracked
smile?

BEER DROPS

because beer tingles
like tear drippings
and deceives relief
from the heat
and the hate,
he spent his afternoons
pushing the rusty
lawn mower
for just enough
change.

his ashy legs
slumped into
rusty raw ankles
and rough ridden shoes
that curled away from
the cracks in the
sidewalk
and pointed up to
the naked pot belly,
wet with sweat,
glistening across
a scar that sneered
stronger than
his yellow gaze
searching the streets
for small treasures
and shaded spaces.

the foam floated further
than the mock bow
and the silent plea
to cut the weeds,
the only green grinning
against the concrete
cage,
but they wiped him away
without changing
their mute stares,

their mouths full
of crushed ice
and diluted lemonade.

he readjusted his slump,
spinning as quick
as the mower blades,
with loud laughter
bursting like
a belch
from his spongy head,
as the empty brown bottle
landed inside
the steel checkered fence,
crushing a dandelion
skull.

COLLEEN J. McELROY

RUTH

And Ruth said Intreat me not to leave
thee, or to return from following after
thee; for whither thou goest, I will go . . .
RUTH 1:16

it took 27 years to write this poem
27 years mama and still I see you falling
like a lump of coal down a chute
arms hands and feathered thighs churning
inside a tumbling hulk of helpless flesh
falling away from me
your dress flying open
until you were finally free form
and without face

Published in *Willow Springs* 7 (Fall 1980). Included in *Lie and Say You Love Me* by
Colleen J. McElroy (Port Orchard, Washington: Circinatum Press, forthcoming).

since then I have counted those stairs
I would like to say there were 27
but significance lies not in exactness
but in the panic of not knowing
which step would claim you
I have saved that morning
the blood-sucking thud of body
against wood the back staircase
of that red brick duplex
where you clawed air

we had fought   I remember that
about what   nothing
grandpa's untimely death
my 16 year old womanish ways
how someday I too would flail
at my own daughter
so many fights   so many stairs
and you tumbling as my terror
claimed me like Venus
without arms or legs to stop you

one moment you were larger than life
your black arms spread like the wings
of some great vulture   the next a step
missed and you fragile   distorted   plunging
in wingless flight toward some evil nucleus
waiting in the space below the steps
but we cannot go back
I cannot correct that split second
when I failed to lean forward
bodies will not reverse and tumble
upward   unwinding into familiar forms
limbs intact   I have hesitated too long
and the landing is too crowded

what dusty things we would find there now
how you quoted Shakespeare for every event
from slamming doors to Sunday walks and bigotry
a broken lamp   your jealousy and mine
too many unspoken holidays
for your one daughter too many

or too many husbands for one daughter
how your senseless plunge into a void
showed me more than all your ominous warnings
how the cycle of blood and pain
has brought us both to this childless time

I have finally faced myself in you
for years I have written poems non-stop
but yours were always more difficult
I have even tried dream language
but your image slips into some zone
of blackness even deeper in color
than your skin when I angered you

how often has the venom from your blueberry
lips stunted the growth of a poem
how often has your voice been with me
wherever I go   you have gone
and sometimes gladly my need to reach out
has pulled you to me
mama for years I have hidden
hundreds of unfinished verses
in the corners of dark closets

read this
and count them

CALEDONIA

Caledonia, Caledonia
What makes your big head so hard . . . .

the way I hear tell aunt jennie
tapdanced on the hood of her husband's
car because she heard he *might*
have smiled at Miz Dora Emma's daughter
Brand new ford baby pink it was
and a convertible right out of days
full of white buck shoes sock hops

and little richard wailing over the local
disc jockey all night party station
Neighbors whooped and laughed seeing her
fly straight out the front door swearing
that nigger would never live another day
seeing mama running down the block
just in time to catch her falling
butt first into the gutter
But mama wouldn't laugh because jennie
knew who had not accidentally put too much
red pepper in daddy's beans and rice
that night he came home smelling
of southern comfort and blue grass
neither of which mama ever touched
And who bought a one way ticket home
for Uncle Brother's first wife
stuck up and full of airs
just because she came from California
in the 40s before it was fashionable

mama and aunt jennie both hardheaded
and lean on words
inhaling and saying humph and um-um-um
to a chorus of head wagging un-huh's
whenever they hear tell I'm having female
problems full of husband troubles
They have been married for as long
as anyone can remember and now so dependent
on their husbands and each other and husbands
on them and the other there's no telling
where one begins and ends
or which sister has religiously whipped
the other into shape
until I've learned that love, like hate
is always acted out

LOOKING FOR A COUNTRY UNDER ITS ORIGINAL NAME

gold will not buy this voyage
and I am but a turning point
a teller of tales who wants all the secrets
but none of the answers
who cries and laughs her way through church
meetings, back rooms, undertaker parlors
behind beauty parlors full of card
players, gin drinkers and good women
who would just as soon cut you another hole
before they'd let you sass grown folks
and now me grown
and waiting to see what furrows
I have turned to line my face
when my children finally remember
to call home

and if you ask yourself why this information
is so freely given
remember it wasn't freely earned
and that this is how I always find
my way home even before I have arrived
and that these words hold more than all
the photographs I can remember
and although you may think I travel
these roads for your pleasure
each one brings me closer to where I am
than all the details in the wide-eyed
picture of my mother at eight
sitting between her younger brother
and now dead sister with her father's
hawk stare pinning them all

on the horizon of the camera's eye
or how I must squint into a waxy copy
of a daguerreotype holding a young girl
who is to be my mother's mother
and who dressed for the occasion
holds fast to the tight blackness
of her skin and the tight kinks
of thick hair piled neatly

into a coil that all
but hides the fake landscape
backdropped behind her
flat and void of sunlight
which is strange yet familiar
as if I've been there before and know
just what is around the next corner

and finally the journey is so easy
you need only prime me with a bit of buttered bread
to find my family
I will unearth them for you as quickly as a strip
miner might tear that hill you're looking at now
and like the earth they will turn up raw
wood brown and blackened by lime and salt
from seas that no longer exist
though I have often wished this weren't so automatic
the lava and loam
of my bearings rising so quickly to the surface
the blood lines veined so neatly to their source
their mysteries so perfect even their undoings
seem as planned as way signs on a map

A WOMAN'S SONG

The land is cold and its men gather earth for no reason. Their
    eyes fail to give them pictures of the inner world. They
    are angered by small changes in clouds.
I am Diamonane, daughter of seven voices, my language as
    old as soft hands across a man's bared chest. Bones
    mean nothing. It is the flesh, hot and sweet, it is there
    you flower and die. You have seen me walking slowly
    at the edge of foreign seas, you have seen me choking
    on diesel fumes of cities, eating muskmelons under the
    striped tents of incense filled bazaars, quarrelling with
    the fishhawkers in the French Quarter, or standing,
    head bowed, at the edge of a clearing among Dutch
    settlers in those first New England snows. But always,
    always, my cape, full and black, billows and flows even
    on windless nights.

My father weeps like his father before him. He weeps for
   fathers yet to be born. He has seen the zebra die,
   watched the blood bubble and spurt from the severed
   head like blue gas from an open pit of volcanic earth.
   Blood erupting with the swift touch of a ubaba's blade,
   a chieftain's weapon, definite and deadly. My father
   knows this ritual sings of other treacheries, the whis-
   pered trading and bartering of bodies that split men
   from their countries and bloat skinny jungle trails with
   long coffle chained rows of people who could build a
   great nation.

My father knows that the dull eyes of the dying zebra will be
   repeated until both chieftain and farmer pray dumbly
   to new gods. The lovely blue waters of the Bight of
   Benin hold a body for three days before it's washed out
   to sea, Dachau is eleven miles from Munich, and the
   slave castles of Madagascar cannot be seen from the
   shores of Mozambique.

My mother was the first Eritrean, too noble and proud for
   deserts. She abandoned me in the courts of Messinessa
   and Syphax, sent me to Carthage where I stayed until
   Hannibal arrived. Later I fled, and still later, sang frail
   lyrics to the strings of Te-kwa-ta's knee harp in the
   courts of Ann Zingha, warrior queen of Matamba. I was
   well groomed for my role, knew the subtle costume, the
   changes in skin, knew the snake-sly eyes of the dancing
   woman and the cow eyes of the wifely woman. I was
   sold for a high price and willingly loved my king.

I have known time and halcyon days. I have learned to pick
   my wounds like a wild bird and to feed on berries in the
   kingdom of Kotoko. I have run with the antelope and
   spoken to the griots. Those wily-faced halfmen and
   she-apes have chased me into the clearing, damned me
   for living like a poet, and forced me into marriage
   rituals.

Once I rowed from a Roman galley, its sails billowing out like
   brim-filled wine gourds, its belly full of women, black
   like me and framed in fear. The Roman, Theallus, keep-
   er of the osprey, cradled and kept me in a coffin of tiles
   and sickly perfumes. He loved me too well and was put
   to death when I left. I still see his eyes, sad and dark as
   the polished wood of the oud. I conjure up his image in

songs that command the strings of the oud, and like
Te-kwa-ta's knee harp, the oud sings melodies of death
as sweetly as a child.

I have bathed in my father's loins and he has called me quela,
bird girl. I have loved daughters and sons, licked the
hollows of their skin, the wrinkles holding sweet am-
ber smells. We have slept fitfully under the eyes of
slavers, and later watched weary sunsets among the
red bricks of cold cities where north winds rust the
wood and tears its still-sharp claws into the doors. On
hungry nights we lay naked, listening to the sounds of
rats and lice scurrying about in the dark.

I have tamed the flames of my body to get food for my man,
auctioned its lust to keep his mask of manhood in
place, smiled as I lay with strangers so that he would
never know loneliness. And when he left me, I
reshaped the images of Theallus into new songs. In the
hot days of Harlem, I sang in rat-hole bars. I was
Chelsea and Bessie, blues and gospel, heroin in the
blood and coke in the nostrils. I have buried my babies
in swamplands and under cottonwood trees. I have
kissed off my men like forgotten toys and spent my
motherhood in kitchens suckling babies who were not
mine.

I brought dark songs to piss-stained hallways, aborted un-
named children in cluttered alleys, and loved diseased
men. I have sweated under the smoothness of my sis-
ter's flesh, driving her into full heat like the demon I
am, tasted the sweet sperm from my brother's penis,
and rose from both beds refreshed and without guilt. I
have watched hate dance against black skin, turning
and jumping just so, watched it sleep on the sidewalks
of Frisco and wake to the tune of Jim Crow.

Today I walk into hurried streets where exhaust-fumed faces
of so-called world travelers are as pale as the moun-
tains they have fled. They speak to me with voices like
stone against stone. I answer in words stolen from the
dark underside of the brightly plumed touraco. I have
sold my secrets to survive. I am Diamonane, beloved
daughter, bird child of obsidian and serpent. I am the
egg, the sperm.

BIBLIOGRAPHY

POETRY ANTHOLOGIES

Adam, William, Peter Conn, and Barry Slepian, eds. *Afro-American Literature: Poetry.* Boston: Houghton Mifflin Company, 1970.

Adoff, Arnold, ed. *Black Out Loud: An Anthology of Modern Poems by Black Americans.* New York: Macmillan, 1970.

Bell, Bernard W., ed. *Modern and Contemporary Afro-American Poetry.* Boston: Allyn & Bacon Inc., 1972.

Blacksong Series I: Four Poetry Broadsides by Black Women. Detroit: Lotus Press, 1978.

Bontemps, Arna, ed. *American Negro Poetry.* Rev. ed. New York: Hill and Wang, 1974.

Boyd, Sue Abbott, ed. *Poems by Blacks.* 2 vols. Fort Smith, Arkansas: South and West, 1970-72.

Breman, Paul, ed. *Sixes and Sevens: An Anthology of New Negro Poetry.* London: Paul Breman Ltd., 1962.

Brooks, Gwendolyn, ed. *A Broadside Treasury, 1965–1970.* Detroit: Broadside Press, 1971.

———, ed. *Jump Bad: A New Chicago Anthology.* Detroit: Broadside Press, 1971.

Brown, Patricia L., Don L. Lee, and Francis Ward, eds. *To Gwen with Love: An Anthology Dedicated to Gwendolyn Brooks.* Chicago: Johnson Publishing Company, 1971.

Burroughs, Margaret Goss and Dudley Randall, eds. *For Malcolm: Poems on the Life and the Death of Malcolm X.* Detroit: Broadside Press, 1967.

Collins, Marie, ed. *Black Poets in French.* New York: Charles Scribner's Sons, 1972.

Coombs, Orde, ed. *We Speak as Liberators: Young Black Poets, An Anthology.* New York: Dodd, Mead & Co., 1970.

Cullen, Countee, ed. *Caroling Dusk: An Anthology of Verse by Negro Poets.* New York: Harper & Brothers, 1927. Reprint. New York: Harper & Row, 1974.

Culver, Eloise Crosby, ed. *Great American Negroes in Verse: 1723–1965.* Washington, D.C.: Associated Publishers, 1965.

Cunard, Nancy, ed. *Negro: An Anthology.* 1934. Reprint. New York: Frederick Ungar Publishing Company, 1970.

Danner, Margaret, ed. *The Brass House.* Richmond, Virginia: privately printed, 1968.

———, ed. *Regroup.* Richmond, Virginia: privately printed, 1969.

Dee, Ruby, ed. *Glowchild, And Other Poems.* New York: Third Press, Joseph Okpaku Publishing Co., 1972.

Dunbar-Nelson, Alice, ed. *The Dunbar Speaker and Entertainer.* Naperville, Illinois: Nichols Publishing Company, 1920.

———, ed. *Masterpieces of Negro Eloquence.* New York: The Bookery Publishing Co., 1914. Reprint. Chicago: Johnson Reprint Corporation, 1970.

Gibson, Donald B., ed. *Modern Black Poets.* Englewood Cliffs, N.J.: Prentice-Hall, Inc. 1973.

Giovanni, Nikki, ed. *Night Comes Softly: Anthology of Black Female Voices.* New York: Nik-Tom Publications, 1970.

Hayden, Robert, ed. *Kaleidoscope: Poems by American Negro Poets.* New York: Harcourt, Brace & World, Inc. 1967.

Hughes, Langston, ed. *New Negro Poets: U.S.A.* Bloomington: Indiana University Press, 1964.

Jones, Patricia, ed. *Ordinary Women: An Anthology of New York City Women.* New York: Ordinary Women Books, 1978.

Jordan, June, ed. *Soulscript: Afro-American Poetry.* New York: Doubleday, 1970.

Kendricks, Ralph, ed. *Afro-American Voices: 1770's–1970's.* New York: Oxford Book Company, 1970.

Kerlin, Robert T., ed. *Negro Poets and Their Poems.* 1923. Reprint. Washington, D.C.: Associated Publishers, 1935.

King, Woodie, ed. *Blackspirits: A Festival of New Black Poets in America.* New York: Random House, 1972.

———, ed. *The Forerunners: Black Poets in America.* Washington, D.C.: Howard University Press, 1975.

Lane, Pinkie Gordon, ed. *Poems by Blacks.* 2 vols. Fort Smith, Arkansas: South and West, 1973–75.

Locke, Alain, ed. *The New Negro: An Interpretation.* 1925. Reprint. New York: Johnson Reprint Corporation, 1968.

Lomax, Alan and Raoul Abdoul, eds. *Three Thousand Years of Black Poetry: An Anthology.* New York: Dodd, Mead & Co., 1970.

Major, Clarence, ed. *The New Black Poetry.* New York: International Publishers, 1969.

Miller, Adam David, ed. *Dices or Black Bones: Black Voices of the Seventies.* New York: Houghton Mifflin, 1970.

Murphy, Beatrice, ed. *Ebony Rhythm.* Rev. ed. New York: Exposition Press, 1968.

———, ed. *Negro Voices: An Anthology of Contemporary Verse.* New York: Harrison-Hilton Books Inc., 1938.

Peplow, Michael W. and Arthur P. Davis, eds. *The New Negro Renaissance: An Anthology.* New York: Holt, Rinehart & Winston, 1975.

Pool, Rosey E., ed. *Beyond the Blues: New Poems by American Negroes.* London: Hand and Flower Press, 1962.

Randall, Dudley, ed. *The Black Poets.* New York: Bantam Books, 1971.

Robinson, William H., ed. *Early Black American Poets.* Dubuque, Iowa: William C. Brown Co., 1969.

Rodgers, Carolyn M., ed. *For Love of Our Brothers*. Chicago: Third World Press, 1970.

Sanchez, Sonia, ed. *Three Hundred and Sixty Degrees of Blackness Comin' at You*. New York: Bantam Books, 1971.

Shuman, R. Baird, ed. *Nine Black Poets*. Durham, North Carolina: Moore Publishing Co., 1968.

Watkins, Mel, ed. *Black Review, No. 1*. New York: William Morrow & Company, 1971.

White, Newman Ivey and Walter Clinton Jackson, eds. *An Anthology of Verse by American Negroes*. 1924. Reprint. Durham, North Carolina: Moore Publishing Co., 1968.

Wilentz, Ted and Tom Weatherley, eds. *Natural Process: An Anthology of New Black Poetry*. New York: Hill and Wang, 1970.

Wormley, Beatrice and Charles W. Carter, eds. *An Anthology of Negro Poetry by Negroes and Others*. n.p., n.d. Work Progress Administration (W.P.A.), Shomburg Collection, New York City.

CRITICAL WORKS

Books

Bell, Roseann P., Bettye J. Parker, and Beverly Sheftall, eds. *Sturdy Black Bridges: Visions of Black Women in Literature*. New York: Doubleday & Company, 1979.

Bowles, Juliet, ed. *In the Memory and Spirit of Frances, Zora and Lorraine: Essays and Interviews Relating to Black Women and Writing*. Washington, D.C.: Institute for the Arts and Humanities, 1979.

Brawley, Benjamin. *The Negro Genius: A New Appraisal of the Achievement of The American Negro in Literature and Fine Art*. Rev. ed. New York: Dodd, Mead, & Company, 1944.

Cade, Toni, ed. *The Black Woman: An Anthology*. New York: New American Library, 1970.

Carson, Josephine, ed. *The Southern Negro Woman Today*. New York: Delacorte Press, 1969.

Christian, Barbara. *Black Women Novelists: The Development of a Tradition, 1892–1976*. Westport, Conn.: Greenwood Press, 1980.

Culp, D.W., ed. *Twentieth Century Negro Literature*. Naperville, Ill., and Toronto: n.p., 1902.

Davis, Arthur P. *From the Dark Tower: Afro-American Writers, 1900–1960*. Washington, D.C.: Howard University Press, 1974.

Evans, Mari, ed. *Black Women Writers 1950–Present*. New York: Doubleday & Company, 1981.

Fisher, Dexter, ed. *The Third Woman: Minority Women Writers of the United States*. Boston: Houghton Mifflin, 1980.

Gayle, Addison, Jr. *The Way of the New World: The Black Novel in America*. New York: Doubleday & Company, 1973.

Harley, Sharon and Rosalyn Terborg Penn, eds. *The Afro-American Woman: Struggles and Images*. Port Washington, N.Y.: Kennikat Press, 1978.

Henderson, Stephen E. *Understanding the New Black Poetry: Black Speech and Music as Poetic Reference*. New York: William Morrow & Company, 1972.

Huggins, Nathan. *Harlem Renaissance*. New York: Oxford University Press, 1971.

————, ed. *Voices From the Harlem Renaissance*. New York: Oxford University Press, 1976.

Johnson, Willa D. and Thomas Green, eds. *Perspectives on Afro-American Women*. Washington, D.C.: Ecca Publications, 1975.

Kunitz, Stanley Jasspon, ed. *Twentieth Century Authors: A First Supplement*. New York: Wilson Press, 1955.

Lowenberg, Bert and Ruth Bogin, eds. *Black Women in Nineteenth Century American Life*. University Park: Pennsylvania State University Press, 1972.

Perry, Margaret. *Silence to the Drum: A Survey of the Literature of the Harlem Renaissance*. Westport, Conn: Greenwood Press, 1976.

Redmond, Eugene B. *Drum Voices: The Mission of Afro-American Poetry*. New York: Doubleday & Company, 1976.

Sanchez, Sonia, ed. *We Be Word Sorcerers*. New York: Bantam Books, 1973.

Sherman, Joan. *Invisible Poets: Afro-Americans of the Nineteenth Century*. Urbana: University of Illinois Press, 1974.

Sims, Janet L. *The Black Woman in the United States*. Westport, Conn.: Greenwood Press, 1980.

Singh, Amrityit. *The Novels of The Harlem Renaissance: Twelve Black Writers, 1923–33*. University Park, Penn.: Pennsylvania State University Press, 1976.

Sterling, Dorothy. *Black Foremothers: Three Lives*. Old Westbury, N.Y.: The Feminist Press, 1979.

Wagner, Jean. *Black Poets of the U.S.* Urbana: University of Illinois Press, 1973.

Walker, Alice, ed. *I Love Myself When I am Laughing . . . And Then Again When I am Looking Mean and Impressive*. Old Westbury, N.Y.: The Feminist Press, 1979.

Whitlow, Roger. *Black American Literature: A Critical History*. Totowa, N.J.: Littlefield, Adams, & Co., 1974.

Williams, Ora. *American Black Women in The Arts and Social Sciences: A Bibliographic Survey*. Metuchen, N.J.: The Scarecrow Press, 1973.

Articles

Dandridge, Rita. "On Novels by Black American Women: A Bibliographic Essay." *Women's Studies Newsletter* 6 (Summer 1978): 28–30.

Giddings, Paula. "A Special Vision, A Common Goal." *Encore* 12 (June 23-July 4, 1975): 44–48.

Hoffman, Nancy. "White Woman, Black Woman: Inventing an Adequate Pedagogy." *Women's Studies Newsletter* 5 (Winter/Spring 1977): 21–24.

Hull, Gloria T. "Black Women Poets from Wheatley to Walker." *Negro American Literature Forum* 9 (Fall 1975): 91–96.

———. "Re-Writing Afro-American Literature: A Case for Black Women Writers." *The Radical Teacher* 6 (December 1977): 10–13.

Parker, Bettye. "Black Literature Teachers: Torch Bearers of European Myths." *Black World* 24 (December 1975): 12–15.

Rushing, Andrea Benton. "Images of Black Women in Afro-American Poetry." *Black World* 24 (September 1975): 18–30.

Russell, Michele. "Black-Eyed Blues Connection: Teaching Black Women." *Women's Studies Newsletter* 4 (Fall 1976): 6–7; 5 (Winter/Spring 1977): 24–28.

Smith, Barbara. "Doing Research on Black American Women." *Women's Studies Newsletter* 4 (Spring 1976): 4–7.

———. "Teaching about Black Women Writers." *Women's Studies Newsletter* 2 (Spring 1974): 2.

———. "Toward a Black Feminist Criticism." *Conditions: Two* 1 (October 1977): 25–44.

Smitherman, Geneva. "The Black Idiom and the New Black Poetry." *Black Creation* 6 (1974–75): 81–86.

Washington, Mary Helen. "Black Women Myth and Image Makers." *Black World* 23 (August 1974): 10–18.

———. "Teaching Black-Eyed Susans: An Approach to the Study of Black Women Writers." *Black American Literature Forum* 2 (Spring 1977): 20–24.

WORKS BY THE POETS

ADA, "A YOUNG WOMAN OF COLOR"

No published volume of poetry.

ALLAH, FAREEDAH [RUBY C. SAUNDERS]

American Born Black (unpublished)
Singing Praises to the Lamb (unpublished)

ANGELOU, MAYA

And Still I Rise. New York: Random House, 1978.
Gather Together in My Name. New York: Random House, 1974.
I Know Why the Caged Bird Sings. New York: Random House, 1970.
Just Give Me a Cool Drink of Water 'Fore I Diiie. New York: Random House, 1971.
Oh Pray My Wings Are Gonna Fit Me Well. New York: Random House, 1975.
"Rehearsal for a Funeral." *Black Scholar* (June 1975): 3–7.
Singin' and Swingin' and Gettin' Merry Like Christmas. New York: Random House, 1976.

BENNETT, GWENDOLYN B.

No published volume of poetry.

"*The Ebony Flute.*" Literary column for *Opportunity* (August 1926–May 1928), a quarterly journal of the National Urban League headquartered in New York City from 1910–1946.

BIRD, BESSIE CALHOUN

Airs From the Woodwinds. Philadelphia: Alpress, 1935.

BOYD, MELBA JOYCE

Cat Eyes and Dead Wood. Highland Park, Michigan: Fallen Angel, 1978.
Wild Strawberries in the Onion Field (unpublished)

BROOKS, GWENDOLYN

Aloneness. Detroit: Broadside Press, 1971.
Annie Allen. 1949. Reprint. Westport, Conn.: Greenwood Press, 1972.
The Bean Eaters. New York: Harper & Row, 1960.
Beckonings. Detroit: Broadside Press, 1975.
Bronzeville Boys and Girls. New York: Harper & Row, 1956.
Family Pictures. Detroit: Broadside Press, 1970.
Foreword to *New Negro Poets: USA.* Edited by Langston Hughes. Bloomington: Indiana University Press, 1964.
In the Mecca: Poems. New York: Harper & Row, 1968.
Introduction to *The Poetry of Black America: Anthology of the 20th Century.* Edited by Arnold Adoff. New York: Macmillan, 1973.
"The Life of Lincoln West." In *New Writings by American Negroes, 1940–1962.* Edited by Herbert Hill. New York: Knopf, 1968. (Short story)
Maud Martha. New York: Harper & Row, 1953. (Novel)
"Of Flowers and Fire and Flowers," *Black Books Bulletin* 3 (Fall 1975): 16–18. (Criticism)
Report from Part One. Detroit: Broadside Press, 1972. (Autobiography)
Riot. Detroit: Broadside Press, 1970.
Selected Poems. New York: Harper & Row, 1963.
A Street in Bronzeville. New York: Harper & Row, 1945.
The Tiger Who Wore White Gloves, or What You Really Are, You Are. Chicago: Third World Press, 1974.
The Wall. Broadside Series number 19. Detroit: Broadside Press, 1967.
We Real Cool. Broadside Series number 6. Detroit; Broadside Press, 1966.
The World of Gwendolyn Brooks. New York: Harper & Row, 1971. (Includes selections from *A Street in Bronzeville, Annie Allen, Maud Martha, The Bean Eaters, In the Mecca.*)

BURROUGHS, MARGARET GOSS

Africa, My Africa. Chicago: DuSable Museum, 1970. (Short stories)
Did You Feed My Cow? New York: Crowell, 1955. Rev. ed. Chicago: Follett
    Publishing Company, 1969. (Street games, chants and rhymes.)
Jasper the Drummin' Boy. New York: Viking, 1947. Rev. ed. Chicago: Follett
    Publishing Company, 1970.
" 'Strawberry Blonde,' That Is." *Black World* 19 (July 1970): 78–81. (Short
    story)
"Tribute to Paul Robeson." *Freedomways* 11 (First Quarter 1971): 16–18.
What Shall I Tell My Children Who Are Black? Chicago: DuSable Museum,
    1968. (Short stories)
*Whip Me Whop Me Pudding and Other Stories of Riley and His Fabulous
    Friends.* Praga Press, 1966; Chicago: DuSable Museum, n.d.

BURT, DELLA

No published volume of poetry.

CLIFFORD, CARRIE WILLIAMS

The Widening Light. Boston: Walter Reid Company, 1922.

CLIFTON, LUCILLE

All Us Come Across the Water. New York: Holt, Rinehart and Winston, 1973.
Amifika. New York: E.P. Dutton, 1977.
The Black B C's. New York: E.P. Dutton, 1970.
The Boy Who Didn't Believe in Spring. New York: E. P. Dutton, 1973.
Don't You Remember? New York: E.P. Dutton, 1973.
El Nino Que No Creia en la PrimaVera. New York: E. P. Dutton, 1976.
Everett Anderson's Christmas Coming. New York: Holt, Rinehart & Winston,
    1971.
Everett Anderson's Friend. New York: Holt, Rinehart & Winston, 1976.
Everett Anderson's Nine Month Long. New York: Holt, Rinehart & Winston,
    1978.
Everett Anderson's 1-2-3. New York: Holt, Rinehart & Winston, 1977.
Everett Anderson's Year. New York: Holt, Rinehart & Winston, 1974.
Generations: A Memoir. New York: Random House, 1976.
Good News About the Earth. New York: Random House, 1972.
Good, Says Jerome. New York: E. P. Dutton, 1973.
Good Times. New York: Random House, 1970.
The Lucky Stone. New York: Delacorte Press, 1979.
My Brother Fine With Me. New York: Holt, Rinehart & Winston, 1975.
An Ordinary Woman. New York: Random House, 1974.

Some of the Days of Everett Anderson. New York: Holt, Rinehart & Winston, 1970.

Three Wishes. New York: Viking Press, 1976.

Two Headed Woman. Amherst, Mass.; University of Massachusetts Press, 1980.

COBB, ALICE S.

Blood of Africa. Madison, Wisconsin: FAS Publishers, 1975.

To Break These Chains (unpublished)

CORTEZ, JAYNE

Festivals and Funerals. New York: Phrase Text, 1971.

Mouth on Paper. New York: Bola Press, 1977.

Pissstained Stairs and the Monkey Man's Wares. New York: Phrase Text, 1969.

Scarifications. New York: Bola Press, 1973.

COWDERY, MAE V.

We Lift Our Voices and Other Poems. Philadelphia: Alpress, 1936.

CUMBO, KATTIE M.

No published volume of poetry.

DANNER, MARGARET

The Down of a Thistle: Selected Poems, Prose Poems, and Songs. Waukesha, Wisc.: Country Beautiful, 1976.

Impressions of African Art Forms in the Poetry of Margaret Danner. Detroit: Broadside Press, 1961.

Iron Lace. Kerhonkson, NY: Poets Press, 1968.

To Flower: Poems. Nashville, Tenn.: Hemphill, 1963.

DAVIS, THADIOUS M.

Emergence (unpublished)

DUNBAR-NELSON, ALICE RUTH MOORE

No published volume of poetry.

The Goodness of St. Rocque and Other Stories. 1899. Reprint. New York: Dodd, Mead & Company, 1969.

"People of Color in Louisiana." *Journal of Negro History* 2 (January 1917): 51–78.

"The Poet and His Song." *AME Church Review* 13 (1914): 6–9.

Violets and Other Tales. New Orleans: Monthly Review, 1895.

EVANS, MARI

"Black Writer's Views on Literary Lions and Values." *Negro Digest* 17 (January 1968): 22.

"Contemporary Black Literature." *Black World* 19 (June 1970): 4.

I Am a Black Woman. New York: William Morrow & Company, 1970.

I Look at Me. Chicago: Third World Press, 1974.

J.D. New York: Doubleday & Company, 1973.

Singing Black. Indianapolis: Reed Visuals, 1976. (Videotape)

"The Third Stop in Caraway Park." *Black World* 26 (March 1975): 54–62. (Short story)

Where is All the Music? London: Paul Breman Ltd., 1968.

FABIO, SARAH WEBSTER

Black Images/Black Resurrection. San Francisco: Julian Richardson, n.d.

Black Is/A Panther Caged. San Francisco: Julian Richardson, n.d.

"A Black Paper: An Essay on Literature." *Negro Digest* 18 (July 1969): 26–39.

"Black Writer's Views on Literary Lions and Values." *Negro Digest* 17 (January 1968): 39.

A Mirror: A Soul. San Francisco: Julian Richardson, Success Publishers, 1969.

Review of *Let's Go Somewhere*, by Johari Amini. *Black World* 20 (December 1970): 68.

"A Tribute to Owen's Song." *Black World* 24 (July 1975): 76-96.

"Tripping with Black Writing." In *The Black Aesthetic*, edited by Addison Gayle, Jr. New York: Doubleday & Company, 1971.

"Who Speaks Negro? What Is Black?" *Negro Digest* 17 (September-October 1968): 33–37.

FAUSET, JESSIE REDMON

No published volume of poetry.

The Chinaberry Tree. New York: Frederick A. Stokes, 1931. Reprint. New York: Negro Universities Press, 1969. (Novel)

Comedy: American Style. New York: Frederick A. Stokes, 1933. Reprint. New York: Negro Universities Press, 1969. (Novel)

"The Gift of Laughter." In *The New Negro*, edited by Alain Locke, pp. 161–67. New York: Atheneum Press, 1938.

Literary editor of *The Crisis* 18–25 (February 1919–May 1926), a quarterly journal (1910-present) published under the auspices of the NAACP headquartered in New York City.

"Mary Elizabeth." *The Crisis* 19 (December 1919): 51–56. (Short story)
"Nationalism and Egypt." *The Crisis* 6 (April 1920): 310–16.
"New Literature on The Negro." *The Crisis* 19 (June 1920): 78–83.
"Pastures New." *The Crisis* 5 (September 1920): 224–26.
Plum Bun. New York: Frederick A. Stokes, 1929.
Review of *The Big Sea*, by Langston Hughes. *Negro History Bulletin* 2 (December 1938): 20, 23.
The Sleeper Wakes. In *The Crisis* 20 (August-October 1920): 168–73; 226–29; 267–74. (Short novel)
There is Confusion. New York: Boni and Liveright, 1924. (Novel)
Translation of "Joseph and Mary Come to Bethlehem." *Crisis* 21 (November 1920): 72.

FORTEN, CHARLOTTE L. [MRS. FRANCIS GRIMKÉ]

No published volume of poetry.
"Interesting Letter from Miss Charlotte L. Forten." *Liberator* 19 (December 12, 1862): 7.
The Journal of Charlotte L. Forten. Edited with an introduction by Ray Allen Billington. New York: Dryden Press, 1953. Reprint. New York: Macmillan, 1961.
"Life on the Sea Island." *Atlantic Monthly* (May–June 1864): 11.
"Personal Recollections of Whittier." *New England Magazine* 8 (June 1893): 472.
Translation of Erckmann, Emilie and Alexander Chatrian, *Madame Therese; or the Volunteers of '92.* 13th ed. New York: Scribner & Sons, 1869.

GIOVANNI, NIKKI

Black Feeling Black Talk/Black Judgement. Detroit: Broadside Press, 1968; New York: William Morrow & Co., 1970.
Black Judgement. Detroit: Broadside Press, 1969.
"Black Poems, Poseurs and Power." *Negro Digest* 18 (June 1969): 30–34.
Cotton Candy on a Rainy Day. New York: William Morrow & Company, 1978.
A Dialogue: James Baldwin and Nikki Giovanni. New York: J.B. Lippincott Company, 1972.
Ego Tripping and Other Poems for Young Readers. New York: Lawrence Hill & Co., Pubs., Inc. 1973.
Gemini: An Extended Autobiographical Statement. Indianapolis: Bobbs-Merrill Company, Inc. 1971.
Like a Ripple On A Pond. Niktom Ltd: Atlantic Records, 1973. (Record)
My House. New York: William Morrow & Company, 1972.
Poem of Angela Yvonne Davis. Newark: Niktom Ltd., 1970.
A Poetic Equation: Conversations Between Nikki Giovanni and Margaret Walker. Washington, D.C.: Howard University Press, 1974.
Re-Creation. Detroit: Broadside Press, 1970.
Truth is On Its Way. Right On Records, 1971. (Record)

Spin a Soft Black Song. New York: Hill and Wang, 1971.
The Way I Feel. Niktom Ltd.: Atlantic Records, 1975. (Record)
The Women and the Men. New York: William Morrow & Company, 1975.

GREGORY, CAROLE C.

No published volume of poetry.

GRIMKÉ, ANGELINA WELD

No published volume of poetry.
"A Biographical Sketch of Archibald H. Grimké." *Opportunity* 3 (February 1926): 44–47.
"Let There Be Light." Lincoln Centennial Phonodisc, New York: National Council of the Churches of Christ in the United States of America Broadcasting and Film Commission, 1954. (Radio Program)
Rachel. Boston: Cornhill Publishing Company, 1921. Reprint. Washington, D.C.: McGrath Publishing Co., 1969. Produced by the NAACP at the Neighborhood Theatre in New York in 1921.
Review of *Gertrude of Denmark*, by Tillie Buffum Chase Wyman. *Opportunity* 5 (December 1924) 378–79.
"Struggle Against Race Prejudice." *Journal of Negro History* 48 (October 1963): 277–91.

HALL-EVANS, JO ANN

No published volume of poetry.

HARPER, FRANCES E.W.

Atlanta Offering Poems. Philadelphia: George S. Ferguson, 1895. Reprint. Miami, Fla.: Mnemosyne, 1969.
Eventide [pseudonym. Effie Afton] Boston: Ferridge, 1854. (Poems and stories)
Forest Leaves. Baltimore: By the author, 1855.
Idylls of the Bible. Philadelphia: By the Author, 1901. Reprint. New York: AMS Press, 1975.
Iola Leroy: Or Shadows Uplifted. Philadelphia: Garrigues Bros., 1892. Reprint. New York: AMS Press, 1969. (Novel)
"Is Money The Answer?" In *The Anglo-African* I (May 1859): 283–87.
Moses: A Story of the Nile. Philadelphia: Merrihew and Sons, 1869. 2nd ed. Philadelphia; By the Author, 1889.
Poems. Philadelphia: Merrihew and Sons, 1871. Reprint. New York: AMS Press, 1975.
Poems. Philadelphia: George S. Ferguson, 1895. Reprint. Freeport, New York: Books for Libraries Press, 1970.

Poems. Philadelphia, 1900.
Poems on Miscellaneous Subjects. Philadelphia: J.B. Ferrington & Son, 1854. Revised. Philadelphia: Merrihew & Sons, 1864.
Sketches of Southern Life. Philadelphia: Merrihew & Sons, 1872; Philadelphia: George Ferguson, 1888, 1891.
The Sparrow's Fall and Other Poems, n.p., n.d.

JOHNSON, GEORGIA DOUGLAS

An Autumn Love Cycle. 1928. Reprint. New York: Books for Libraries Press, 1971.
Bronze: A Book of Verse. 1922. Reprint. New York: Books for Libraries Press, 1971.
The Heart of A Woman and Other Poems. 1918. Reprint. New York: Books for Libraries Press, 1971.
Share My World. Washington, D.C.: Privately printed, 1962.

JOHNSON, HELENE

No published volume of poetry.

JONAS, ROSALIE M.

No published volume of poetry.

JONES, GAYL

No published volume of poetry.
Corregidora. New York: Bantam Books, 1975. (Novel)
Eva's Man. New York: Random House, 1976. (Novel)
"White Rat." In *Norton Anthology of Short Fiction,* edited by R.V. Cassill. New York: W.W. Norton and Company, 1978. (Short story)

JONES, PATRICIA

No published volume of poetry.

JORDAN, JUNE

Dry Victories. New York: E.P. Dutton, 1972. Rev. ed. New York: Avon Books, 1975.
Fannie Lou Hamer. New York: Thomas Y. Crowell Co., 1972. (Biography)
"For Beautiful Mary Brown." *Freedomways* 11 (Second Quarter 1971): 191–93 (Short story)

His Own Where. New York: Dell Publishing Company, 1971.
New Days: Poems of Exile and Return. New York: Emerson Hall Publishers, 1973.
"On Richard Wright and Zora Neale Hurston: Notes toward a Balancing of Love and Hatred." *Black World* 23 (August 1974): 4–8.
Passion. Boston: Beacon Press, 1981.
"Second Thoughts of a Black Feminist." *Ms.* 5 (February 1977): 113–15.
Some Changes. New York: E.P. Dutton, 1971.
Things That I Do in The Dark: Selected Poems. New York: Random House, 1977.
"Thinking about My Poetry." *Chrysalis* 4 (Winter 1977): 105–109.
The Voice of the Children. New York: Holt, Rinehart and Winston, 1970.
Who Look at Me. New York: Thomas Y. Crowell, 1969.

KUNJUFU, JOHARI M. [JOHARI AMINI; JEWEL C. LATIMORE]

An African Frame of Reference. Chicago: Institute of Positive Education, 1972. (Essays)
Black Essence. Chicago: Third World Press, 1968.
Common Sense Approach to Eating. Chicago: Institute of Positive Education, 1975. (Essays)
Folk Fable. Chicago: Third World Press, 1969.
A Hip Tale in the Death Style. Detroit: Broadside Press, 1972.
Images in Black. Chicago: Third World Press, 1969.
Let's Go Somewhere. Chicago: Third World Press, 1970.
Re-Definition: Concept as Being. Chicago: Third World Press.
Review of *Good Times*, by Lucille Clifton. *Black World* 19 (July 1970): 51–53.
"Statement on the Black Arts." *Black World* 24 (February 1975): 80–81.

LANE, PINKIE GORDON

The Mystic Female. Fort Smith, Arkansas: South and West, 1978.
Wind Thoughts. Fort Smith, Arkansas: South and West, 1972.

LORDE, AUDRE

Between Ourselves. Point Reyes, California: Eidolon Editions, 1976.
The Black Unicorn. New York: W.W. Norton, 1978.
Cables to Rage. Heritage Series, Vol. 9. London: Paul Breman Ltd., 1970.
Coal. New York: W.W. Norton, 1978.
The First Cities. New York: The Poets Press, 1968.
From a Land Where Other People Live. Detroit: Broadside Press, 1974.
The New York Head Shop and Museum. Detroit; Broadside Press, 1974.
"Scratching the Surface: Some Notes on Barriers to Women and Loving." *The Black Scholar* 7 (April 1978): 31–35.

Uses of the Erotic: The Erotic as Power. New York: Out and Out Pamphlet Inc., 1978. (Essay)

MADGETT, NAOMI LONG

Exits and Entrances. Detroit: Lotus Press, 1978.
One and the Many. New York: Exposition Press, 1956.
Pink Ladies in the Afternoon. Detroit: Lotus Press, 1972.
Songs to a Phantom Nightingale. New York: Fortuny's, 1941.
Star by Star. Detroit: Harlo Press, 1965. Rev. ed. Detroit: Lotus Press, 1970 and 1972.
"Woman with Flower." *Black Song Series I.* Detroit: Lotus Press, 1977. (Broadside)

McCLAURIN, IRMA

Black Chicago (unpublished)
Song in the Night (unpublished)

McELROY, COLLEEN J.

Lie and Say You Love Me. Port Orchard, Washington: Circinatum Press, forthcoming.
The Mules Done Long Since Gone. Seattle: Harrison-Madrona Publishers, 1973.
Music from Home: Selected Poems. Carbondale, Ill.: Southern Illinois University Press, 1976.
Winters Without Snow. San Francisco: Ishmael Reed Books, 1979.

MILLER, MAY

"Christophe's Daughters." In *Negro History in Thirteen Plays*, edited by Willis Richardson and May Miller. Washington, D.C.: Associated Publishers, 1935.
The Clearing and Beyond. Washington, D.C.: The Charioteer Press, 1974. (Including *Into the Clearing* and other poems.)
Dust of Uncertain Journey. Detroit: Lotus Press, 1975.
"Graven Images." In *Plays and Pageants From the Life of the Negro*, edited by Willis Richardson. Washington, D.C.: Associated Publishers, 1930.
"Harriet Tubman." In *Negro History in Thirteen Plays*, edited by Willis Richardson and May Miller. Washington, D.C.: Associated Publishers, 1935.
Into the Clearing. Washington, D.C.: The Charioteer Press, 1959.
Not That Far. Washington, D.C.: The Charioteer Press, 1973.

Poems. Washington, D.C.: The Charioteer Press, 1962.
"Riding the Goat." In *Plays and Pageants From the Life of the Negro,* edited by
Willis Richardson. Washington, D.C.: Associated Publishers, 1930.
"Samory." In *Negro History in Thirteen Plays,* edited by Willis Richardson
and May Miller. Washington, D.C.: Associated Publishers, 1935.
"Scratches." *The Carolina Magazine* 3 (April 1929).
"Sojourner Truth." In *Negro History in Thirteen Plays,* edited by Willis
Richardson and May Miller. Washington, D.C.: Associated Publishers,
1935.

MURRAY, PAULI

Dark Testament. Norwalk, Conn.: Silvermine Publishers, 1970.
Proud Shoes: The Story of an American Family. New York: Harper & Row,
1956. (Novel)

ODEN, GLORIA C.

The Naked Frame. Privately printed, 1952.
Resurrections. Homestead, Fla: Olivant Press, 1979.
The Tie That Binds. Homestead, Fla.: Olivant Press, 1980.

PARKER, PATRICIA

Child of Myself. Oakland, Calif.: Diana Press, 1972, 1974.
Movement in Black: The Collected Poetry of Pat Parker. Oakland, Calif.:
Diana Press, Inc., 1978.
Pit Stop. Oakland, Calif.: Diana Press, 1973.
The Poetry of Pat Parker and Judy Grahn: Where Would I Be Without You.
Olivia Records: 1975. (Record)

PIPER, LINDA

No published volume of poetry.

PLATO, ANN

Essays Including Biographies and Miscellaneous Pieces in Prose and Poetry.
Hartford, Conn.: n.p., 1841.
Poems. South Carolina: 1834.

RAY, HENRIETTA CORDELIA

Poems. New York: The Grafton Press, 1910.

RODGERS, CAROLYN M.

"Black Poetry-Where It's At." Negro Digest 18 (September 1969): 7–16.
"Black Writer's Views on Literary Lions and Values." Negro Digest 17 (January 1968): 14.
"Breakforth, In Deed." Black World 19 (September 1970): 13–22.
For Flip Wilson. Detroit: Broadside Press, 1971.
The Heart as Ever Green. New York: Doubleday & Company, 1978.
How I Got Ovah. New York: Doubleday & Company, 1976.
"The Literature of Black." Black World 19 (June 1970): 5–11.
Now Ain't That Love. Detroit: Broadside Press, 1970.
Paper Soul. Chicago: Third World Press, 1968.
Songs of a Black Bird. Chicago: Third World Press, 1969.
"Uh Nat'chal Thang, The Whole Truth, Us." Black World 20 (September 1971): 11.

SANCHEZ, SONIA

The Adventures of Fathead, Smallhead and Squarehead. Chicago: Third World Press, 1973.
"After Saturday Night Comes Sunday." Black World 20 (March 1971): 53–59. (Short story)
A Blue Book for Blue Black Magical Women. Detroit: Broadside Press, 1974.
Homecoming. Detroit: Broadside Press, 1970.
It's a new day: poems for young brothas and sistuhs. Detroit: Broadside Press, 1971.
I've Been a Woman. Sausalito, Calif.: The Black Scholar Press, 1978.
Love Poems. Chicago: Third World Press, 1973.
Review of Black Essence, by Johari Amini. Negro Digest 18 (April 1969): 91–92.
"Sister Son/Ji." In New Plays from the Black Theatre, edited by Ed Bullins. New York: Bantam Books, 1969.
"Uh, Huh; But How It Free Us?" In The New Lafayette Theatre Presents: Plays with Aesthetic Comments by Six Black Playwrights, edited by Ed Bullins. New York: Anchor Press, 1974.
We a baddDDD people. Detroit: Broadside Press, 1971.

SHANGE, NTOZAKE

For Colored Girls Who Have Considered Suicide When the Rainbow is Enuf. New York: Macmillan, 1977.
Nappy Edges. New York: St. Martin's Press, 1978.
Sassafrass. San Lorenzo, Calif.: Shameless Hussy Press, 1976.

SPENCER, ANNE

No published volume of poetry.

TERRY, LUCY [PRINCE]

No published volume of poetry.

THOMPSON, CLARA ANN

Songs from Wayside. Rossmoyne, Ohio: By the author, 1908.

TRUTH, SOJOURNER
[ISABELLA BAUMFREE, ISABEL STONE]

No published volume of poetry.

WALKER, ALICE

"The Black Writer and the Southern Experience." *New South* 25 (Fall 1970): 23–26.

"But Yet and Still, the Cotton Gin Kept on Working." *Black Scholar* 1 (January/February 1970): 17–21.

"Eudora Welty: An Interview." *Harvard Advocate* 106 (Winter 1973): 68–72.

Goodnight, Willie Lee, I'll see you in the morning. New York: Dial Press, 1979.

In Love and Trouble. New York: Harcourt Brace Jovanovich, Inc., 1973. (Short stories)

"In Search of Our Mothers' Gardens: The Creativity of Black Women in the South." *Ms.* 2 (May 1974): 64–70, 105.

"In Search of Zora Neale Hurston." *Ms.* 3 (March 1975): 74–79.

Langston Hughes. New York: Thomas Y. Crowell Company, 1974. (Biography)

"Lulls." *Black Scholar* 7 (May 1976): 3–12. (Essay)

Meridian. New York: Harcourt Brace Jovanovich, Inc., 1976. (Novel)

Once. New York: Harcourt, Brace and World, 1968.

Revolutionary Petunias and Other Poems. New York: Harcourt Brace Jovanovich, Inc., 1972.

The Third Life of Grange Copeland. New York: Harcourt Brace Jovanovich, Inc., 1970. (Novel)

"To Hell with Dying." In *The Best Short Stories by Negro Writers: An Anthology from 1899 to the Present*, edited and introduced by Langston Hughes. Boston: Little, Brown and Company, 1967.

"The Unglamourous but Worthwhile Duties of the Black Revolutionary Artist or of the Black Writer Who Simply Works and Writes." *The Black Collegian* 1 (October 1971).

"Women on Women." *American Scholar* 41 (Fall 1972): 599–622.

WALKER, MARGARET

For My People. New Haven, Conn.: Yale University Press, 1942.

How I Wrote Jubilee. Detroit: Broadside Press, 1971.
Jubilee. Boston: Houghton Mifflin, 1966. (Novel)
"New Poets." *Phylon* 11 (1950): 345–54; also in *Black Expression*, edited by
　　Addison Gayle, Jr. New York: Weybright and Talley, 1969.
*A Poetic Equation: Conversations between Nikki Giovanni and Margaret
　　Walker.* Washington, D.C.: Howard University Press, 1974.
Prophets For a New Day. Detroit: Broadside Press, 1970.
"Some Aspects of the Black Aesthetic." *Freedomways* 16 (Second Quarter,
　　1976): 95–103.

WHEATLEY, PHILLIS [PETERS]

Memoir and Poems of Phillis Wheatley, A Native African and A Slave.
　　Boston: Isaac Knapp, 1838. Reprint.
Poems on Various Subjects, Religious and Moral. London: Bell 1773 1st
　　British ed.; 1st American edition, Philadelphia: 1786.
The Poems of Phillis Wheatley edited by Julian D. Mason, Jr., Chapel Hill,
　　North Carolina: University of North Carolina Press, 1966. Includes a
　　reprint of 1786 American edition.

WILLIAMS, LUCY ARIEL [HOLLOWAY]

Shape Them Into Dreams: Poems. New York: Exposition, 1955.

WILLIAMS, SHERLEY ANNE

Give Birth to Brightness: A Semantic Study of Neo-Black Literature. New
　　York: Dial Press, 1972. (Literary criticism)
The Peacock Poems. Middletown, Conn.: Wesleyan University Press, 1977.